Andrew Ingham was born in Leeds in
1945. He emigrated to Rhodesia with his
family in 1957. He has lived in London
since 1968, where he practised as a
graphic designer and studied architecture
at the Architectural Association.

SELF HOUSE
HELP REPAIRS
MANUAL

Andrew Ingham

PENGUIN BOOKS

Penguin Books Ltd,
Harmondsworth, Middlesex, England
Penguin Books, 625 Madison Avenue,
New York, New York 10022, U.S.A.
Penguin Books Australia Ltd,
Ringwood, Victoria, Australia
Penguin Books Canada Ltd, 2801 John Street,
Markham, Ontario, Canada L3R 1B4
Penguin Books (N.Z.) Ltd,
182-190 Wairau Road, Auckland 10,
New Zealand

First published 1975
Revised edition 1980

Made and printed in Great Britain by
Butler & Tanner Ltd, Frome and London

Preface

This manual is intended to help anyone wanting to do their own house repairs. It concentrates on the most basic practical aspects, assuming no prior specialised knowledge, and gives information and instruction in enough detail to enable most people to acquire the basic techniques needed in such things as plumbing and electrical repairs.

It is primarily intended for those involved in the repair of short-life housing and, consequently, focuses on the basic repairs needed to get a house habitable as quickly and as cheaply as possible. However, the nature of the information given makes it just as useful to anyone, owners or tenants, wishing to do their own repairs, renovations and improvements - thereby filling a gap often left by the more glossy books intended for the home owner. Anyone doing repairs should realise that it need not be just a way of saving money, but can be a joy as well. It's an opportunity for gaining experience, seeing that to increase your knowledge of the things around you is to increase your freedom and effectiveness, and enjoying what to a professional would be just another job.

In the last ten years, there has been such a shortage of housing that many people have taken direct action to house themselves. Paradoxically, the worst housing areas often contain an immense number of empty and temporarily abandoned houses. Either through individual action or through organised groups, with or without the consent of the owners, these abandoned houses have been brought back into use by the people who most need them. However, instead of seeing this as a creative force in a decaying urban environment, the media - and especially the newspapers - have condemned squatters as lawless vandals and have helped to make a difficult situation worse. Indeed, the media-generated hysteria has been a strong factor in the introduction of new legislation to control squatting. It remains to be seen whether this will be used against the genuine homeless and will prevent the use of abandoned council and private property.

The new legislation does not make squatting illegal, but much more difficult. The process of obtaining eviction orders against squatters has been greatly speeded up, making it easier for owners to regain their property. Moreover, as a squatter, you can be prosecuted for criminal damage (in such cases even some repairs can be seen as damage) or for trespassing with an offensive weapon (including anything from a bread knife to a bag of flour). To avoid legal problems, therefore, it is best to try to reach an agreement with the owner. This may mean joining a squatting group who already have a 'licence', or forming your own group and negotiating with the owner yourself.

The basis of such agreements are generally as follows: the houses can be used until they are genuinely required for redevelopment or demolition, and will be vacated at such time; reasonable notice will be given before the property is wanted back; all repairs and maintenance will be carried out by the squatters; and rates will be paid, and possibly a nominal rent will be charged. As a 'licensee' under this type of agreement, you have some security and an idea of when you will have to move. If you want more details about making agreements or forming groups, get in touch with an established local group, or the Advisory Service for Squatters (see 3. 10. 02 - 03).

The prime concern of this manual, however, is the repair of short-life housing, cheaply and quickly. In general, abandoned houses are in a bad state of repair, and often lack even basic amenities by the time they are reoccupied. Years of neglect whilst still in use are followed by vandalisation as soon as the houses are emptied. Inevitably, old lead pipes, lead flashing and roof coverings, and copper pipes and cable are stripped and sold for their scrap value. Moreover, the houses are sometimes purposely gutted by the owners (including councils) in order to discourage their re-use.

Repairing such houses - taking into account their short life and the uncertainty of your 'tenure' -

is, to say the least, extremely difficult. There are some precautions that can be taken, but in the end the project will always be something of a risk. It is important, for instance, to ensure as early as possible that the main services - gas, water and electricity - have only been disconnected, and not cut in the road. The worse the condition of the house, the surer you must be that the length of time you can stay will justify the effort you put into it. For repairs to be 'economic', you should not spend more on them than you would otherwise have spent on rent over the same period of time.

In general, the best materials are those in common use by the building industry. Their availability - especially second-hand - often outweighs any advantages of materials that are cheaper but more difficult to get. However, in seeking advice from tradesmen and professionals, remember that they are concerned with a much longer life and higher degrees of finish and performance than you need in short-life housing. Always seek more than one opinion: advice tends to vary, even among people with years of experience. Avoid buying at D.I.Y. shops: their small pre-packed quantities are very expensive. Find your nearest builders' merchant or electrical wholesaler, where, even if you can't get a trade discount, things are a lot cheaper. They are also good places for picking up advice and finding sources of cheap materials. Let people know that you don't mind shop-soiled or second-hand fittings, odd pairs, or last year's models.

If you intend to make the use of short-life property into something of a way of life, think of recovering materials and fittings put into one house for use in another. It may mean spending more to start with, but could be cheaper in the long run. The manual covers all the materials in common use and some that are not, and in general emphasises cheapness. Nevertheless, the final decisions will depend on you and your own particular circumstances.

This manual covers all aspects of basic repairs and will not leave you in mid-stream or advise calling in a tradesman when the explanations run out. It's our basic assumption that most people, given enough information and encouragement, can do all the repairs necessary to rehabilitate a house. But, although it helps to have as much information as possible, in the end one has to have the courage to make a start: it's often this move from thinking about doing it to actually doing it that's the hardest part of all.

I would like to thank the many people who have helped in the preparation of this manual, but especially Ian Litterick and Student Community Housing.

All information given in this manual is given in good faith. Care has been taken to make sure it is accurate; however, changes and variations do occur from time to time. If you're at all in doubt, then refer to the relevant regulations. All installations which could involve risk are normally subject to inspection and under no circumstances should you try to avoid or interfere with these inspections. If you disregard any advice given by the inspecting authority, it is entirely your own responsibility - this manual cannot be used to justify such disregard. No liability can be accepted for any loss, damage or injury, however it arises, as a result of any of the recommendations, instructions or suggestions set out in this manual. All information in the manual is based on the regulations of England, Scotland, Wales and Northern Ireland only.

Contents

CONTENTS (cont'd.)

ELECTRICITY

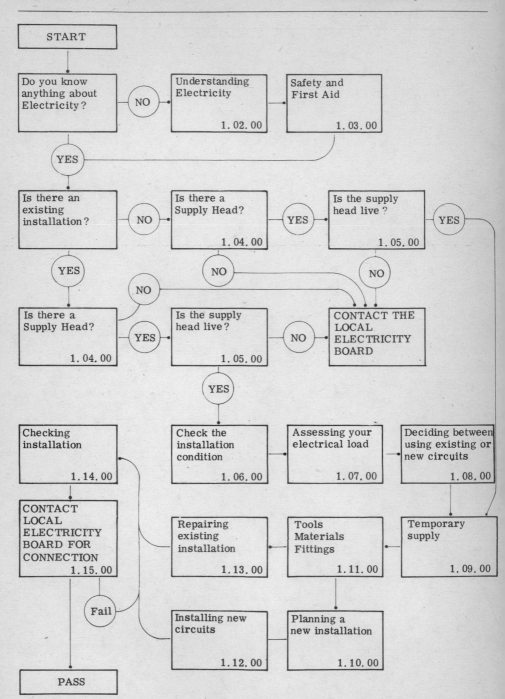

1. 01. 00 INTRODUCTION

1. 01. 01 One of your first needs will be for a
supply of electricity. For this you are
almost totally dependent on the Electricity Board. They expect a certain
standard from your electrical installation
and can, under certain circumstances,
refuse to reconnect a supply. These
standards are concerned mainly with
safety and for this reason alone should
be adhered to.

1. 01. 02 If you move into your house shortly after
the previous tenant has left, you can go
to the local Electricity Board's showroom and ask for the supply to be reconnected. If there has been a lapse, or
the board knows changes to the old circuits have been made, or if they know
the house is in an area with old wiring,
they may insist on inspecting the installation.

1. 01. 03 In any case you want to have a safe
electrical installation, so it will be
necessary to run through some checks.
The type and the condition of an installation varies from house to house. To
allow for these differences, and to make
working from this section simple, we've
devised a flow chart which is on the
opposite page . Although at first this
may seem complicated , if you take it
step by step, it will provide a sequence
which allows you to deal with one thing
at a time. In each box there is a simple
instruction or question with a choice of
two (or sometimes three) alternative
paths to the next stage. In some instances you will not be able to answer a
question or follow an instruction, and in
these cases the number in the box
refers to the section which carries the
necessary information.

1. 01. 04 The text uses as few technical terms
as possible, but where one cannot be
avoided an explanation accompanies its
first appearance in the text.
It's intended that the drawings read as
a cartoon strip providing similar information as in the text, but in a visual
form. If this is your first attempt at
electrical work, then read through the
whole of Part One to get some idea of
what is involved. The information is
based on the regulations affecting
electrical installations for the United
Kingdom only.

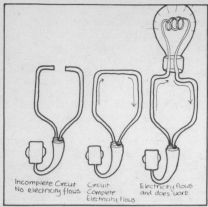

Incomplete Circuit   Circuit   Electricity flows
No electricity flows   Complete   and does work
                      Electricity flows

Electricity needs a circuit to flow

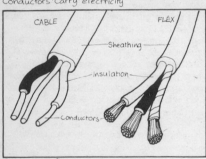

Copper   Insulation
Conductor   Material

Conductors 'Carry' electricity

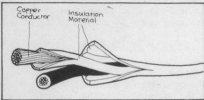

CABLE   FLEX

—Sheathing—

—Insulation—

—Conductors—

Cable and flex

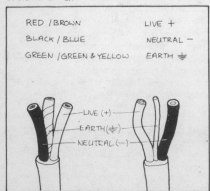

RED / BROWN   LIVE +

BLACK / BLUE   NEUTRAL —

GREEN / GREEN & YELLOW   EARTH ⏚

—LIVE (+)—
—EARTH (⏚)—
—NEUTRAL (—)—

Colour Code for conductors

1. 02. 00 UNDERSTANDING ELECTRICITY

1. 02. 01 Electricity is generated in power stations all over the country. It's fed into a system of cables, transformers and switches - the national grid - and eventually arrives at each house through a mains or service cable.

1. 02. 02 In order for electricity to flow, it must have a circuit or pathway from the source back to the source. This circuit is provided by the wires or conductors in cables and flex. The electricity does work (gives light, or heat, or works a radio) when an appliance is connected into the circuit and the circuit is completed.

1. 02. 03 Conductors are made from materials which offer little resistance to the flow of electricity; the less the resistance the better the conductor. Good conductors are copper, silver, aluminium and most metals. Bad conductors, which don't allow electricity to flow in them, are used as insulation, keeping the conductors apart from each other and their surroundings; such as P. V. C., rubber, paper, ceramic, etc.

1. 02. 04 The form of conductor you'll probably be most familiar with is flex or flexible cable. The conductors themselves are made from several thin strands of copper (or aluminium) held together and insulated by a covering of P. V. C. (or other insulating material). Three of these wires are then insulated and held together by a second coat of P. V. C.. Flex is intended for use when there will be constant movement and handling.

1. 02. 05 Cable is another type of conductor which is fixed in position so there is no constant handling. The conductors in modern domestic cable are of one thick strand of copper, with two conductors insulated and a third bare, held together by a covering of P. V. C., usually oval or flat in cross section.

1. 02. 06 The colours of the insulation are used to identify the particular use of the conductor. Recently this colour code has been changed to conform to an international standard, but these new colours are used only on flex. Cable uses the old colours.

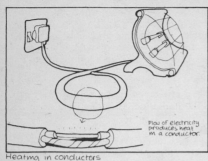

Flow of electricity produces heat in a conductor.

Heating in conductors

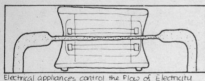

Conductors overloaded.

Take care not to overload conductors

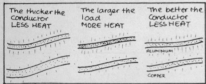

The thicker the conductor LESS HEAT

The larger the load MORE HEAT

The better the conductor LESS HEAT

ALUMINIUM

COPPER

Overheating depends on the load, the material & thickness of conductor

Short circuit

Electrical appliances control the Flow of Electricity

Fuse wire heats and melts if overloaded

Fuse wire
Fuse Bridge

Fuses protect conductors from overloading

The colour code (old first) and the function of the conductors are:

1) Red or brown for the 'live' conductor which carries electricity from the source to the appliance.

2) Black or blue for the neutral conductor, which carries electricity from the appliance back to the source.

3) Green (or bare) or green and yellow stripes identifies the earth conductor which acts as a safety device.

1. 02. 07 In any conductor there is some resistance to the flow of electricity. This resistance tends to generate heat. The amount of heat generated depends on the amount of current flowing, the material being used for the conductor and the thickness or cross-sectional area of the conductor. This generation of heat can be dangerous: if a conductor is greatly overloaded (i. e. carrying too much electricity) it may become so hot as to melt the insulation, and start a fire. Or over a long period with less heat the insulation will slowly disintegrate (especially rubber) and eventually let electricity 'leak'. If electricity is allowed to run freely (i. e. in the case of the live wire touching directly the neutral wire) you have a short circuit, and the conductors would heat up rapidly. Electrical appliances have a resistance, which in effect controls the amount of electricity that flows through them. (Note: damage to flex or cables can cause danger of fire or electrocution.)

1. 02. 08 There is, of course, a safety device to prevent conductors overheating – the fuse. The fuse is simply a short piece of wire (conductor) which has a certain resistance and thickness such that, at a certain load (amount of current) it will melt, and in so doing, break the circuit, and prevent all electricity flowing. Fuse wire is graded to take differing loads, e. g. 5 amps, 10 amps, 15 amps etc.

So the flex from a modern socket to an appliance is protected by the 13 amp fuse in the plug. The cable on which all the sockets are connected is protected by the 30 amp fuse in the consumer

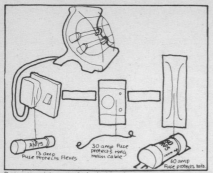

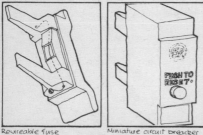

Domestic wiring is protected in three places

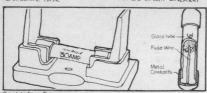

Rewireable fuse

Miniature circuit breaker

Cartridge fuse

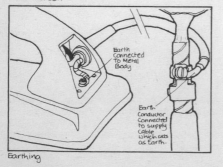

Electric shock

Earthing

unit, and the cable on which the lights are, is connected by a 5 amp fuse. The cables between the consumer unit and the service cable are protected by a fuse of between 35 and 150 amps (often 60 amps).

1.02.09 There are three types of fuse; they all do the same job.

Rewireable -
uses fuse wire held in a ceramic (or plastic) holder. When the fuse blows the old wire is removed and new secured in its place.

Cartridge -
The fuse wire is held between two metal caps in a glass tube filled with an insulating powder. When the fuse blows you replace the whole thing. 13 amp plug fuses are this type.

Miniature Circuit Breaker (MCB) -
These are an automatic switch or button which disconnects with any overload. The switch or button is simply reset by hand when the overload is removed.

1.02.10 There's one other way for electricity to complete a circuit, and that is by earthing. This literally means the electricity flows into the ground. Electricity will take any opportunity to earth, and one way is if you come into contact with a live wire while standing on the ground: you get an electric shock, which can give burns or even stop the heart. The earth wire acts as a safety device by offering an alternative path (with less resistance than you) to earth. One end of the earth wire is connected to the metal sheathing of the service cable, or in some cases a metal water pipe, which gives good contact with the earth. The earth wire follows the live and neutral to each appliance where it is securely attached to any metal part of the appliance. Then if the live part of the appliance shorts onto the metal case the electricity is safely carried to earth. This is usually such an unrestricted flow as to blow the fuse, although this is not always the case.

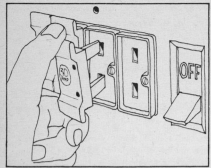
Turn off at mains and remove fuses

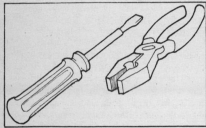
Use Insulated tools

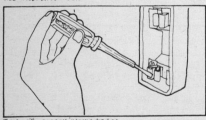
Test with a neon mains tester

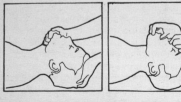

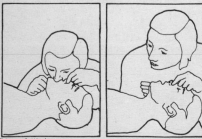
'Kiss of life'

1. 03. 00 SAFETY and FIRST AID

1. 03. 01 If simple precautions are taken there is no reason why electricity should be any more dangerous than crossing the road. The more you know about it, the safer it is.

1. 03. 02 Before attempting any repairs or inspection of electrical circuits, turn off the main switch and remove all the fuses. Do it yourself or work with someone who you know is familiar with what to do. If it's possible that someone may try to turn the mains back on while you're working, then keep the fuses with you.

1. 03. 03 Always work with insulated tools, tools with plastic or wooden handles. Keep a neon mains tester with you at all times (see 1. 11. 01). Use it as a personal tool and remember it's possible for it to break and to indicate no current when there may be one.

1. 03. 04 The degree of shock depends on the surface you're in contact with.
A dry wooden floor - only a slight or no shock.
A concrete floor - moderate shock.
A wet concrete floor, garden soil, or contact with metal pipes - a severe shock. So when working in these conditions, take extra precautions. Work with dry hands, keep away from metal pipes or metal fixtures and stand on dry ground or on an insulated mat.

1. 03. 05 If someone does receive an electric shock:

Turn off the current or remove them from contact with the live part. Use some insulating material such as dry wood or paper, plastic or rubber to move them with. Don't just grab them with bare hands.
Send someone for a doctor or ambulance in the meantime.
If their breathing has stopped, apply mouth-to-mouth artificial respiration. Treat for shock - keep them lying down with legs slightly elevated. Don't move them unnecessarily or disturb them by questioning. They should be kept warm but without external heat; give liquids sparingly even though they may be thirsty. Dress any minor burns.

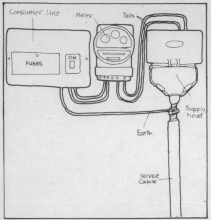

Typical Distribution Board.

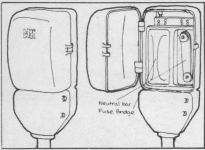

One type of single phase supply head.

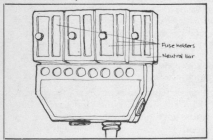

One type of three phase, or three way head.

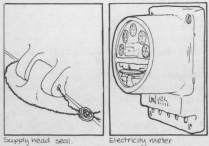

Supply head seal.   Electricity meter

1. 04. 00 LOCAL ELECTRICITY BOARD'S SUPPLY HEAD

1. 04. 01 The service or mains cable coming in from the street terminates in a box called the supply head. It is normally found high up, near the front door, or in a central hall or stairwell, under stairs, in a hall or porch cupboard, in the cellar or basement. It is fairly easily recognised even though it may be surrounded by other electrical equipment. A thick, slightly oily looking cable will enter the head, probably in the bottom, coming up from the ground (the service cable). A red cable and black cable (the tails) will leave the top and be connected to the meter or to where the meter was. And possibly an earth wire (green) will be attached to a clip on the metal of the service cable. In multi-occupied houses there will be more than one head. The supply heads on upper floors are often supplied by MICC (see 1. 11. 24).

1. 04. 02 The heads vary in design, but are usually black and made of Bakelite (plastic) or occasionally have a metal cover. Inside the head is an oil seal for the main cable, the main fuse (one for a single phase head, three for a three phase head) and a neutral bar. The bottom compartment contains the seal and the top compartment, which has a removable cover, the main fuse or fuses and the neutral bar. The fuses can be ceramic rewireable type or cartridge type.

1. 04. 03 The head and the meter belong to the L. E. B. and normally the cover over the main fuses will be sealed with a wire seal. This is supposed to prevent people opening the head and taking an unmetered supply. Occasionally the meter is removed when a house is disconnected, but will be returned when the supply is reconnected.

1. 05. 00 <u>CHECKING THE L.E.B.'s SUPPLY HEAD</u>

1. 05. 01 The most important thing to check is that there is still an electricity supply connected to the house. The L.E.B. have three ways of disconnecting a supply to a vacated house:

By severing the service cable in the road. To reconnect a severed service cable can cost between £10 and £100.

By disconnecting the live wire (tail) from the head or from the meter.

By removing the mains fuse. (It will probably be left on the top of the head). Or by removing the fuse wire or cartridge. The tails and meter may also be missing.

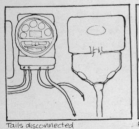 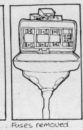

Tails disconnected.   Fuses removed.

1. 05. 02 There are several other signs that may indicate if the head is dead: Freshly dug earth or fresh tar macadam between the house and the road (in line with the head). 'LEB OFF' painted on the wall. Call the L.E.B. and ask for 'meter department', who should have records. Even if you think, or are told, that the cable is dead, under no circumstances try to remove it. The cable may be live although the head is dead and it will give you a very big fright indeed if you try to cut it. The cable is the property of the L.E.B. and they will remove it if required.

1. 05. 03 The only sure way to tell, though, is by testing with a neon mains tester (see 1.11.01   ). The seal on the fuse cover will have been broken when the supply was disconnected. Remove the fuse cover and remove the fuse (or fuses) if they haven't already been removed.

Fresh digging may indicate a severed service cable.

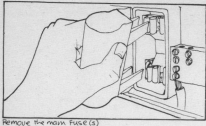

Remove the main fuse(s)

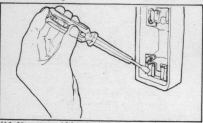

Check its rating

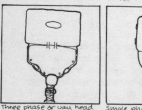

Use neon mains tester to test for electricity

Three phase or way head　　　Single phase head

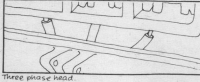

Three phase head.

Three way head.

Look for the amperage marked either on the fuse bridge itself or on the fuse cartridge.

1. 05. 04　The neutral bar looks similar to a fuse holder without the fuse bridge. The top and bottom contacts are connected by a thick brass bar. In some old heads the neutral is also fused. If this is so, it must carry a higher rated fuse than the live, otherwise the neutral fuse could blow, breaking the circuit but leaving everything live. If this is the case, get the L. E. B. to change the neutral fuse when they reconnect the supply.

1. 05. 05　With the fuse or fuses removed, the top fuse contacts will be dead. To test if the bottom contacts are live, touch them with the neon mains tester. If the neon bulb lights, the head is live. Be especially careful while doing this; the tester should not slip, or any uninsulated part of the shaft touch the metal casing (or other metal) while the tip is on or near any live part. Use only a tester you know works, that you're familiar with, and that is insulated for the whole length of the shaft. Remember there is no fuse between you and the nearest sub-station. If there are three fuses, test each one separately. The neutral bar will not give a positive reading.

1. 05. 06　Three phase head -
In three phase heads there are three fuses and a common neutral bar. Occasionally a single head is split into three fuses. This can be distinguished from a proper three phase head by care-fully looking at the bottom row of fuse contacts. If each has a separate cable attached, then it is a true three phase head. If each is connected to one another, then it is a single phase split into three fuses or 'ways'.

1. 05. 07　Where there's a large load the L. E. B. may often put in a three phase supply for their own convenience. Don't for-get that there are 415 volts (not 240) across a three phase head, so that it is important to treat it with respect. You must never have circuits run from two different phases in the same room. Keep different phases to different parts of the house.

1. 06. 00 ASSESSING THE EXISTING INSTALLATION

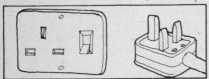
Make sure the installation is dead before inspecting

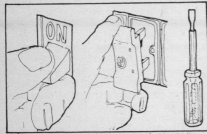
13 amp square pin socket and plug

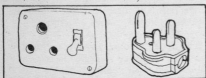
15 amp round pin socket and plug

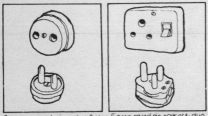
2amp round pin socket & plug 5amp round pin socket & plug

1. 06. 01 There are several clues to the condition of an existing installation. But before you go poking around behind sockets, just make sure that there is no current. Turn off at the mains or remove the main fuse from the head. Use your neon tester to make sure no wires are live.
What to look for and at:

    Age
    Damage
    Insulation
    Under floor
    Distribution board

1. 06. 02 Age - A rough guide to the age of an installation can be got from the type of sockets used. Of course, different parts of an installation may have been done at widely different times. The two round pins (2 amp) are the earliest type. They don't have any earth protection and couldn't be used for more than a light or a radio. The 5 amp round three pin plug has been in use since before the war, and might be considered borderline. The 15 amp round three pin is usable for most loads. The square pin 13 amp socket came into use in the 50's and could possibly indicate a good circuit in good condition.
But, it must be remembered that this can only be a rough guide. All these types of sockets are still sold today,

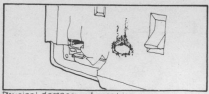

Physical damage and scorching

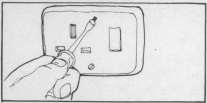

Remove the socket cover

Inspect the cables

look for perished insulation

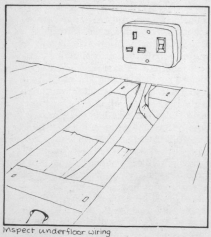

Inspect underfloor wiring

and there's nothing to stop people putting new sockets on old wiring which may not be of sufficient size.

1. 06. 03 Damage - Look for damage to various fittings, those on the distribution board, sockets, light switches, light sockets, ceiling roses and any special fittings (cooker switch for example). They should all be securely fastened to the wall. On sockets look for scorching around the holes; this indicates a bad connection causing overheating which may have perished the insulation.

1. 06. 04 Insulation - It is important to check the insulation of the hidden cable. Remove the socket from its box and carefully pull the attached cable out. If the insulation on these conductors (wires) is hard and brittle, and if it breaks off when the wire is flexed, then the insulation has perished. Try and pull more cable from the box and test the insulation again as far from the socket as possible - it may be that heat generated in the socket has perished just the ends of the conductors. If this insulation is good, then you will be able to cut back to the good insulation and reconnect the old socket. Repeat this with as many sockets as you can (if they are all of the same type and have the same wiring, then they are likely to be in the same condition. If they vary in type and fitting, you should check all of them). Check the insulation in the switches and ceiling roses in the same way.

1. 06. 05 Underfloor - You should have a look at the condition of the wiring under the floor. It's probably the case that there will be loose or easily removed boards under the sockets, and above ceiling roses of the room below. There are several types of cable:

PVC covered, twin and earth - It's either gray or white in colour, and usually has its size and what it is marked on it. It's flat in section. A modern cable that should be in good condition.

Lead covered rubber insulated cable - If you scratch the surface of lead, a bright metallic mark should be left.

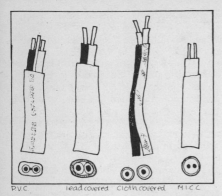

P.V.C.   lead covered   cloth covered   M.I.C.C

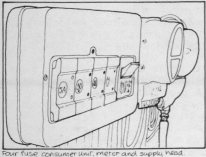

Four fuse consumer unit, meter and supply head.

Switched Fuse box
Main Switch (isolator)
Meter
Supply head
Switched Fuse Box
Henley box

Separate switched fuse boxes

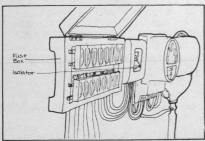

Fuse Box
Isolator

Fuse box and main switch

This is an old type of cable, no longer used, but it has a long life. The rubber insulation may perish where it has been stripped for connection to fittings. However, the rubber covered by the lead is usually good. The lead is used as the earth conductor.

Cloth covered rubber insulated cable – The rubber tends to perish all along the cable and may have to be replaced.

Mineral Insulated Copper Covered (MICC or Pyro) is very new and not used for most domestic installations (see 1.11.24 to 1.11.28).

There may be a number of different cables in use in a single house. Cables are often damaged or taken by vandals for the lead or copper they contain.

1. 06. 06 Distribution board –

a. Consumer unit
If a consumer unit is fitted, the circuits should be fairly new (unless it's been fitted to old circuits). A consumer unit would indicate 30 amp ring mains for the sockets. Remove the fuse cover and look for the rating (amps) of each fuse. 5 amp are for light circuits, 30 for ring mains, any others will be used for radial circuits to cookers or immersion heaters, or other types of sockets. You should check that all the circuits are using the correct size cable, and are not fitted to more than the required number of sockets (see 1.10.00).

b. Switched fuses
These are most common in old houses, and tend to have been added to over the years. Again, check their fuse ratings and see that they are connected to the correct size cable, and to the right number of sockets. Each separate switch fuse box is connected to a Henley box and then to the meter. There may be a separate mains switch.

c. Fuse board and switch
These are usually very old and should be replaced. It is probably connected to radial circuits which may be inadequate for the sockets or load you wish to use.

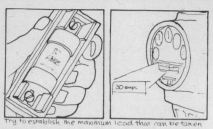

Try to establish the maximum load that can be taken

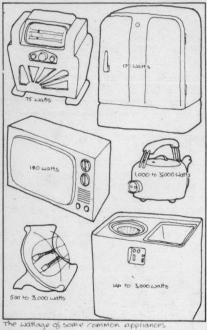

75 watts

175 watts

180 watts

1,000 to 3,000 Watts

500 to 3,000 watts

up to 3,000 watts

The wattage of some common appliances

Example
2 lighting circuits at 5 amps = 10 amps
    66% of 10 amps   6.6 amps
3 Power circuits at 30 amps each
    100% of the first   30 amps
    80% of the second   24 amps
    50% of the third   15 amps
Electric cooker 30 amps with a socket
    30% of 30 amps = 10 + 10 + 5   25 amps
                               100.6 amps

Working out load from each circuit

Example

6 100 watt bulbs   600 watts
2 1000 watt electric fire   2000 watts
1 1000 watt fan heater   1000 watts
2 T.V.s   360 watts
2 Record players   200 watts
                       4160 watts

$Amps = \dfrac{Watts}{Volts}$ Volts = 240

$Amps = \dfrac{4160}{240} = 17.3$

Working out load from appliances

1. 07. 00 ASSESSING YOUR ELECTRICAL LOAD

1. 07. 01 When you make an application for a supply of electricity to the L. E. B. you may be asked to write down all the electrical appliances you will be likely to use. From this the L. E. B. works out the likely maximum load in amps, and compares this with the load that the particular service cable entering your house will carry. In most cases it is 60 amps, although in old houses it might be less.

1. 07. 02 Before committing yourself to a house it may be worth checking that your need for electricity can be met by the incoming service cable. If it can't, it may mean not using electricity for heating or cooking, or having a new larger capacity service cable laid. (Up to £100).

1. 07. 03 Finding the load of the service cable - This may be marked on the L. E. B. head, on the cartridge in the fuse bridge. The meter is often marked with its load. The L. E. B. will also have a record. Any equipment marked with amps may not in fact represent the maximum load that the cable can take.

1. 07. 04 Calculating your own needs - If the house is occupied by a family then it's reckoned that at any one time only a percentage of the appliances will be in use:
Lighting circuits take 66% of each circuit's capacity.
Power circuits take 100% of first 80% of second 50% of remainder.
Cooker takes 10 amps + 30% (+ 5 amps if there is a 13 amp socket incorporated into the cooker switch).
Lighting circuits are taken as 5 amps, power ring main at 30 amps, while cooker can be anything up to 60 amps.

1. 07. 05 Or if the house is occupied by single people, who each might, say, have their light, an electric fire, a record player, and the kitchen in use all at the same time, it's better simply to total all the appliances you've got (see the diagrams for approximate watts for each appliance). The amps may be marked on the appliance, or the watts. To work out the amps from the watts:

Watts = Voltage x Amps ∴Amps = $\dfrac{Watts}{Voltage}$

1. 08. 00 DECIDING BETWEEN USING OLD CIRCUITS OR INSTALLING NEW ONES

1. 08. 01 It's only possible to give a rough guide to this as each case will depend on the individual circumstances, the condition, life of the house and money available.

1. 08. 02 Is there a supply of electricity? If the head is dead, is it worth paying the £50 - £100 for reconnection? This largely depends on the life of the house and on negotiations with the L. E. B. as to price. If they think there will be a large return from the reconnection, they may share the costs.

1. 08. 03 Is the supply adequate? If the main fuse in the supply head is less than 60 amps you should check that your electrical needs will be met by, or modified to, the capacity of the incoming service cable. Check with the L. E. B. - the fuse may not represent the full capacity of the service cable. They can advise you on the maximum load that might be safely taken.

1. 08. 04 Safety - If you're in any doubt about the safety of the circuits, then replace them. Remember that the cost of material is slight compared to the potential damage a fault might cause.

1. 08. 05 Cost - The amount you spend can be linked to the life of the house. The longer the life, the longer you can spread the cost over. However, don't let this interfere with a minimum of safety no matter how short the life is.

1. 08. 06 Damage - If there is obvious damage to the electrical installation - the fittings smashed and cables ripped out - then you'll have to replace it. Don't try to patch up extensive damage; it will be easier to start from scratch.

1. 08. 07 Age - If the circuits are old and in doubtful condition, then trying to repair them may start more faults.

1. 08. 08 Lighting circuits - On the whole, lighting circuits are usually in good condition. The small load needed by lights is less demanding on the cable, and if there is a fault, less dangerous. The pendant flex may need changing and check that the circuit is correctly fused.

1. 08. 09 Power circuits - Old power circuits are much more likely to have been overloaded, the insulation perished and any fault will be potentially more dangerous.

1. 08. 10 Checking circuits - If still in doubt, you can do a more thorough check (see 1. 14. 00). In the meantime you can ask for a temporary supply.

1. 09. 00 <u>TEMPORARY ELECTRICAL SUPPLY</u>

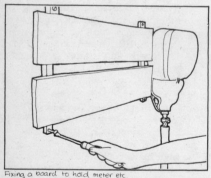

Fixing a board to hold meter etc

1. 09. 01 The L. E. B. will supply electricity without inspecting the installation if it is
what they call a temporary supply. The
charge per unit of electricity that you
use is about 4 times that normally
charged.

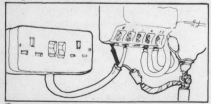

Temporary sockets

1. 09. 02 However, a supply of electricity can be
invaluable when getting a house habit -
able, allowing the use of 'wander leads',
electric power tools and for testing circuits. The L. E. B. will need a board
onto which they can attach a meter (if
there isn't one already) and which should
be big enough to carry a consumer unit
(2' - 2'6" square). The board should be
attached to the wall as near to the head
as possible. The L. E. B. don't like
long 'tails'.

Wander light

1. 09. 03 You can make up extension leads and
wander lights yourself, perhaps attaching temporary sockets to the distribution
board.

1. 10. 00 PLANNING A NEW ELECTRICAL
INSTALLATION

1. 10. 01 There are three types of circuit in
common use for domestic purposes:

The power circuit - supplies socket
outlets

The lighting circuit - for lights

Special circuits - for appliances such as
cookers, or off-peak storage heaters,
immersion heaters, etc.

1. 10. 02 The power circuit -

This can use two types of circuit, the
radial circuit, or the ring circuit.

1. 10. 03 In a radial circuit, the cable is run from
a fuse box or consumer unit to the first
socket outlet, from the first to the second,
from the second to the third, stop-
ping at the last socket outlet. As the
cable between the fuse and the first
socket will carry the cumulative load of
all the sockets, it needs to be a hefty
cable. In fact, using cable with a conductor of 2. 5mm in cross-section, one
is allowed to attach no more than six
sockets in one room (if not a kitchen)
using a 20 amp fuse in the consumer
unit, or no more than two sockets if in
2 rooms or a kitchen using a 20 amp
fuse.

1. 10. 04 In a ring circuit or ring main, the
sockets are attached in the same way as in
the radial circuit except from the last
socket the cable is returned to the consumer unit where the live wire is inserted into the same terminal as the first
live wire and the neutral into the same
neutral terminal. This forms a ring
into which electricity flows to a socket
from two directions. Using the same
2. 5mm cable the regulations allow an
unlimited number of sockets on a ring
which serves an area of not more than
1000 sq. ft. For larger areas you have
to run separate rings, one for each 1000
or part of 1000 sq. ft. In addition, one
can run spurs (or a radial circuit) from

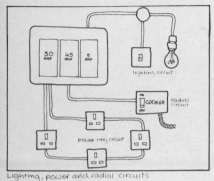

Lighting, power and radial circuits

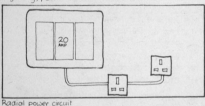

Radial power circuit

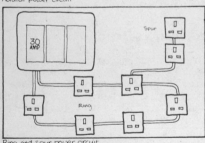

Ring and spur power circuit

How a ring is connected to a Consumer Unit

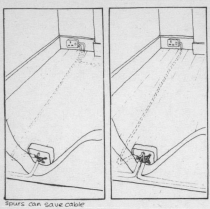

Spurs can save cable

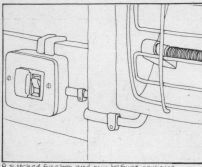

A switched fuse box and spur to fixed appliance.

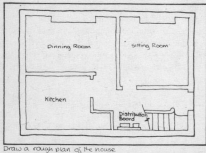

Draw a rough plan of the house.

any point on the ring. The spur cannot have more than two sockets on it (a double socket in this case counts as one) but one may not have more sockets on spurs than there are on the ring.

1. 10. 05 For example: a house of 1800 sq. ft. would need two rings.

If there were 10 sockets on one ring, one could have no more than 10 sockets on as many as five spurs.

1. 10. 06 Spurs have many advantages if used well.

They save cable where a socket is required some distance from the main ring - only one run of cable is then used.

They enable sockets to be added later with much less trouble.

They are used with fused junction boxes for fixed appliances.

1. 10. 07 Designing a power circuit -

Draw a rough plan of the house, one for each floor and work out roughly the area of each floor. For a small house two floors might be just about 1000 sq. ft. while a large house is not likely to exceed 1000 sq. ft. per floor.

1. 10. 08 Decide on the number of sockets you will need for one room. Local authorities recommend 5 in the kitchen, dining room 4, sitting room 6, bedroom 3 or 4. Or simply add up the appliances which you are likely to use in each room. If you're feeling generous, decide one socket for each, with maybe an extra one for something you didn't think of. If that's too expensive, allow one socket for each appliance that must be on all the time (e. g. fridge) plus one for all

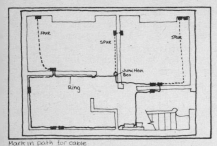
Mark in path for cable

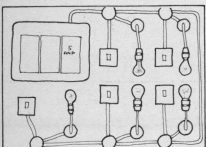
Junction box lighting circuits

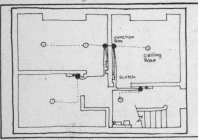
Plan for junction box lighting circuit

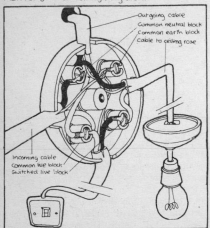
Junction box wiring

the things you're unlikely to have on together (e.g. T.V. and stereo). Remember a socket costs about the same as a
double adaptor.

1. 10. 09   No sockets are allowed in bathrooms, or
in fact any electrical appliance or switch
which can be touched with one hand while
holding a tap with the other. Use a pull
switch for the light. There are special
sockets for shavers which can be fitted.

1. 10. 10   Once you've decided on the number,
decide on the position of each one in
each room. This will relate to the likely position of the appliances, but keep in
mind that the more central the sockets
in relation to each other, the less cable
you use. Use a spur for sockets that
you want on 'outside' walls. It's probably wise to leave some lee-way on the
number of spurs you use, as it's
relatively easy to run a spur at any time
later, while breaking into the ring may
be more difficult. Double sockets are
cheaper than two single and slightly
easier to fit.

1. 10. 11   Once the position of each socket is
marked on your drawing, you can work
out the shortest distance between each
one, joining them together to show the
intended path of the cable.

1. 10. 12   Lighting circuits -

The lighting circuit uses a much smaller
load than that of the power circuit. The
lighting circuit uses a modified radial
circuit which is designed to take in the
provision for wall switches. There are
two ways of doing this.

1. 10. 13   Junction Box System -
A cable is run from the distribution
board to a junction box under the floor
(which is just above the ceiling the light
hangs from). From the first junction
box another cable is run to a second,
from the second to the third, and so on.
From each junction box a cable is run to
a wall switch (or a pull switch). The
live (red) and neutral (black) of this
cable act as two live wires with the returning (black) live controlled by the
switch. From the junction box a fourth
cable connected to the neutral and

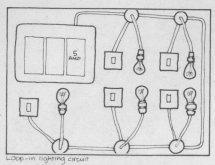

Loop-in lighting circuit

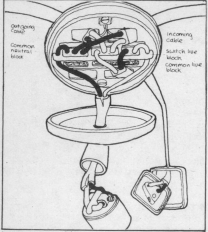

Plan for loop-in lighting circuit

Loop-in lighting wiring

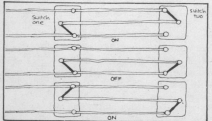

Wiring diagram for two way switching

switched (black) live is taken to the ceiling rose, and from the ceiling rose flex is hung with a bulb holder connected. The positioning of the junction box in this system is critical for the minimum use of cable.

1. 10. 14 Draw a rough diagram of each floor of the house, mark the positions of each ceiling rose, and each wall or pull switch (which are usually near the door). From these positions, work out the position of each junction box (one for each ceiling rose and switch). The optimum position will probably be near the switches, as these are usually fairly central around a hall or corridor. Try for a short run of cable between each one, a short run to the switch, with probably the longest run to the ceiling rose. The ease of removing floorboards - some may already be loose - may influence you on positioning junction boxes and ceiling roses. Once you're satisfied with the junction box's position, mark in the intended cable runs.

1. 10. 15 Loop-in System -
This method is the same as the one above except the junction box is incorporated into the ceiling rose. The cable runs from ceiling rose to ceiling rose, with the cable running to the switch and the flex for the bulb holder both connected into the rose. This system probably uses more cable but leaves you with fewer fittings to buy.

1. 10. 16 Again, draw a diagram of each of the floors and mark in the ceiling rose and light switches and show the path for the cable from rose to rose and from each rose to switch.

1. 10. 17 There's no reason why the two systems cannot be used together, if it happens that you have a mixture of fittings.

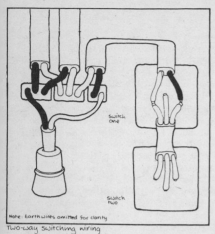

Note: Earth wires omitted for clarity

Two-way switching wiring

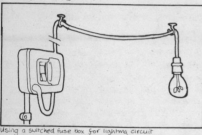

Using a switched fuse box for lighting circuit

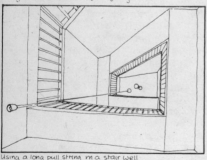

Using a long pull string in a stair well

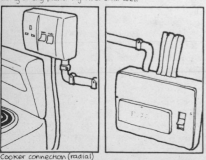

Cooker connection (radial)

1.10.18 Two-way switches -
These are used when a single light (or a number of lights on the same switch) needs to be controlled from two points. Special switches are needed (called two-way switches) which have three terminals instead of two. You have a special three core and earth cable running between the two switch positions. (see 1.12.26). This is coded red, yellow, and blue.

1.10.19 There are several alternatives to lighting circuits. You could, for instance, have a spur from the ring mains running to a switched fuse box (2 amp fuse) by the door, with a flex running to a lamp holder in any part of the room. (For the bathroom you would need a separate pull switch). This way you would need no separate lighting circuit. In place of two-way switches you could hang a long cord down a stairwell so allowing the light to be operated from any point on the stair. Pull switches can be used for all switches, but are rather more expensive than wall switches.

1.10.20 Other Circuits -
Cookers and immersion heaters use a radial circuit run from the appropriate fuse in the consumer unit to the appliance. For fixed electric fires, a switched fuse box can be run from the power ring (appliances which are rated over 13 amps cannot be taken off the power ring but need a separate circuit of their own). Special circuits for white meters (cheaper rate at night) for use with storage heaters, are probably not worth installing for short periods.

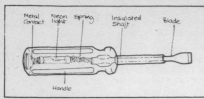

Metal Contact · Neon light · Spring · Insulated Shaft · Blade · Handle

Neon Mains Tester

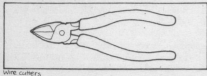

Wire cutters

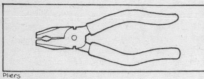

Pliers

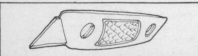

Stanley knife

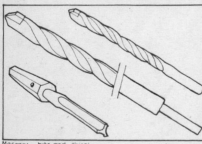

Masonry bits and chisel

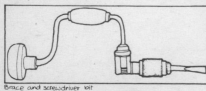

Brace and screwdriver bit

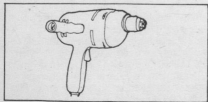

Electric Drill

1.1i. 00 TOOLS, MATERIALS AND FITTINGS

1. 11. 01 Neon Mains Tester -
Indispensable. It consists of a screw-driver which contains a neon bulb and one megohm resistor in the handle. By touching a live terminal with the blade, and holding the metal stud in the handle against your finger, you complete a circuit with the earth. The bulb lights, indicating power, while the 1 megohm resistor prevents you getting a shock. Buy a good make with a long shaft insulated the whole of its length. Keep it as a personal tool. It's worth checking it regularly with something you know to be live.

1. 11. 02 Wire Cutters,
pliers, or heavy duty side-cutters, for cutting flex, cable and conductors.

1. 11. 03 Stanley Knife
or other sharp knife for stripping off insulation. Good wire strippers are also useful. In using a knife, take care not to damage the conductors as this leads to overheating and eventual breakage.

1. 11. 04 Masonry Bits
and/or cold chisels (star drill) for making holes through brickwork. A half-inch masonry bit (durium tip) with a 16" shaft can be bought to fit a $\frac{1}{4}$-inch jaw of an electric drill. Otherwise, use hammer and $\frac{1}{2}$-inch star drill, or as a last resort, iron gas pipe and a lot of bashing.
For fixing fittings to the wall:
No. 8 masonry bit for electric or hand drill, or a No. 8 rawl plug chisel for use with a hammer;
a range of wood bits for making holes in wood.

1. 11. 05 Screwdrivers -
Heavy screwdriver or screwdriver bit for a brace.
For electrical terminals use neon mains tester or medium-sized insulated screwdriver.

1. 11. 06 General Tools -
Hammer; 10" tenon saw; floorboard saw (not essential); chisels; plane; file; bolster chisel; tape measure; torch; pencil, etc.

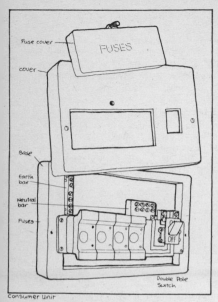

Consumer Unit

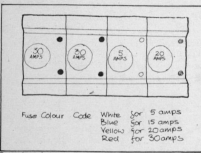

Fuse Colour Code   White   for 5 amps
                     Blue   for 15 amps
                     Yellow for 20 amps
                     Red   for 30 amps

Rating (amps) of each fuse

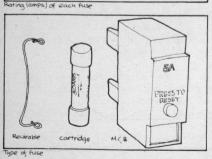

Type of fuse

5amp Fuse wire

15 amp Fuse Wire

20 amp Fuse Wire

30 amp Fuse Wire

Approximate thickness of fuse wire

1. 11. 07 The Consumer Unit -
The consumer unit is where the incoming electrical supply is split between the various circuits of the house. The tails enter the unit and are connected to the live and neutral terminals of a two pole or isolator switch. This is the mains switch from which you can cut off electricity from the whole installation. A two pole switch breaks both live and neutral connections, thereby completely isolating the house circuits. From the live side of the mains switch a brass or copper conductor is connected to the base of the set of fuse holders and fuses. The neutral side is connected to a neutral bar, a brass bar with several terminals. A similar bar, the earth bar, is attached to one side of the box.

1. 11. 08 The number of fuses needed in the consumer unit is one per circuit. One for each power circuit rated at 30 amps each (if a ring main). One for the lighting circuit rated at 5 amps. One for each electric cooker rated between 30 - 45 amps (look on the cooker for amps or its wattage, and work out amps from that - see 1.07.00). One for each appliance rated over 15 amps. You might consider having one spare.

1. 11. 09 The number of fuses in a consumer unit goes up in twos (2, 4, 6, 8, etc.) and you will need to state the number of fuses (circuits) that you want and the rating (or amps) for each one. There are three types of fuse: rewireable, cartridge, and the miniature circuit breaker (M. C. B.).

1. 11. 10 The Wylex is a good cheap consumer unit that takes rewireable fuses (these are more difficult to mend than the cartridge type, but cheaper). The 'ON' 'OFF' labelling becomes confusing when the cover is removed so take care.

1. 11. 11 Fuse holders are designed so that only the correctly rated fuse will fit. In the Wylex the holders can be changed, so once you've ordered a particular fuse, it can only be altered by buying another holder to replace it. There is a colour code for the amps rating of fuses. Buy a supply of fuse wire of the correct amps.

1. 11. 12 Isolator -
An isolator is similar to a consumer unit but has only one fuse. The switch is double pole. The size of the fuse needs

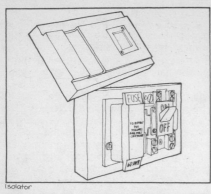

Isolator

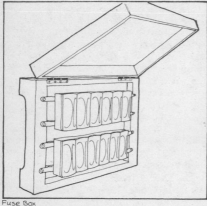

Fuse Box

to be specified depending on the type of circuit you use with it. An isolator can be used to add a new circuit when there is no spare fuse in the consumer unit. Or where a separate mains switch is needed for each circuit (e. g. for supplies to separate households in one house).

1. 11. 13 Fuse Box -
A fuse box contains a number of fuses but no switch. They have generally been replaced by the consumer unit. If you do use one, use it with a double pole switch (an isolator).

1. 11. 14 Cables and Flexes -
The conductors in cables and flexes are usually made of copper, but you can get them with aluminium conductors. Aluminium is not as good a conductor as copper and so thicker conductors are needed to carry the same load. All the sizes given here are for copper.

1. 11. 15 The size of the conductor, its cross-sectional area, is directly related to the amount of current it can safely carry and therefore to the fuses to be used with it.

1. 11. 16 The table (opposite) shows this relationship. You will notice too that there is a voltage drop for each cable depending on length. L. E. B. regulations forbid more than a 6 volt drop. If, due to the length of a cable, there is likely to be more than a 6 volt drop, then the next larger cable size should be used. This applies to radial circuits only.

1. 11. 17 The cross-sectional area of the conductors in general use in domestic installations are:
For lighting - 1mm^2 cable protected by a 5 amp fuse.
For 13 amp sockets - 2.5mm^2 cable protected by a 30 amp fuse when in a ring (or 20 amp fuse when in a radial circuit).
For 15 amp (round pin) sockets - 2.5mm^2 cable protected by a 20 amp fuse (radial circuit).
The tails (the cable between the head, meter and C. U.) are 16mm^2 cable protected by a 60 amp fuse.

FLAT TWIN AND EARTH
PVC COVERED CABLE

Usual Circuit rating Amp.	Cable Size mm^2	Maximum length (approx.) at circuit rating	
		metres	Feet
5	1.0	36	118
5	1.5	45	150
20	2.5	18	59
30	4.0	16	52
30	6.0	29	95
45	10.0	32	105
60	16.0	38	125

Cable ratings

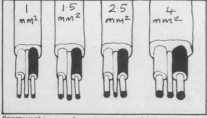

Approximate size of conductors in cables

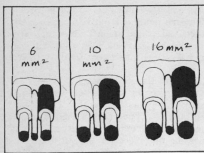
Approximate size of conductors in cables

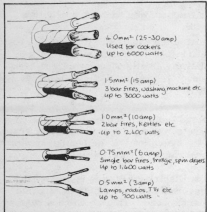
Approximate size of conductors in flexes

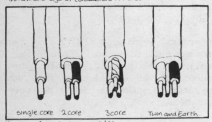
single core   2 core   3 core   Twin and Earth
Number of conductors in cables

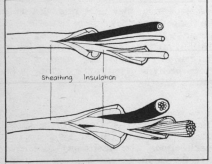
Sheathing   Insulation

Insulation and sheathing

Other appliances should be worked out and appropriate cable and fuse used.

1. 11. 18   If the cable is thicker than it need be for the fuse protecting it , then it's a waste of the cable's capacity (but not dangerous).

If the cable is thinner than it should be for the fuse protecting it (or as more often happens, the fuse is too large for the cable) then the cable can be overloaded long before the fuse will blow.

If the electrical load is too great for the cable used, the fuse will keep blowing (fuses usually blow a few amps over their rating).

1. 11. 19   The size of the conductor in flexes also varies. They are usually not sold according to their cross-sectional area (although this may be marked) but as lighting flex, or electric fire flex, etc. If you're using 13 amp sockets you can change the cartridge fuse in the plug for one appropriate to the flex on the plug – 2 amp for lights to 13 amp for an electric fire, etc.

1. 11. 20   Cable is referred to as being single core, double core, or triple core, etc. , depending on the number of conductors it carries. But for domestic wiring where the earth conductor is uninsulated and sometimes smaller than the live and neutral conductors, it's referred to as Twin and Earth.

1. 11. 21   It's also necessary to state the type of insulation and sheathing. The insulation being the immediate covering on the conductor and the sheathing being the thing that binds them all together. The most common is PVC insulated, PVC sheathed. This is commonly referred to as 'PVC' or 'PVC sheathed' (or, if it's only single core cable, 'PVC double sheathed' or 'PVC double insulated, or just 'PVC PVC').

1. 11. 22   Generally cables are referred to as flat – having an oval cross-section. Flex is referred to as round, having a circular cross-section.
So when ordering cable or flex, state:
the size of the conductor,
the number of conductors,
the type of insulation.
E. g. 1mm^2 Round 3 core PVC flex 'x' metres.

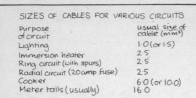

SIZES OF CABLES FOR VARIOUS CIRCUITS

Purpose of circuit	usual size of cable (mm²)
Lighting	1.0 (or 1.5)
Immersion heater	2.5
Ring circuit (with spurs)	2.5
Radial circuit (20 amp fuse)	2.5
Cooker	6.0 (or 10.0)
Meter tails (usually)	16.0

Uses of cables

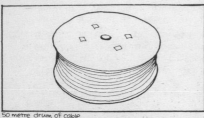

50 metre drum of cable

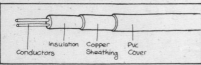

Mineral Insulated Copper Cable
Conductors   Insulation   Copper Sheathing   Pvc Cover

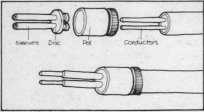

Sealing MICC from moisture
sleeves   Disc   Pot   Conductors

Cable in conduit   Cable buried under plaster

Plastic staple (Flex)   Plastic staple (Cable)

1.11.23   Cable usually comes on 50 metre or 100 metre drums (1 metre is just over a yard) but you shouldn't have difficulty in getting shorter lengths, although you may have to pay an extra 'cutting charge'.

1.11.24   Mineral Insulated Copper Cable - MICC or pyro is an expensive, very high quality fire resistant cable. The outer sheathing is copper and the insulation is a special heat resistant mineral. Sometimes the outer copper sheath is also covered with PVC. The copper sheath acts as an earth conductor while there can be one, two, or three conductors inside.

1.11.25   Because the cable is heat resistant, very much higher loads can be carried on relatively small conductors. The conductors heat up, but do no damage to th insulation.

1.11.26   Special tools are needed to seal the ends of the cable to prevent moisture getting to the insulation. If the insulation gets wet it causes a short circuit.

1.11.27   Most Electricity Boards insist on MICC being used when the meter is separate from the head. This would be necessary where the head is inaccessible (e. g. on someone else's property) to the household using the supply.

1.11.28   Otherwise, avoid using MICC; it's expensive and difficult to use. There is no real need for it in most domestic installations. It may often be possible to move the meter to a position next to the company head.

1.11.29   Cable Fixing
The traditional method of getting cable from one place to another is by running it under the floorboards, down steel tubes (conduit) buried in the wall, or hidden under plaster. While it might in some cases be quick to run cable under the floor, where it isn't it can easily be fixed to the surface of the wall or skirting.

1.11.30   There are two types of cable fixings for doing this - plastic cable clips and buckle clips. The plastic ones are made to fit the various common sizes of Twin

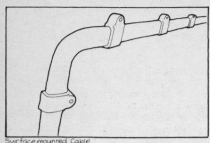

Surface mounted Cable

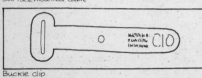

Buckle clip

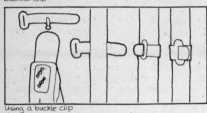

Using a buckle clip

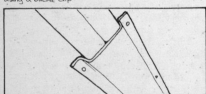

Plastic or metal channel

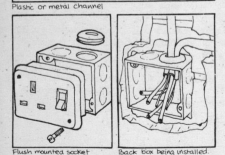

Flush mounted socket   Back box being installed.

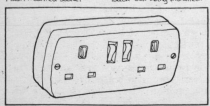

Surface mounted double switched socket.

and Earth PVC cable and others which fit various size flexes. Some are made to hold two cables side by side. They carry a steel nail which can be hammered into wood or masonry. These steel nails are not always satisfactory; if the plaster is an inch or more deep, then you'll have to change them for longer steel nails.

1. 11. 31 Buckle clips seem somewhat less attractive than the plastic, though they are more versatile. One size fits a range of sizes of cables and flexes. They are cheap.

1. 11. 32 There are a number of types of metal conduit, the best type use threaded joints. The split tube type is not recommended. Metal conduit can be used with two single core cables (the conduit is used as earth) or with PVC twin and earth. Plastic conduit is also available. Surface mounted cables can be protected by metal or plastic channel which comes in different widths to cover one, two or three widths of cable.

1. 11. 33 Electrical Fittings -

Most electrical fittings are available as surface-mounted or flush-mounted. Flush-mounted fittings need a hole made in the wall, and a metal 'back' box inserted. They are normally used with hidden wiring but can be used with surface wiring. Generally though it's much easier to use surface mounted sockets and switches with surface mounted wiring.

1. 11. 34 Surface-mounted socket outlets are designed to take a square three pin plug which carries a 13 amp fuse. The actual socket mechanism is contained in the body of the socket, covered with a front plate which is attached by two screws. They come switched or unswitched, double unswitched or double switched. It's probably worth the slight extra cost for the switched version. They are made in various materials and colours, but the plastic type are probably robust enough for most purposes.

1. 11. 35 Surface-mounted wall light switches come with one, two, three or more switches, or gangs. A switch can be one-way or two-way. Two-way switches are necessary when two switch positions are needed. A two-way switch can be used as

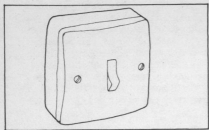

Surface mounted switch

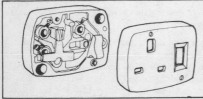

Surface mounted switched socket

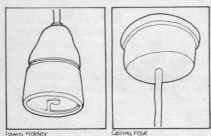

lamp holder   Ceiling rose

Pull switch   Fused spur box

                             Junction box

Connection strip   Green sleeving

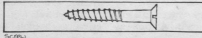

Screw

one-way, but not a one-way as a two-way. The switch mechanism is attached to the front plate which fits into a box or patress.

1.11.36 Ceiling roses for use with a loop-in lighting circuit have eight terminals plus an earth terminal. Ceiling roses for use with junction boxes have three terminals. Both consist of a back plate which holds the terminals and a separate cover which screws on.

1.11.37 Bulb holders can be for use with ceiling roses or be screwed directly to a wall or ceiling (batten holders). They normally have a ring, the skirt, which is intended to hold a lampshade.

1.11.38 Pull switches. For use in bathrooms. The switch is attached to the ceiling and operated by a long cord.

1.11.39 Junction box looks similar to a ceiling rose in size, contains a set of four separate terminals for use with a junction box type of lighting circuit or for joining cables together. The terminals are covered with a screw-on plastic top.

1.11.40 Connection strips - these are for making connections between cable and flex. They are bought in strips and you cut off as many as you need. They should not be used in places where dust or water could 'short' them.

1.11.41 Green sleeving is used inside the fittings to insulate and identify the bare earth wire.

1.11.42 Fuse spur boxes - about the size of a 13 amp socket outlet, they are used where a permanent connection to an appliance is needed. They can be switched and unswitched.

1.11.43 Screws and rawl plugs - A variety of screws and rawl plugs and nails are needed. If you standardise to no. 8 (gauge number of the thickness of screws) you only need one set of rawl plug tools and masonry bits. You'll need $1\frac{1}{2}$-inch to 2-inch screws for fixing sockets, etc., to masonry walls with thick plaster, $\frac{3}{4}$-inch to 1-inch screws for fixing to wood.

Prepare the consumer unit to take the cables.

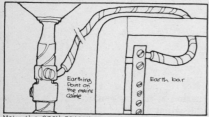
Make the earth connection

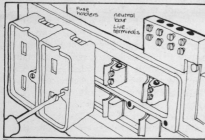
Fixing the fuse holders in place

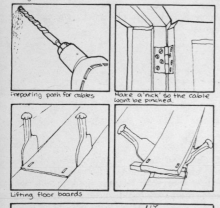
Preparing path for cables

Make a 'nick' so the cable won't be pinched.

Lifting floor boards

Floor board should be cut over the floor joists

1. 12. 00 INSTALLING NEW CIRCUITS

1. 12. 01 Installing a consumer unit -
You should mount a board onto the wall
next to, or as near as possible to, the
supply head. It needs to be big enough
to hold the consumer unit and the meter
with space around them (about 2ft to 2ft
6" sq.). $\frac{3}{4}$-inch blockboard would be
ideal, or two short lengths of floorboard
nailed to two battens and screwed and
rawl-plugged to the wall.

1. 12. 02 Before attaching the base to the board,
cut a long slot through which the cables
can come. There may be a partly cut
section, or knock-out holes (metal) or
break off pieces (plastic).

1. 12. 03 Screw the base to the board and fix the
fuse-holders in place. Leave the connection of the unit to the meter until
all the circuits have been installed.

1. 12. 04 The earth bar should be connected to an
earthing point. This is usually on the
metal sheath of the mains cable (see
1. 02. 10). Use single core green
sheathed cable, 6mm^2 or 10mm^2.
You should fix a label "SAFETY ELEC-
TRICAL EARTH - DO NOT REMOVE"
(available from your wholesalers) to
the earth lead at the earth clamp.

1. 12. 05 Installing surface-mounted cable -
Mark the position of each of the sockets
and prepare a path for the cable. Where
you have to go through a masonry wall
use a $\frac{1}{2}$-inch masonry bit in an electric
or hand drill (use the slowest speed). A
star drill and hammer can be used; rotate
the drill $\frac{1}{4}$ of a turn each time you hit it.
Clean off any loose wallpaper, flaking
paint or anything which will prevent the
cable laying flat. If there are any parts
which don't give a solid surface (e. g.
plasterboard) on which to attach the
cable, then you could first attach a strip
of wood. If you take cable through a
door opening, nick the architrave or
door to make sure the cable is not
pinched when the door is closed.

1. 12. 06 Cable cannot be laid on top of the floor
or under carpets. It must go under the
floorboards or round the top of doors.
When laying cable under floorboards,
you should not simply take a nick out of

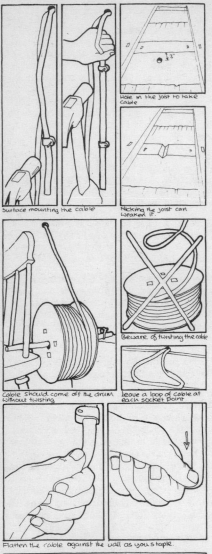

Surface mounting the cable

Hole in the joist to take cable

Nicking the joist can weaken it.

Beware of twisting the cable

Cable should come off the drum without twisting

Leave a loop of cable at each socket point

Flatten the cable against the wall as you staple.

the top of the joist (this also weakens the joist - reducing the effective thickness by the depth of your cut), but drill a $\frac{1}{2}$-inch hole about 3 inches from the top. Joists are often so close that you may need an 'electrician's ratchet'. You might get away with drilling at a slight angle. Don't put the cable in any place where it is in danger of being nailed (e. g. when you replace the floorboards). Where cable runs with the joists it can be left loose.

1. 12. 07 Starting at the consumer unit, thread the cable along the route, leaving a loop at each socket position, and back to the consumer unit. Pull through enough cable to enable you easily to connect it into the consumer unit or fuse box later. Don't at this stage cut the cable from the rest of it on the drum. As you go round you'll probably find you have an excess which can be worked back and rewound. While unwinding the cable, be very careful that it comes straight off. If the drum lies flat and the cable spirals off, it will introduce twists or kinks to the cable which make laying it flat impossible. Stick a broom handle through the drum so it's free to turn as you pull off cable.

1. 12. 08 Secure the loose end of cable and pull the cable taut and flat and staple it at 3 foot intervals. Come back to add two intermediate staples later. You'll find the cable hard to flatten; with the smaller ones, use your thumb or palm to run along the cable while keeping it bent and taut with the other hand. With heavier cables, link your fingers together and run the cable through your hands, under the little fingers and over the thumbs.

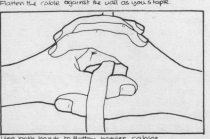

Use both hands to flatten heavier cables

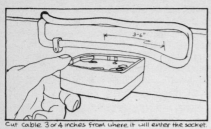

Cut cable 3 or 4 inches from where it will enter the socket.

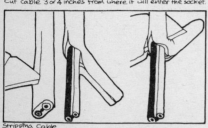

Stripping cable

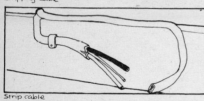

Strip cable

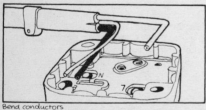

Bend conductors

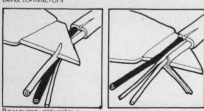

Removing insulation

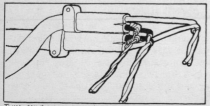

Twist conductors together

1. 12. 09 Flat, well mounted cable tends to staple easier, is less likely to be damaged by kinks and gives the impression to the L. E. B. inspectors that you took trouble and knew what you were doing.

1. 12. 10 When you have stapled to the first socket position, cut the cable so there is enough to reach to the socket and 3 or 4 inches beyond. Cut off the sheathing to a point about $\frac{1}{2}$-inch inside the socket when it will be in place. Don't cut round the cable; slice along the middle, peel back and then cut off. Look at the back of the socket and you'll see the terminals marked 'L' (live), 'N' (neutral) and 'E' (earth). Hold the socket against the partly stripped cable so the end of the sheath is $\frac{1}{2}$-inch inside the back, and bend the conductors at the point where they go into the terminals of the socket. It's from this bend that the insulation needs stripping from the conductors. Strip the live and neutral by slicing off the PVC, do not cut round, as a nick in the copper could lead to an eventual break. Sheath the earth in green sheathing.

1. 12. 11 Staple the end of the second loose cable and strip off the insulation in the same way. (If it comes from the other side, measure again how much you have to cut back). Bend both sets of conductors out and twist them together:
The live with the live;
the neutral with the neutral;
the earth with the earth.

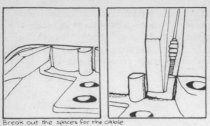
Break out the spaces for the cable

1.12.12 Break out the plastic holes in the appropriate places, loosen the terminal screws and slip the socket over the conductors. Make sure the conductors go into the correct terminal. Screw the socket to the wall (if you're rawl-plugging, mark the position of the holes and fit rawl plugs, etc.).

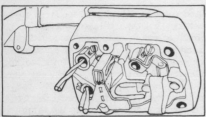
Thread the conductors into the correct holes.

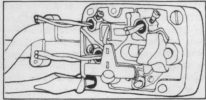
Secure the socket to the wall.

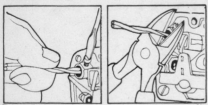
Tighten the terminal screw against the conductor & cut off the rest

1.12.13 Pull the conductor so it's taut and screw down the terminal screw tightly. Snip off the excess copper and screw on the socket cover.

1.12.14 Staple the cable to the next socket position and repeat.

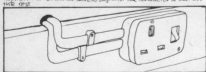
Replace the front cover.

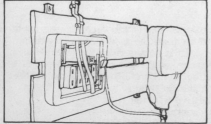
Staple both cables back to the consumer unit.

1.12.15 When you have the two cables stapled back to the C. U. cut off the rest of the cable still attached to the reel. Strip the PVC and test for continuity to see that there is no break in the conductors (see 1.14.16). Then secure the two live conductors into the 30 amp fuse terminal, the two neutrals into the neutral bar and the sheathed earths to the earth bar.

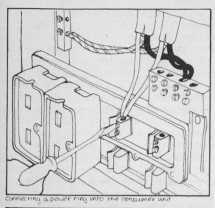

Connecting a power ring into the consumer unit

1. 12. 16 Repeat for other power rings.

Cables prepared for a spur.

1. 12. 17 Spurs -

Connect the spurs as you fit the ring
sockets. Take a third cable from the
back of the nearest socket to where you
want the spur (or from a junction box
inserted into the ring if no socket is
conveniently placed). Strip the cable in
the normal way and twist three conductors together - all the lives together, the
neutrals together, and earths together.

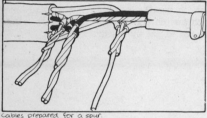

Double over conductors when a single cable is attached to a
socket

1. 12. 18 Staple the cable to the spur socket position and strip the cable. When connecting a single cable to a socket bend the
conductors over so that there is a double
thickness of conductor entering the
terminals. Secure the socket to the wall.

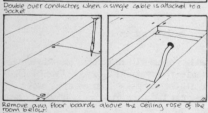

Remove any floor boards above the ceiling rose of the
room below.

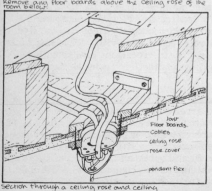

Joist
Floor boards.
Cables
ceiling rose
rose cover
pendant flex

Section through a ceiling rose and ceiling

1. 12. 19 Installing a lighting circuit -

The cable for the lighting circuit is laid
under the floor of the room above (or in
the loft). If for any reason you don't have
access to that floor, or the floor is difficult to remove, then you may have to
run cable over the surface of the walls
and ceiling. It may be difficult to nail
into ceilings as they are usually made of
soft materials - plasterboard, laths and
plaster, etc.

Secure the ceiling rose to the joist.

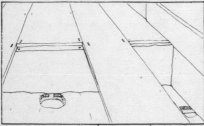

Make holes in the ceiling for the rose and switch cable

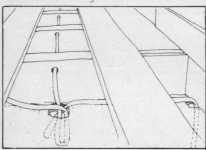

lay cables to each rose and switch position

Identify the switch cable with a nick and strip all the cables.

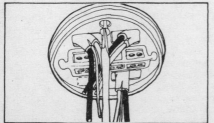

Attach rose

1. 12. 20 Prepare the route for the cable by removing floorboards and marking the position of ceiling roses and switches. If you use existing positions, you might find that the floorboards in these areas are already cut and easily taken up. Lift a small section of floorboard above each rose position and switch position. You may need to remove boards where you may be threading the cable from one room to another. The ceiling rose should be screwed to a piece of wood fastened across the joists, just above the ceiling plaster. This may still be there, or you might fix the rose close to the joist so that you can screw straight into it, but leaving enough room for the cable. Make a small hole at each rose and above each switch position in the plaster - big enough to get the cable through.

1. 12. 21 Loop-in lighting roses -

These roses will have four separate terminals or terminal blocks. One block is for all the earths. The neutral block connects the incoming and outgoing neutral and the neutral of the hanging flex. The centre live block connects the incoming and outgoing lives and the live wire going to the switch. The last block connects the returning live from the switch and the live from the hanging flex.

1. 12. 22 In the junction box system a junction box is screwed to the joist just above the switch (or a more convenient place). The incoming and outgoing cables are connected together, a live to the switch is taken down and back, and a cable running to the ceiling rose is connected to a common neutral and the switched (black) live.

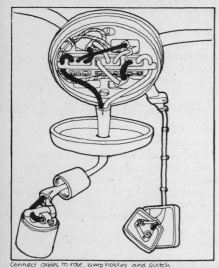

Connect cables to rose, lamp holder and switch.

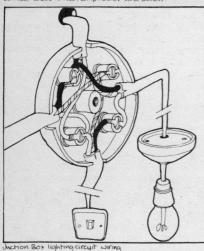

Junction Box lighting circuit wiring

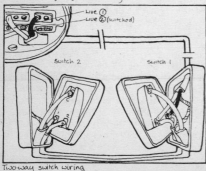

Two-way switch wiring

1. 12. 23 If the light fitting or the bulb holder has a metal frame, you must run a three-core flex to it and connect the earth to the metal frame. Otherwise the earth should be run to the ceiling roses and light switches, but a two-core flex can be used to hang the bulb holder.

1. 12. 24 Starting at the consumer unit (or switch fuse) thread the cable to each rose position, leaving a small loop sticking through the ceiling. End the cable at the last rose - don't return it to the consumer unit. Run separate lengths of cable from the ceiling rose to the light switch (make a nick in the covering to identify this). Cut and strip the cable at the ceiling rose, break out the holes to get the cable in through the back of the rose. Be careful not to confuse the cables. Secure the rose to the joist or ceiling with two screws. Strip and connect the cable to the switch and secure that to the wall. Connect the flex to the bulb holder, thread on the cover of the holder and ceiling rose and connect flex to the rose. Screw on the covers.

1. 12. 25 You can test the circuit with a bulb and battery (see 1. 14. 00) before connecting the cable into the 5 amp fuse, neutral and earth bar of the consumer unit.

1. 12. 26 Two-way switching -

Where you have a light which needs to be operated from two separate switch positions, use two-way switching.

The incoming and outgoing cables are connected into the rose normally. The outgoing live (1) and switched live (2) are run to the first switch. (1) and (2) are connected to the two bottom terminals. A three core and earth cable (or use two twin and earth) is run to switch two. Live (3) and live (4) are connected to the two terminals in each of the two switches. Live (5) is connected to the common (c) in both switches. Connect all earths together.

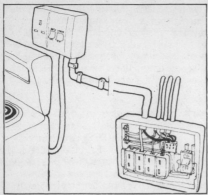

Radial circuit

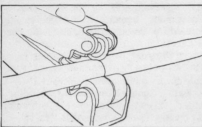

Score copper sheathing

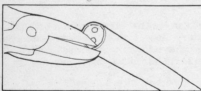

Snip the end of the sheathing...

...and peel back towards the score.

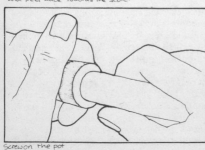

Screw on the pot

1. 12. 27 Installing other circuits -
Cooker -
Fix a switched fuse box (cooker box) by
the cooker and run the appropriate cable
from the C. U. to it (6mm for 30 amp,
10mm for 45 amp) (see table p. 32).
You can use a special flexible conduit
between the cooker and cooker box, with
asbestos covered cable inside. The
asbestos insulation doesn't deteriorate
with the heat from the cooker.

1. 12. 28 Immersion heater -
Needs a separate switched fuse box,
preferably with a neon indicator to show
when it's on. This can be a spur if the
immersion heater is less than 13 amps.
If it's more, it should have a circuit of
its own from the consumer unit.

1. 12. 29 Using MICC or Pyro -
When ordering Pyro state the length of
cable, the number of conductors (two
for most domestic purposes) and their
cross-sectional area. You also need
pots or seals for each termination of the
cable, glands for where the cable enters
any metal fuse or switch boxes, sheathing for the exposed conductors in the
boxes, sealing compound, a ringing tool
and a crimping tool.

1. 12. 30 When buying a short length of Pyro, the
ends should be sealed to prevent water
getting into the insulation (moisture
from the air is enough) unless you're
going to use the cable right away. This
can be done by fitting a pot (see
1. 12. 32) filling it with a compound
and covering them with waterproof tape.
Store in a dry airy place. If when you
come to use the cable there is the
slightest chance that the insulation has
absorbed moisture, cut back at least 6"
(150mm) before making a seal. Or the
last few feet can be heated by a blow
lamp or over a gas stove to drive out
any moisture.

1. 12. 31 Stripping Pyro -
Work out the length of conductor you
need to expose (add a few inches to be
safe) and mark the place on the sheathing. Put the cable between the two
rollers and the cutting disc of the ringing tool and tighten the cutter onto the
cable; it shouldn't be so tight as to
deform the cable. Rotate the tool round
the cable making sure the cutter keeps

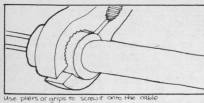

Use pliers or grips to screw it onto the cable

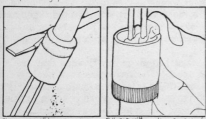

Clear away all loose insulation   Fill pot with sealing compound

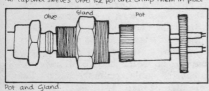

Put cap and sleeves onto the pot and crimp them in place

olive   gland   Pot

Pot and Gland.

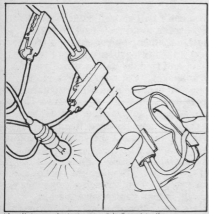

Identifying conductors using a bulb and battery.

to the same score line. Tighten the tool more, rotate again. Repeat this till a deep score is made in the sheathing. Don't cut through the sheathing but make sure it's deep enough to be easily torn away cleanly. With a pair of side cutters, nick the end of the sheathing and peel it back, tearing the sheathing in a spiral toward the score. Knock away any of the remaining insulation.

1.12.32 Fitting a seal -
File the end of the copper sheathing to a slight bevel and engage the thread of the pot (if you're using a gland with the seal this should be slipped on the cable first). Make sure it engages squarely and with a pair of pliers screw it on till the shoulder in the pot is level with the end of the sheathing. Knock out any loose insulation powder. From one side only push the compound in with your thumb till the pot is full. If you try to push the compound in from more than one side air pockets will be formed in the pot and a good seal won't be made.

1.12.33 Assemble the disc and sleeves and thread them onto the conductors and push the disc into the mouth of the pot. Place a crimping tool round the pot, engage the three points on the outside of the pot in line with the three marks on the disc. Tighten the crimping tool till the disc is secured in position. The gland can then be tightened over the pot (it uses an olive similar to that of a compression fitting used in plumbing, see 2.11.04) and secured through a knock-out hole to the switch gear.

1.12.34 Because there is no individual insulation on the conductors in Pyro they have to be identified when they are being sealed. Using a bulb and battery tester (or a megger) use the copper sheathing as one conductor and one of the conductors as the other- make a circuit, mark this conductor live at both ends - the other will be neutral.

1.12.35 Before using Pyro it should be tested for polarity and for the effectiveness of the insulation. This can only be done with a megger (if you haven't got one then ask the L. E. B. to test it).

Turn off at mains...   and remove fuses

Replace damaged fittings   Test bulb holders

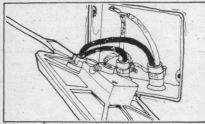

Remove socket from perished cable

Pull more cable into the back box

Strip off sheathing to fresh insulation

Strip back to fresh insulation and replace socket.

1.13.00 **REPAIRING AN EXISTING**
INSTALLATION

1.13.01 The existing circuit will need to be
brought to a standard which will pass the
L. E. B. inspection as well as being
made safe for one's own use.

1.13.02 Before doing any repairs, always make
sure the mains are off, and the fuses are
out of the consumer unit. Always switch
off before removing or replacing fuses.

1.13.03 Damage: Replace any fittings that are
damaged. The front panels of sockets
and switches often break and expose
live parts. Bulb holders become brittle
with heat and often need replacing.
Always replace with similar fitting.
Light drop flex usually needs replacing.
Mark where conductors are connected
before removing the old fitting. If you
are at all in doubt about getting them
back in the right place, see 1.12.00.

1.13.04 Insulation -
If you discovered any perished insulation
in your first inspection, you should
either renew the cable or cut back the
old. Remove the socket from its back
box (or pattress), pull the cable from
the hole as far as possible. Disconnect
the conductors (there may be one, two
or three conductors in each terminal).
Cut back the sheathing on each cable,
and strip the insulation to where it is
not perished. If it's perished under the
sheathing as well, then you'll have to
replace the cable, or more likely, the
whole circuit (see 1.12.00).

1.13.05 If you can't pull enough cable through
the pattress to strip it back to fresh
insulation, then you can attach a fresh
piece. Lift a floorboard next to the
socket and find the cables which run out
to the socket. Cut the cable, strip it
back, and connect it to a junction box
screwed to a joist. Connect a new longer
piece of cable to the same box (if the
old cable is lead covered, then use an
earth clip to connect the earth conductor
of the new cable). Run the cable to the
socket position, strip, and connect it
into the socket. Replace the socket and
floorboards. Don't attach a new piece
of cable unless you're sure the old
cable's insulation is in good condition.

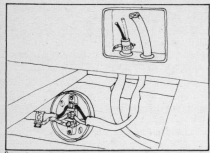

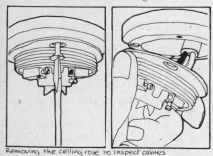

Replacing perished end of cable

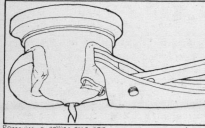

Removing a ceiling rose cap

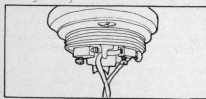

Pendant flex connections in a ceiling rose

Removing the ceiling rose to inspect cables

Light switch....

Removed to inspect cable

1. 13. 06 It's often necessary to change the pendant or drop flex on light fittings. This flex is exposed to the heat from light bulbs and quickly deteriorates.

1. 13. 07 Unscrew the ceiling rose cap. This may be difficult as they are often painted over or simply jammed with age. Try using a wrench covered with a cloth. If the cap breaks, then you'll have to replace the whole rose, as old type ceiling roses are no longer made. If the ceiling rose itself loosens and twists, then it may have to be replaced.

1. 13. 08 Inside the cap, the live and neutral conductors can be disconnected. Remove the old bulb holder (replace if broken) and connect it onto the new flex. Slip the rose cover over the flex, connect it back into the rose and screw on the rose cap.

1. 13. 09 Replacing a Ceiling Rose -
Remove the cap and loosen the two screws holding the rose to the ceiling. Pull down the rose and the connecting cables. If it is a loop-in system, there will be three cables not including the pendant flex. If it is a junction box system, there will be just one cable. Mark them if there is any doubt about getting them back into the right terminals. Strip back any perished insulation, and connect to a new ceiling rose. Screw the rose back to the ceiling and replace the pendant flex and rose cap.

1. 13. 10 It's worth checking that the lights are correctly switched. That is, that the switch is connected into the live conductor and not the neutral conductor. If the neutral has been switched, the bulb will go out when the switch is "off", but the live contact in the bulb holder will still be live and could give a shock (while changing a bulb, for instance). The conductors inside the switch should be red (although one may be black, one red, if a normal piece of cable is used for the incoming and outgoing live). Otherwise, when the circuit is on turn the light out, remove the bulb, and carefully test each of the contacts in the bulb holder with a neon mains tester.

1. 13. 11 Make sure that all the sockets are correctly fused for the size of the cable. Check the thickness of the conductor against the diagram (page 32/33) and check the size fuse needed to protect

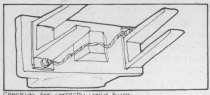
Checking for correctly wired fuses

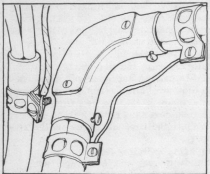
Checking for correctly earthed lead cable & split tubing

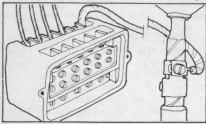
Henley box with earth connection

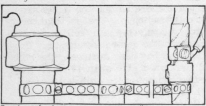
Bonding of metal service pipes to earth

Pull string through when removing old cable

that size cable. Fuse wire is often replaced with the wrong size wire. Buy a selection of fuse wire and rewire each fuse if in doubt. Make sure that there are not more sockets attached than the regulations allow (see 1. 10. 03 and 1. 10. 04).

1. 13. 12   Earthing -
One of the things the L. E. B. will check is the earthing. On old lighting circuits, there is often no earthing. Provided there are no major changes to the circuit, they will let this pass. If a new lighting circuit is installed, it should be earthed.

1. 13. 13   If lead sheathed cable is used, then the sheathing is used as an earth conductor. Use earth clips to make any earth connection. If split tube conduit has been used, the conduit acts as an earth conductor. The joints of this conduit often become 'dry', that is, no longer make a good electrical connection. Tighten the connecting screw, or clean a section of the tube and clip a conductor across each joint.

1. 13. 14   For power circuits, the earth conductor is carried in the cable as a third conductor or as lead sheathing. Uninsulated earths should be insulated in green sleeving inside each fitting. Each earth conductor is connected to an earth bar in the consumer unit (or together in a Henley box) and a $10mm^2$ or $16mm^2$ earth cable connected from this to an earth clip on the metal sheathing of the service cable (see 1. 14. 04).

1. 13. 15   Bonding -
All metal water pipes and gas pipes should be connected to the earth circuit. Usually a perforated copper strip is connected to the water pipe, to the gas pipe, and to the service cable sheath or to the main earth connection. The L. E. B. don't always insist on pipes being bonded.

1. 13. 16   Replacing Cable -
Disconnect both ends of the cable which needs replacing. If it is run under the floor or through a conduit, attach a cord to one end before removing it. Wrap the join with tape to prevent it snagging. Use the cord to pull the new cable through. If the cable is plastered into the wall, then simply chop it off as close as possible, and relay the new

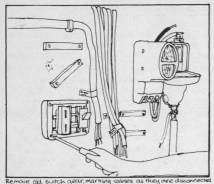

Remove old switch gear, marking cables as they are disconnected

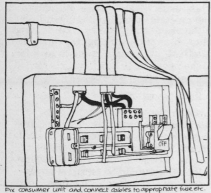

Fix consumer unit and connect cables to appropriate fuse etc.

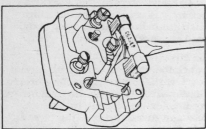

Remove plug top and 13 amp fuse.

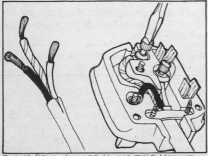

Prepare flex and connect to appropriate terminals.

cable on the surface using cable clips (see 1. 12. 05).

1. 13. 17 Distribution Board -
If the circuits and the cable are in good condition and the distribution board is a collection of switched fuses and Henley boxes, it may be worth replacing them with one consumer unit. Although this might not be strictly necessary (unless some switches are damaged), it tends to give a good impression to the L. E. B. It's probably a bit safer too.

1. 13. 18 Check the rating of each fuse and the number of circuits you need, and order a consumer unit accordingly (see 1. 11. 07). Disconnect all the old circuits marking each one with its fuse rating. Place the consumer unit in a position such that all the cables will be able to reach their connection in the unit. Prepare the box (see 1. 12. 01) and secure it to the wall. Strip each cable and connect the live conductors to the appropriate fuse terminal, all the neutrals to the common neutral bar, and the earths to the common earth bar. If there is any doubt about the circuits working, test them before finally conecting them to the consumer unit (see 1. 14. 00).

1. 13. 19 Wiring a 13 amp Plug -
Remove the cover by loosening the screw in the centre of the base of the plug. Loosen the two screws holding the cable grip, and remove the 13 amp fuse and loosen the terminal screws. Strip the sheathing off the flex (see 1. 12. 10) and cut the conductors approximately to the right length (the earth usually needs to be $\frac{1}{4}$-inch longer than the other two). Strip the insulation off the conductors (about $\frac{1}{2}$-inch) and twist the ends of each conductor so the small wires stay together. Bend over the bare part of the conductor and push it into the terminal (or they may be wrap-around terminals). Screw down the terminal screws tightly. The earth (green and yellow stripes or green) is always connected to the largest pin. The live (brown or red) is always connected to the terminal with the fuse holder. The neutral (blue or black) is always connected to the left-hand terminal. Replace the fuse, screw down the cable; clamp and replace the cover.

1.14.00 CHECKING CIRCUITS

1. 14. 01 It's essential to check circuits before you use them even for a temporary supply (see 1. 09. 00). The L. E. B. are obliged, under the Electricity Act to test all major alterations or new circuits for their safety. They do this when they come to make the final connection between the meter and the C. U. (or when going from a temporary to a normal supply - see 1. 15. 00). It saves time if you test the circuits yourself, correct any faults, and then call the L. E. B. (the first visit is free). However they have test equipment that allows them to test quickly and do certain tests it's otherwise difficult to do. If the circuits seem in good condition then call them in straight away, but if you've had to do a lot of work on them then do the tests first. The main faults to look for, and the ones the L. E. B. will check are given below (1. 14. 02 - 08).

1. 14. 02 Faults to Look For -

Short circuits -
This is usually caused by the live wire being in direct contact with the neutral or earth wire or some metal object which is earth. In most cases the flow of electricity would be enough to overload the circuit and blow the fuse. This is not always the case, though: if the electricity is using a path with a high resistance (such as along damp wood), then the fuse will not blow.

1. 14. 03 Dead circuit or fitting -
in which the whole or part of the circuit doesn't work, can be caused by a broken or loose wire. In a ring where there are two paths for the electricity, a single break may go unnoticed. This is why it's important to test rings for continuity (see 1. 14. 16). If there's a break , a single $2.5mm^2$ cable may have a load of 30 amps - enough to make it get hot and cause a fire.

1. 14. 04 The earth wire will be tested for continuity and effectiveness.
If no earthing point is provided, then it's possible to earth to a metal water pipe, providing it's metal all the way to the ground, or by driving a 6'(2m) copper pipe into the ground and connecting to that. In either case the L. E. B. will test for resistance.

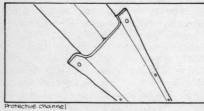

Protective channel

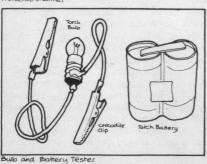

Torch Bulb

crocodile clip   Torch Battery

Bulb and Battery Tester.

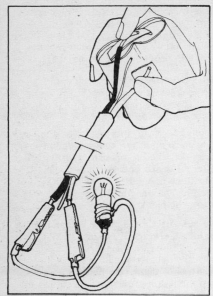

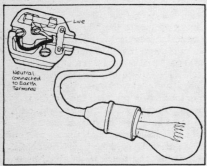

Testing for continuity in a cable with a bulb and Battery

Polarity tester

1. 14. 05 Insulation -
Apart from very obvious breaks in the insulation, where a short circuit occurs, there is also a more gradual seepage of electricity from live to neutral and earth conductors through the insulation. With new insulation this is minimal, but as it becomes older, the seepage increases. The amount of seepage can be accurately measured with a 'megger', but when the seepage is bad enough to become dangerous, the deterioration of the insulation can be seen and felt.

1. 14. 06 Polarity-
In some instances the sockets or lights could be incorrectly wired so the neutral is switched and not the live; this should be tested for and corrected (see 1. 14. 10).

1. 14. 07 Exposed conductors -
If there is any danger, however, slight, from exposed conductors or parts of a fitting which carry electricity (e. g. naked wires) this must be remedied - even if they are not causing a short or discontinuity.

1. 14. 08 Surface cables -
Surface cables are supposed to be protected from mechanical damage up to 4'6" from the floor - the L. E. B. don't seem to be very strict on this, but it's wise to protect any cables which are likely to be kicked or knocked with metal channel ('top-hat capping') or plastic capping.

1. 14. 09 A Home-Made Circuit Tester -
Most of the components can be taken from a torch, or bought separately. You need a battery (3 volt), a torch bulb and two crocodile clips (or any type of metal clips), solder (or tape) and two short pieces of wire. Solder a short piece of wire to each of the bulb contacts with a clip on the other end. With this you can place any conductor between the battery and the bulb and so test for continuity and shorts.

1. 14. 10 A Polarity Tester -
For sockets- using a normal 13 amp plug, attach a flex with the live connected to the live pin and the neutral wire to the Earth pin. Attach a 240 volt bulb and bulb-holder to the other end. If the live and neutral have been confused, or if the earth is not continuous, then the light won't work. Testing a light circuit for

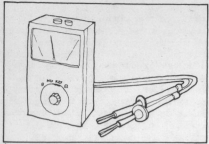

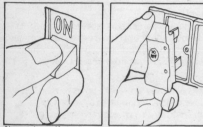

An insulation tester or megger

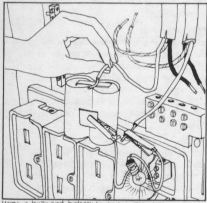

Always turn off at mains befor testing circuits

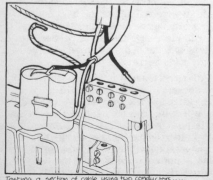

Using a bulb and battery to test a ring main

Testing a section of cable using two conductors......

polarity is more difficult. The best way is to test both terminals in the bulb-holder with a neon mains tester with the switch 'off' - if one remains live the switch is connected to the neutral.

1. 14. 11 The insulation tester or megger - The megger is a useful piece of equipment if you can borrow one, but not worth buying for a single job.

1. 14. 12 It consists of an ohm meter which can be used to measure resistance between wires designed to operate with certain potential drops between them. The test conditions are set to a very high factor of safety. The megger is operated by a battery or hand dynamo.

1. 14. 13 The megger should never be used while the mains electricity is on.

1. 14. 14 They are usually used for testing the condition of insulation but can also be used for testing for short circuits and earth resistance.

1. 14. 15 Testing Insulation - Set the meter onto the 500 volt scale and zero the needle by touching the two crocodile clips together and adjusting the needle until it registers zero. Attach the positive clip to the live and the negative clip to the neutral conductor. Press the button (or turn the handle). If the needle shows infinite resistance (or 1 megohm) then the insulation is good. If it measures less than $\frac{1}{2}$ megohm the insulation is perished, or there is a short circuit, or there is an appliance connected into the circuit. An all-out short will register as 0 (zero) resistance.

1. 14. 16 Testing a Ring Main - Using a bulb and battery tester. Turn off at the mains and remove all the fuses. Disconnect the cable of the ring you wish to test (or test before it's finally connected).

Connect one of the crocodile clips to the battery, the other to one of the two lives. Touch the other live to the other battery contact. If the bulb lights, the live is continuous. (Make sure the battery is charged and the bulb works). Test the neutral in the same way, and finally the earth.

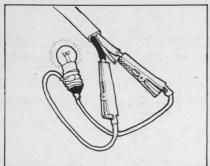

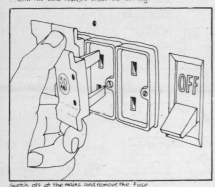

...with the bulb remote from the battery.

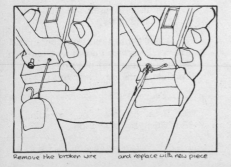

Switch off at the mains and remove the fuse

Test the fuse wire to see if it is still intact

If the bulb doesn't light, you either have a disconnection or the conductors have been confused.

With one clip on the live, put the other onto the neutral and then the earth. If the bulb lights on either the earth or the neutral, there is a short somewhere.

1. 14. 17 For testing sections of a ring or a lighting circuit, you have to use two of the conductors. Connect the battery to the live and neutral at the consumer unit and take the bulb to the end of the cable or circuit and attach the bulb to the live and neutral. Then swap one set of clips to the earth to test that for continuity.

1. 14. 18 An alternative is to attach a wanderlead to one of the conductors and test one conductor at a time. If you do find discontinuity, isolate it down to a single length of cable - i.e. eliminate by testing the possibility of a disconnected terminal in a fitting. If you're sure there is a break in a piece of cable (and that you're tester is working properly), then remove and replace with a new piece of cable - retest. It is possible for a conductor to be broken without it being apparent on the outside. If, however, there is an obviously damaged or badly kinked section, then you could cut the cable at that point and insert a junction box and retest.
(Note: all these tests are to be done on the consumer unit side of the installation; tests on the meter, head or mains cable are the responsibility of the L. E. B.)

1. 14. 19 Mending a Fuse -

Turn off the mains, remove each of the fuses and look to see if the wire running between the two brass contacts is intact. Attempt with a screwdriver or pointed object to pull the fuse wire out of the corner - it may be broken out of sight. Remove any remains of the old wire, and clear off any residue left in the porcelain. Cut off a short piece of fuse wire - make sure it's the correct rating- thread it through or round the porcelain and secure at each end with the screws.

Remove the broken wire   and replace with new piece

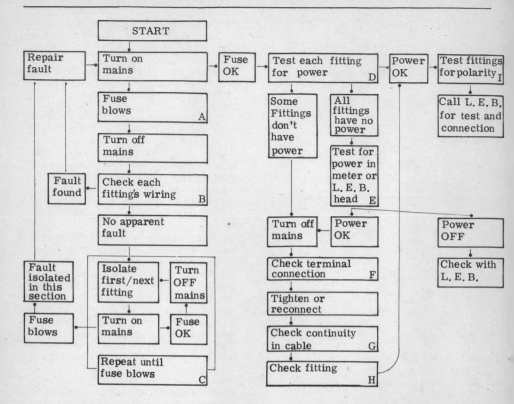

1.14.20 If you have a supply of electricity (perhaps a temporary supply) then you can test the circuits using that supply. Do the continuity tests first with a battery (see 1.14.16). Then follow flow chart above.

Make sure the circuit you are testing has no appliances plugged in (including light bulbs). Remove all fuses in the C.U. except for the one to the circuit you're testing. Check that the fuse wire or cartridge is the right amps.

A. Repair the blown fuse but do not replace till you have completed any work on the circuit.

B. When looking for a short circuit, open each of the fittings and check that the conductors are in the right terminals, that the insulation is intact where the conductors leave the terminals and that there is no possibility of bare conductors being forced to touch as the fitting is closed.

C. To test part of the circuit, disconnect the outgoing cable from the first fitting and turn on the power to that section. If the fuse doesn't blow, reconnect the outgoing cable and disconnect the outgoing cable on the second fitting; repeat till you find the section that blows the fuse.

D. Use a neon mains tester or bulb, or bulb on a plug.

E. Use a neon mains tester (see 1.11.01 and 1.05.05).

F. Check that terminal connections are well screwed down and insulation is clear from that part of the conductor inside the terminal.

G. (See 1.14.16).

H. If the cable is OK, try changing the fitting for a new one.

I. See Polarity Tester 1.14.10.

1. 15. 00 THE L. E. B. 's INSPECTION

1. 15. 01 When the L. E. B. arrive to check and
connect your meter, they expect you to
provide the tails. Enough live and neutral single core (16mm^2 PVC PVC cable)
to reach easily from the head via the
meter to your C. U. There should be
room for the meter to be mounted if it's
not already there. The earth should
already be in place. (See 1.13.12).

1. 15. 02 If they refuse to pass your installation,
or find faults in it, they'll send you a
report (ask for it to be sent to you).
These reports are fairly unhelpful,
couched in very broad electrical jargon.
They will use a megger to check the
installation, which can save you the
trouble of buying or borrowing one yourself.

1. 15. 03 Interpreting the Report –

The L. E. B. may say the following things
in their report (they call cables conductors):

1. 15. 04 "The insulation resistance is zero" –
i.e. there is a short circuit. This could
be a fault (see 1.14.02), but it could
also be due to an appliance being connected into the circuit, e. g. a light bulb
or fire, etc. , or it could be a coin meter
in another part of the house. The L. E. B.
may not bother to check that there is no
appliance connected in, or that the circuit isn't metered in another place.

1. 15. 05 "All services should be efficiently bonded to the earthing system. " 'Services'
means water and gas pipes that are
metal.

1. 15. 06 "Mechanical damage" means something's
broken.

1. 15. 07 The L. E. B. ALWAYS recommends a
complete overhaul and renewal; don't
worry – they will be satisfied if the
faults are corrected.

PLUMBING

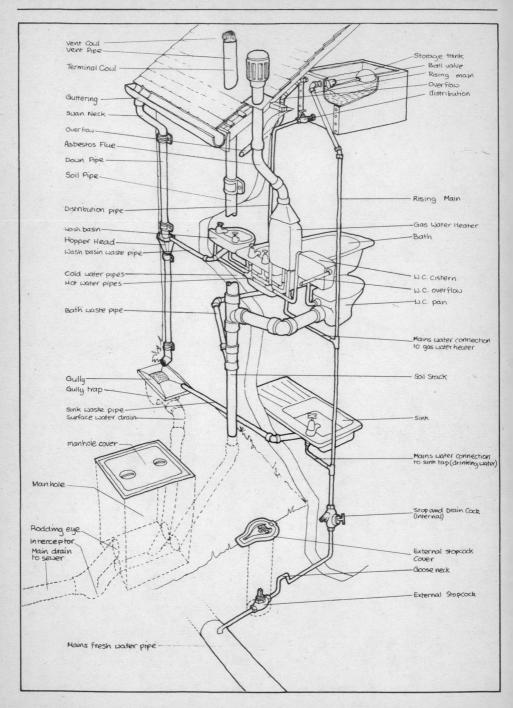

Vent Cowl
Vent Pipe
Terminal Cowl
Guttering
Swan Neck
Overflow
Asbestos Flue
Down Pipe
Soil Pipe
Distribution pipe
Wash basin
Hopper Head
Wash basin waste pipe
Cold water pipes
Hot water pipes
Bath waste pipe
Gully
Gully trap
Sink waste pipe
Surface water drain
manhole cover
Manhole
Rodding eye
Interceptor
Main drain to sewer
Mains fresh water pipe

Storage tank
Ball valve
Rising main
Overflow
distribution
Rising Main
Gas Water Heater
Bath
W.C. Cistern
W.C. overflow
W.C. pan
Mains water connection to gas water heater
Soil Stack
Sink
Mains water connection to sink tap (drinking water)
Stop and Drain Cock (Internal)
External stopcock Cover
Goose neck
External Stopcock

2. 01. 00 <u>INTRODUCTION</u>

2. 01. 01 A supply of fresh water is a first neces-
sity when living in a house. It's also the
most vulnerable of the services: a target
for vandals and thieves.

2. 01. 02 Plumbing has a long history, and until
recently required very skilled workmanship for its installation and maintenance.
But now, with the wide use of copper and
plastic pipes, many simple methods of
joining and bending have been introduced.
Using these methods, and some specially
developed for 'short-life' situations, it's
possible for a person with no previous
experience to install a simple but effective plumbing system.

2. 01. 03 In many ways, installing plumbing is
easier than electricity - after all, if
you make a mistake the worst that might
happen is that you get a little wet.
What's difficult, or confusing, about
plumbing is the vast range of materials
used for piping, and the methods of joining and bending them.

2. 01. 04 It would be possible to simplify the matter
by describing only the most common
or 'best' materials and methods, but
this might leave you high and dry should
you come across, or want to use, some
other material. So at the risk of making
this section look complicated, there is
a description of all the materials and
methods you're likely to come across or
use.

2. 01. 05 It's also impossible to imagine or
describe every situation that's likely to
confront you, so rather than describe
the most common situation, there is a
description of particular repairs. The
idea is that you can then string each of
these particular repairs together as
your own situation demands, using the
methods and materials most convenient
to your situation.

2.02.00 DOMESTIC PLUMBING SYSTEM

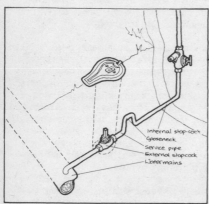

Water mains supply to a house

2.02.01 In a house there are three distinct
systems for handling water:

The mains water supply - all fresh
water for drinking, cooking, etc., can
be subdivided into cold water supply and
hot water supply.

Waste system - the disposal of 'used'
water from sinks, bath, W.C. etc.

Surface water - the disposal of rainwater, is linked with the waste system
but will be more fully explained in Part
Three.

2.02.02 Mains Water Supply -

Fresh water is supplied from a water
main running under the road or pavement, through a small service pipe running into each house. The service pipe
is buried two to three feet underground
to protect it from damage and frost. It
enters the house in the basement or
cellar. In a modern installation it then
runs up to the loft (called the rising
main) probably passing close to the
kitchen. In the loft it is connected to a
small storage tank.

2.02.03 There are usually two stop-cocks on the
service pipe. (A stop-cock is similar to a
tap, in that it is used to shut off water in a
pipe). The external stop-cock is usually
covered by a cast iron cover and at the
the bottom of a three-foot hole. It's the
responsibility of the local Water Board
and can only be operated by a special
'key' - a sort of box spanner on the end
of a long rod. The second stop-cock is
placed inside the building as near to
where the service pipe enters as is convenient. It's the responsibility of the
householder and can be hand-operated.

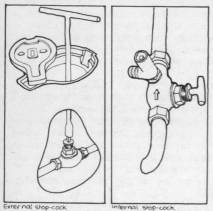

External stop-cock   Internal stop-cock

Water storage tank

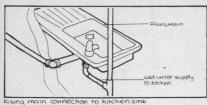

Rising main connection to kitchen sink.

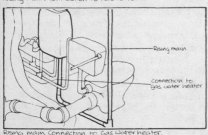

Rising main connection to Gas Water heater.

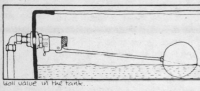

Ball valve in the tank.

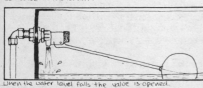

When the water level falls the valve is opened.

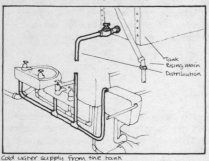

Cold water supply from the tank

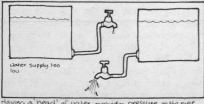

Having a 'head' of water provides pressure in the pipe

2. 02. 04 There is usually one connection to the rising main - to the cold water tap in the kitchen, which is intended to supply drinking water to the household. Occasionally there may be other connections to gas water heaters such as an 'Ascot' or 'Main'.

2. 02. 05 However it is quite common in old houses for the service pipe to be connected straight to each fitting without going through a tank. In some cases all the draw-off points are from the tank - in which case it should be kept clean and covered. The rising main empties into the storage tank (strictly speaking it's a cistern, a tank is a closed container). The level of water in the tank is kept constant by a ball valve (a tap) which is opened and closed by a lever on the end of which is a ball. The ball floats on the water - as the level of the water drops it opens the valve as it rises closes the valve.

2. 02. 06 From the bottom of the tank a pipe, the distribution pipe, leaves and runs down the house, branching at each fitting to supply water. There is a third stopcock where the distribution pipe leaves the tank; it's hand-operated and cuts off the supply from the tank.

2. 02. 07 Water in the supply system is under pressure. It's this pressure that forces the water out of the taps and carries it up to the tank. Pressure in the distribution pipes is maintained by having the supply of water in the highest part of the house. If the tank was on the level of the taps in the bathroom, there wouldn't be any pressure to push the water through the pipes and out of the taps. The higher the tank is, the more pressure; you may have noticed that taps on the ground floor have more pressure than those on the first floor.

2. 02. 08 Similarly, the pressure in the rising main, the service pipe and the water main is maintained by having a tank or reservoir on a hill or tower. The pressure in the mains again depends on the height of your house below the reservoir, although there is more and more use of electric pumps to even out these pressure variations.

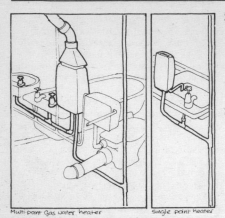

Multi-point Gas water heater   Single point heater

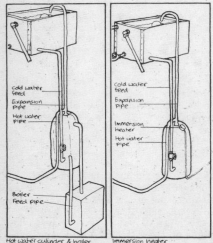

Cold water
feed
Expansion
pipe
Hot water
pipe

Cold water
feed
Expansion
pipe
Immersion
heater
Hot water
pipe

Boiler
Feed pipe

Hot water cylinder & boiler   Immersion heater

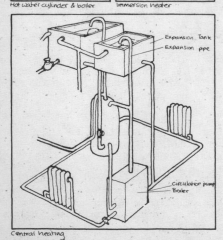

Expansion Tank
Expansion pipe

Circulation pump
Boiler

Central heating

2. 02. 09 Hot Water Systems -

Gas water heaters - these are connected either to the mains or to the distribution system, and either serve one run-off point (single point) or are connected to more than one (multi-point).

2. 02. 10 Hot water cylinder - as well as the cold water system described above, there will be a connection from the storage tank through a stop-cock to a hot water cylinder (the cylinder may be 'lagged', i.e. insulated). The hot water cylinder may be connected by two pipes (both lagged) to a boiler. The pipe from the base of the hot water cylinder goes to the boiler; the pipe from the boiler to the cylinder is connected towards the top of the cylinder. A fourth pipe from the cylinder is connected to each hot tap in the house, with a branch returning to above the cold water storage tank - this is the expansion pipe. The boiler can be oil/gas/solid fuel or built into the back of the fireplace (a 'back-boiler').

2. 02. 11 If the hot water cylinder has an electrical connection it will be electrically heated with an immersion heater and there may be a separate boiler.

2. 02. 12 If central heating is installed it will be similar to having a hot water cylinder and boiler. There will be an expansion tank in the roof space and two pipes leaving the boiler and connected to the radiators, with a circulation pump.

2. 02. 13 Waste System -

Waste pipes don't work under pressure; they are larger than supply pipes, ranging from 1-inch to 6 inches in diameter (28mm to 152mm). From the outlet of the sink, the bath and basin, the waste pipes run out through the wall and are connected into the rain-water down pipes or into the soil stack. The lavatory or W.C. always connects into the soil stack. The soil stack runs up the outside of the house. It's a thick pipe between 4 and 6 inches in diameter (102mm to 152mm) At the top it projects above

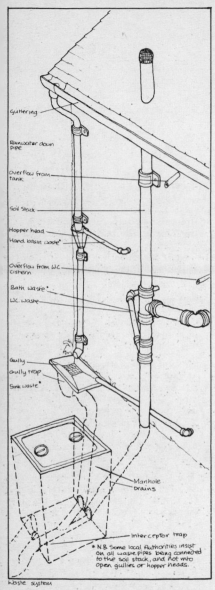

Guttering

Rainwater down pipe

Overflow from tank

Soil Stack

Hopper head

Hand basin waste*

Overflow from W.C. cistern

Bath waste*

W.C. waste

Gully

Gully trap

Sink waste*

Manhole
Drains

Interceptor trap

* N.B. Some local Authorities insist on all waste pipes being connected to the soil stack, and not into open gullies or hopper heads.

Waste system

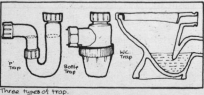

'P' Trap

Bottle Trap

W.C. Trap

Three types of trap.

the eaves, well above the highest windows, and acts as a ventilator for the drains. At the bottom it connects into an underground drain. The drain, usually made of ceramic pipes, runs to the manhole or inspection pit. Other drains connected to gullies or rain water pipes also run into the manhole. A manhole allows access to the drains for cleaning. There may be more than one manhole. The interceptor is a trap in the last manhole which prevents air and to some extent rats from gaining entry to the drains from the sewer to which it discharges.

Regulations vary - in some places waste water cannot be run into rainwater pipes only into the soil stack, while in others, into a separate soil stack.

2. 02. 14 At several points in this system there are traps or water seals. A water seal prevents smells (and rats) from the drains and sewers entering the house. There are several designs, the S-trap, P-trap, and Bottle Trap, but they all work in the same way - by trapping water in a bend in the pipe. This trapped water simply seals or blocks the pipe.

2. 02. 15 There is one under the outlet of the sink, the bath, any basin, and at the outlet of the W. C. - in fact, you can see the 'trapped' water in the W. C. bowl. There is usually one incorporated into the outlet of any open gullies and grates and one in the last manhole between it and the sewer (the interceptor).

2. 02. 16 Overflows -
As a safeguard against flooding, most fittings have an overflow pipe. Baths, sinks and basins can overflow into their own waste pipes (although in older installations they may discharge straight out through the wall). Toilet cisterns and the tank should discharge directly to the outside. This not only prevents water from spoiling the house, but acts as a warning that something is wrong. If you let an overflow run constantly, the Water Board will insist on you carrying out repairs to stop the waste of water.

2. 02. 17 Surface Water - (See Part Three.)

2.03.00 WATER BOARD REGULATIONS

2.03.01 The Water Board enforce by-laws which guard against waste and pollution of fresh water. In the main these are less complex than those for electricity and it's often a question of negotiation with the inspector.

2.03.02 New buildings are usually fitted with a storage tank although this is only strictly necessary where the installation includes a hot water system. If a gas or electric water heater of the non-storage type (e. g. Ascot or Main) is used then again no tank is required. London Water Board is an exception to this, and have the power to insist on a tank regardless of hot water system. In the case of short-life property, especially where there was previously no tank, there is every possibility of getting a waiver.

2.03.03 The main danger that arises from not having a tank is that of polluted W. C. cistern water being syphoned back into the main water supply. For this reason it's important to make sure that the ball valve is well above the water level in the cistern. If a silencer is used then the anti-syphon hole should be well above the water line. Taps should be in no danger of their nozzles being immersed should the sink be full.

2.03.04 Waste water (from bath, sink, etc.) is often run into the hopper heads of the rainwater pipes. This is no longer allowed, and it should be run into ground floor gully traps or into the soil pipe. Again, in short-life houses it may be possible to get a waiver on this.

2.03.05 Great care should be taken to safe-guard the purity of fresh water. The materials used for pipework and joints should conform to British standards (the text indicates if this d not apply to certain materials). Care should be taken not to get dirt or for objects into the pipes while working them.

2.03.06 All pipes should be secured to the wall and supported. Where there is a danger of frost the pipes should be lagged (to outside W. C. , roof space etc.).

2.03.07 Building Regulations
If you are doing long term alterations or conversion then all work will have to be checked by the building inspecto In the case of people obtaining Local Authority grants to help with improvements, payments are often made only after the work has been passed by the inspector.

2.03.08 These requirements are often more detailed or elaborate than those described in the manual. The requirements vary from area to area and are subject to local conditions and to negotiations with the building inspector, so it is advisable to refer queries to them. Before starting any work you will have to submit plans for planning approval and make any alterations required before they are passed. It's wise to keep a close relationship with the inspectors. They can be helpful and give good advice, and they like to feel they are helping to improve the standard of housing, not just putting objections in your way.

2. 04. 00 INSPECTING AN EXISTING PLUMBING
SYSTEM

2. 04. 01 For short-term housing its extremely im
portant to find out the condition of the
plumbing when first seeing a house. De--
pending on your resources and the life of
the house, its condition will be the most
significant factor in deciding if the house
is usable.

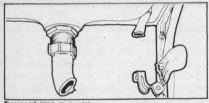

Damaged lead pipe work

2. 04. 02 It's usually painfully obvious when a
house has been vandalised. Old houses
were plumbed in lead pipe, and lead is
now a valuable metal getting a high price
at scrap dealers. (This is also true for
copper pipe used in more modern installations). When a house is vandalised for
the lead, the fittings are usually left intact, but when a house is made unusable
by the council or private owner, the sanitary fittings are the first things to be
smashed. One method is to pour cement
down the W. C. bowl. This blocks the
toilet and may block the soil stack or
even the drains. (Occasionally the council puts sand into the W. C. bowl; this is
to prevent rats from coming up out of the
sewers when the water-seals dry - it's
easily removed.)

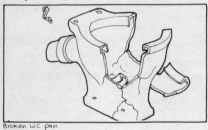

Broken W.C. pan

W.C. pan blocked with cement

2. 04. 03 Once lead pipe is damaged, it takes a lot
of skill to repair it. If you don't have
this skill, join copper to the remains of
the lead (see 2. 10. 05) and go on from
there with copper or some other material.
If there's a lot of lead left, but it's
damaged in several places, then it may
be worth selling the lead to help finance
new cheaper piping.

Damaged pipe work

Find and inspect the tank

Try the kitchen tap

Test the ball valve if the tank is full

Turn on the distribution

The tank may be full

Turn on the Internal stop cock

It may be in the garden

or under front door mat

The external stop-cock is usually in the pavement

2. 04. 04 Turning on the water -

If there is no obvious damage, go carefully through the house, examining the water pipes and waste pipes. Identify the rising main and trace it to the tank and to where it enters the house. Look for damage to pipes, signs of leaks (e.g. staining or rotten wood). As you go round, make sure all the taps are turned off. Examine the tank. It will probably be dry and may eventually need cleaning out. Turn off the distribution stop-cock - clockwise for off.

2. 04. 05 If the tank is full then all the distribution taps should work. If they don't, try turning on the distribution stop-cock. Check if the rising main is working by pushing the ball valve down.

2. 04. 06 When you are familiar with the layout of the plumbing and if it looks intact, try the cold tap in the kitchen. If it works, the tank and the rest of the system should work. If it doesn't, find the main internal stop-cock. It should be a few inches from where the service pipe enters the building, under the front steps, under the front doormat, or out at the back of the house. Occasionally, it may be in the garden under a stone and very rarely there may not be one.

2. 04. 07 Turn it on and try the kitchen tap again. If there is still no water then it's probably turned off in the road at the external stop-cock. To get this turned on you should ask the local Water Board, who should come within 24 hours of being asked. Occasionally there are two external stop-cocks, one outside the boundary and one inside. A key is needed for both, but the inside (your responsibility) can be operated by hammering flat the end of a $\frac{1}{2}$" steel pipe till it fits the shaft of the stop-cock.

2. 04. 08 It's worth finding the cover to the external stop-cock, which is usually in the pavement opposite the house, in line with where the service pipe enters. If there is fresh digging in this area, or you can't find the external stop-cock, or even when it's turned on (as well as the other stop-cock and taps) you still don't get water, then the service pipe may have been cut.

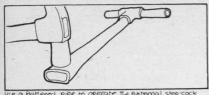
Use a flattened pipe to operate the external stop-cock

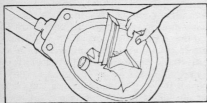
Remove debris from the W.C. pan.

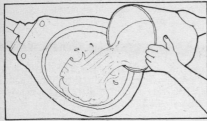
check the pan to see that it clears

Inspection pit or manhole

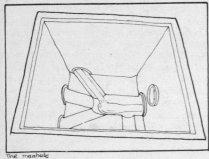
The manhole

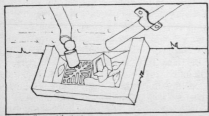
Clear gullies and drains

This is unusual, but if it has been, the Board should have records and you can ask them to reconnect it. Make sure they know it's a reconnection and not relaying a new pipe as a reconnection is cheaper (still £15 to £60).

2. 04. 09 Once you've got the water on, it's important to check the drains. This is critical because blocked drains can become very costly. In old houses, the drains sometimes collapse and replacing them is difficult.

2. 04. 10 Clear the lavatory pan of any debris that has collected there - don't try to flush it clear: you'll only block up the soil stack. If the cistern is working, flush it several times, or if not, use water from a bucket. If more water remains in the pan than is normal, then there's a block just behind the trap. If it runs away fairly quickly, there may still be a block further on, in the stack or in the drain.

2. 04. 11 Find the manhole or inspection pit. It is usually in the front garden, possibly in the back garden or yard, in an out-house, in the pavement or even in the cellar or basement. It's covered by an iron cover about $1\frac{1}{2}$ by $2\frac{1}{2}$ feet (500mm x 750mm). Under the cover is a hole, 3 or more feet (1m) deep. At the bottom several drains will converge.

2. 04. 12 While someone watches the drains in the manhole, send water down the W. C. If there is a sudden rush of water through the manhole, the drain is unblocked; if there is only a trickle or no water, then it's blocked. Test the other drains entering the manhole in the same way (any outside gullies or grates), but always clear away any debris first.

2. 04. 13 If the manhole is full or begins to fill with water, then the drain to the sewer is blocked.

2. 04. 14 Sometimes the drains appear to work, emptying quickly, but after several weeks of working, they begin to block, or the basement begins to flood. Even a collapsed drain may work for weeks. It may be easy to unblock the drain (see 2. 06. 17) but, by testing as early as possible, you may save yourself a lot of trouble.

2. 05. 00 <u>DECIDING ON A HOUSE</u>

2. 05. 01 The quicker a house is used once it's
been emptied, the more likely you are to
find the services intact. If you've been
able to get into a house easily, then it's
quite likely the local wise boys have too.
If you find a house or get one from the
council that's in good nick, don't leave it
for any length of time while you get it
together to move in. Just one night may
be too long. If you have to leave it,
board it up.

2. 05. 02 Don't think if you've got a house from the
council it's safe. There have been many
cases where, while one part of the council is happily making an agreement with
you, the other part is still busily render-
ing houses uninhabitable!

2. 05. 03 If there is a lot of damage to the plumbing or if it's very inadequate (and after
all, many of the houses are empty because of lack of basic facilities) then
you have to consider if there is time to
do the necessary repairs and alterations
and if you can afford it.

2. 05. 04 It's not possible to say here how much a
repair will cost. But on the whole, the
cost of materials is small in comparison
to the cost of labour. Most fittings can
be got for a few pounds second-hand, or
sometimes free if you are prepared to
take them away. The life of the house
is important and the longer you expect
to stay, the more time you can spend on
doing it up. And considering that you
won't be paying normal rents, the more
you should be able to spend.

2. 05. 05 As a rough guide, a year is usually
enough on a house to make the installation of a complete system reasonable in
both time and money. About the only
difficulty is if you suddenly find you have
a collapsed drain - unfortunately, there's
no easy way of knowing - but it's still
quite rare.

2. 06. 00 MINOR REPAIRS

2. 06. 01 If you're lucky, you may only have to do some minor repairs.

2. 06. 02 Minor repairs are those which don't require any major change to the existing system, though you may need to refer to materials and methods described in the rest of Part 2.

2. 06. 03 General cleaning -
Although it's often an unpleasant job, it's important to clear all debris out of the system. Remove (don't try to wash away) debris from sinks, baths, basins and the W.C. bowl. Find the outside gullies or open grates and clear them, make sure the iron grill is in place, or if not, replace it. Clear out the manhole and make sure it's kept covered (sometimes the iron cover is taken for scrap). Before filling the tank, clean out any rust or dirt. If it's particularly rusty then paint the inside with bitumen paint (such as Aquaseal or Synthaprufe). The tank should be covered with a wooden cover. Clean rust and other debris out of the W.C. cistern.

2. 06. 04 Leaking pipes -
Identify the type of material the pipe is made of as follows (also see 2. 10. 00 to 2. 13. 00):

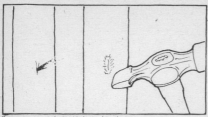

Repairing a pinhole leak in lead pipe

Replace damaged section with copper

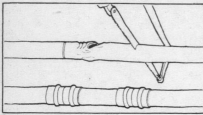

Repairing damaged copper pipe

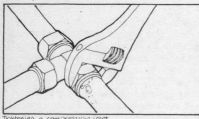

Tightening a compression joint

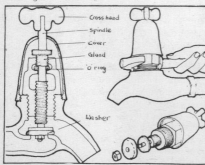

Replacing a tap washer

2. 06. 05 Lead - If it's a very small leak, a drip or a fine spray, you may be able to cure this by carefully tapping the lead around the leak till the hole closes. With more major leaks you can cut out the section of lead and replace it with a piece of copper pipe, taft jointed to the lead at each end (see 2. 10. 05). This is one case where it may be best to call in a plumber to do the repair. (Watch him and see how he does it).

2. 06. 06 Copper - cut out the damaged section and replace it with a new piece of copper, make a compression or capillary joint at each end (see 2. 11. 00).

2. 06. 07 Any other pipe - remove damaged section and replace with a new pipe, using appropriate joints (see 2. 12. 00 to 2. 15. 07).

2. 06. 08 Leaking joints -
Identify the joint (see 2. 16. 00) and tighten or remove and replace. If it's a lead joint, it may be wise to call in a plumber or replace the pipe (see 'taft joints' - 2. 10. 05).

2. 06. 09 Always look for what's causing the leaks. If it's water freezing in the pipe (frost usually splits the pipe longways in lead, or forces the joints apart in copper), then insulate the pipes with lagging (felt strips or a proprietary product).

2. 06. 10 It may be physical damage caused by a door banging into the pipe, or as a result of repairs or changes you've made to the house. Lead pipe may start to leak simply because its old. Or with long unsupported runs its own weight may start a leak.

2. 06. 11 Leaking taps -
Taps leak when the washer in them becomes worn. Turn off the mains, unscrew the chrome cover. Take out the tap mechanism, using a spanner, and remove the worn washer. Use the old washer to make sure you get the right size washer when buying a new one, or ask for a washer for a sink tap ($\frac{1}{2}$-inch) or a bath tap ($\frac{3}{4}$ inch), hot or cold (they differ in that the hot is a fibre washer, and can be used as cold, but the cold is a rubber washer and perishes if used for hot). Replace the new washer, reassemble the tap, and test. You don't need to

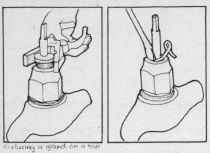

Replacing a gland on a tap

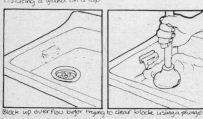

Block up overflow before trying to clear block using a plunger

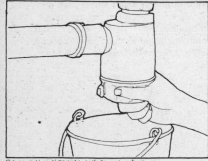

Remove the cleaning nut from the trap

Try using a curtain wire.....or removing other cleaning nuts

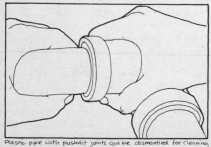

Plastic pipe with pushfit joints can be dismantled for cleaning

turn off the water to replace a 'Supatap' washer, and the washer itself is different from ordinary tap washers.

2. 06. 12 If water leaks around the shaft of the tap then the gland needs tightening or the packing inside needs replacing with an 'O' ring or with hemp or even string. One twist of string is enough, and don't over-tighten the gland.

2. 06. 13 Blocked waste pipe - If water is slow to leave the sink, or remains, then the waste pipe may be blocked. Clear any debris from the outlet grill and block up the overflow with a rag, and with the sink full of water cover the outlet with a rubber plunger. Push the plunger up and down several times and remove it. Repeat until the water runs away.

2. 06. 14 If it still persists, then remove the cleaning nut or cap from the trap under the outlet - have a bucket ready to catch the water. Clean out with a bottle brush or piece of curtain wire. If the block is in some other part of the waste pipe, look for other cleaning eyes. Remove these, take care not to twist the pipe (if lead) while doing this, and poke a long wire, or cane, down the pipe. If it's a particularly bad block, you may need to use a 'metal snake' which is pushed down the pipe while twisting it with a handle.

2. 06. 15 There are drain cleaning fluids (caustic soda) but they are only effective when the block is from vegetable matter and when the drain is free enough to let the fluid get to the block. If your waste has a tendency to block frequently you can use caustic soda regularly to prevent a build-up.

2. 06. 16 If the waste pipes are plastic using push fit joints (see 2.13. 21) then you can disconnect them at any joint and clean out any block.

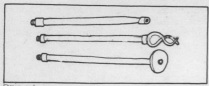

Drain rods

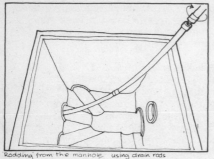

Rodding from the manhole using drain rods

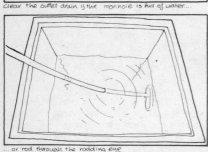

Clear the outlet drain if the manhole is full of water...

2.06.17 Blocked drains -
If water is collecting in the open gullies
or round the manhole or if there's a
permanent bad smell then the drains
may be blocked. Clear out the open
gullies. Remove the cover from the
manhole - there may be more than one
manhole. If it is empty of water then
identify the blocked pipes by sending
water down each of the gullies and the
soil stack. Using drain rods, rod up the
blocked drain. Join the rods together as
they are pushed into the pipe. Always
twist the rods in the same direction as
you screwed them together or they may
become disconnected and that will really
block the drain. Use the corkscrew head
to loosen the block and the rubber plunger
to clear it away. If the manhole is
full of water, then the blockage must be
in the trap or pipe between the pit and the
sewer, or between the first and second
manhole if you have more than one.
Rod back up from the dry manhole to
the blocked pit. Where there's only one
manhole, prod around in the water
till you find the outgoing trap. It's
usually in the middle of the manhole wall,
at the bottom facing the road. Having
found it, agitate it with the rubber disc on
the drain rods. You may find the trap is
full of debris - this should be removed.
If no amount of stirring makes the pit
empty, then remove the cover to the rodding eye (above the trap) and rod through
it. You may need to empty the pit by
bucket in order to find the rodding eye.
If you can't rod through to the main sewer
you may have a collapsed drain, in which
case you'll have to get in touch with the
sewer maintenance department of your
local council.

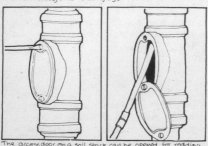

... or rod through the rodding eye

The access door on a soil stack can be opened for rodding

2.06.18 Cleaning drains can be unpleasant. You
can call someone like 'Dyno-Rod' who
have special equipment, but on the whole
they are expensive and it can take hours
to find and remove a block. You can ask
them to quote first, in which case if it's
easy they make good money, if difficult
then they have to work for it.

2.06.19 In some boroughs the engineers' department may come and clear your drains
for nothing. They do tend to be inconsis-
tent and often say it's up to you to have

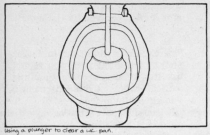

Using a plunger to clear a wc pan.

check for damaged ball   Keep valve closed while replacing ball

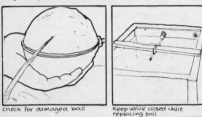

Bend arm to lower level of water in the tank

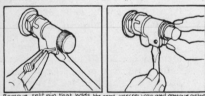

Remove split pin that holds the arm, unscrew cap and remove piston

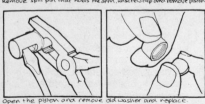

Open the piston and remove old washer and replace.

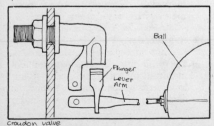

Croydon valve

the drain cleared, or want to charge you. Once the council knows you have a blocked drain they may threaten eviction because of danger to health, or insist that you get it cleared.

2. 06. 20 Blocked W.C. -
Remove as much debris as you can, then use a long plunger (or an old mop) worked rapidly up and down in the bowl. If this does not work try rodding the drains and soil stack as in 2. 06. 17 - 18.

2. 06. 21 Servicing a ball valve -
If there is a constant overflow of water from a tank or a cistern, you may find that the ball valve is not working properly. Check that the ball itself has not been holed or rusted or simply fallen off the lever arm. The lever arm can be held closed by tying it to a piece of wood resting across the top of the cistern or tank while you're out buying a new ball (they are mostly plastic now). Screw it onto the lever arm; there should be a locking nut to prevent it unscrewing itself.

2. 06. 22. If the ball is in good condition try the lever arm to check that it shuts off the water, if so bend the arm so that the ball sits lower in the water. If the leak still persists it may be that a low pressure valve has been connected to a (high pressure) mains supply.

2. 06. 23 There are two old types of valve, the Portsmouth and the Croydon - they both work on a moving piston.

2. 06. 24 Turn off the mains and remove the split pin which holds the lever arm. For the Portsmouth, unscrew the cap from the end of the valve and push out the piston using a screwdriver. Remove the rubber washer and replace it with a new one. Reassemble and clean off any rust or calcium from the piston and valve. Coat the piston with Vaseline. Replace the piston (keep it clean from grit or dirt) and restore the supply of water. The Croydon valve carries the piston on the lever arm, but otherwise can be replaced in the same way.

2. 06. 25 A more recent plastic ball valve - the BRS valve - is now widely used and is the best one to buy when replacing the older type.

2. 07. 00 CHOOSING MATERIALS

2. 07. 01 Should you need to make major repairs or alterations, then you will first need to choose the most suitable methods and materials and to design and plan what you intend to do.

2. 07. 02 It's important that you choose the best material and method to suit your particular purpose and situation. Where it's felt there is a particular method or material that is better than all others, that will be recommended.

2. 07. 03 In any case, no matter what material you choose to work in, at some point it will have to be joined to any of the other materials. In some cases where two materials cannot be joined satisfactorily, a third intermediate material will have to be used.

2. 07. 04 There are seven factors which should be considered when choosing a material.   The factors for each material are described; they are also laid out in a chart in which each factor is given a value so some relative comparison can be made between any materials.

The seven factors:

2. 07. 05 Use -
All materials have a physical limit, and it goes without saying that materials should only be used for the job for which they were intended. e . g. only pipes and joints designed to withstand pressure can be used for cold and hot water systems; only materials that can withstand heat can be used for hot water, etc. (There are exceptions which will be pointed out).

2. 07. 06 Cost -
Some materials are extremely costly and should only be used where nothing else will do - or where you have a cheap or free supply. Always buy as cheaply as you can, providing the material meets up to the standards required by its use.

2. 07. 07 Life -
The expected life of the material should match the time you want to use it. Most materials should be well in excess of this (although if you reuse them it may shorten their life considerably). But always make sure that it will last as long as you need it. Hose, for instance, is very short-lived (see 2. 14. 00).

2. 07. 08 Recoverability -
In short-life housing it's worth remembering that you can recover material and reuse it in another house. So, those materials that are easily demountable, or, especially in the case of pipes, are flexible enough to be rebent, are an advantage.

2. 07. 09 Ease of use -
Where there is a choice, always use the method or material that is easiest to use. In some cases the material is so difficult to use that even had it other advantages, it can be used except by an experienced person (e. g. lead). Or in some cases special tools are needed which are simply too expensive to buy or hire for one small job (e. g. thread cutters for iron pipe). Or it may simply be a case of one material being slightly easier to work with than another.

2. 07. 10 Inter-connect-ability -
Although it's possible to join most materials together in some way, it's always best to choose materials that make it as easy as possible. Copper tends to be a fairly universal material, often acting as an intermediary between other materials.

2. 07. 11 Availability -
It's not unusual - even in London - not to be able to get a particular material or joint and you may have to choose second best. Always have an alternative in mind, especially when buying joints.

Table of Relative Comparison between Materials

KEY: Good · Average · Bad

Material	Component / Joint	Recommended Uses	Possible Uses	Notes
LEAD	Pipe / Joint Weld	Possible: Soil ●, Overflows ●, Waste Water ●, Hot Water ●, Cold Water ●, Life ●		Use for minor repairs to existing system. Can cause lead poisoning in soft water areas.
COPPER	Pipe / Joint Compression / Capillary	Recommended: Soil ○	Possible: Cold Water ○; Soil ●, Overflows ●, Waste Water ●, Hot Water ●, Cold Water ●, Life ●	Use for running gas and hot water services and as intermediate between other materials.
MILD STEEL (IRON)	Pipe / Joint BSP thread	Recommended: Soil ○	Possible: Soil ●, Overflows ●, Waste Water ●, Hot Water ●, Cold Water ●, Life ●	Use for minor changes to gas plumbing unless you have thread cutting equipment.
uPVC (Pressure)	Pipe / Joint Solvent Weld		Possible: Flue Gas ○; Waste Water ●, Hot Water ●, Life ●	Use for cold water when poly is unobtainable.
POLY (Class C) Low Density	Pipe / Joint Compression / Corbyn		Possible: Flue Gas ○; Waste Water ●, Hot Water ●, Cold Water ●, Life ●	Use for cold water supply.
PVC ABS Polypropylene (waste)	Pipe / Joint Push-fit / Solvent Weld	Recommended: Overflows ○, Waste Water ○ ○, Hot Water ○	Possible: Waste Water ●, Hot Water ●, Life ●	Use push-fit joints where possible.
HOSE	Pipe / Joint Patent / Corbyn		Possible: Flue Gas ○; Hot Water ●, Life ●	Use for cold water for life of less than 6 months.
CAST IRON	Pipe / Joint Caulked		Possible: Overflows ●, Waste Water ●	Repairs only.
ASBESTOS	Pipe / Joint	Recommended: Gas Flue ○	Possible: Flue Gas ●	Gas flues.

Category columns: Recommended Uses (Gas Flue, Soil, Overflows, Waste Water, Hot Water, Cold Water); Possible Uses (Flue Gas, Soil, Overflows, Waste Water, Hot Water, Cold Water); Life; Availability; Recoverability; Ease of Use; Cost.

2. 08. 00 PIPES

2. 08. 01 Pipes come in several bore sizes
(internal diameter). The size,
together with the pressure of water,
and the smoothness of the bore, are
directly related to the amount of
water the pipe delivers. The external measure of the pipe does not
necessarily relate to its bore size,
differing materials have different
wall thickness to give them similar
strengths (or performance).

2. 08. 02 For domestic plumbing you need only
worry about some of the sizes:

Hot and cold water supply -
$\frac{1}{2}$" (15mm)
$\frac{3}{4}$" (22mm)
1" (28mm)

Gas pipes -
$\frac{1}{4}$" $\frac{3}{8}$"
$\frac{1}{2}$" $\frac{3}{4}$"

Waste pipes -
$1\frac{1}{4}$" (35mm)
$1\frac{1}{2}$" (42mm)

W. C. pipes and soil stacks -
3" (80mm)
4" (110mm)
6" (160mm)

2. 08. 03 Pipes usually come in 3 or 6 metre
lengths (10 or 20 feet), though you
can usually buy it by the metre for
a small cutting charge from builders'
merchants.

2. 08. 04 Metrication -

U. K. pipe sizes, like other building
materials, have gone or are going
over to metric sizes. Unfortunatel
it is not yet clear exactly what size
are going to be used in the future.
We have, in this handbook, given
metric sizes where we know them,
and made guesses when future con-
versions are uncertain.
In the Autumn of 1973:
Copper pipe has already been
converted and is only available in
metric sizes.

Old Imperial (nominal bore sizes)	New Metric (outside diamete sizes)
3/8"	12mm
$\frac{1}{2}$"	15mm
$\frac{3}{4}$"	22mm*
1"	28mm

Iron pipe (Mild Steel) will remain
exactly the same size (continental
pipe is already the same size). Th
names of the sizes will change to
"mm" although people will probabl
continue to talk of "half-inch" etc.

Old Imperial (nominal bore sizes)	New Metric (nominal bore sizes)
$\frac{1}{4}$"	8mm
3/8"	10mm
$\frac{1}{2}$"	15mm
$\frac{3}{4}$"	20mm
1"	25mm

Plastic pipe - no decision has been
made about sizes after metrication
which means that no change is like-
ly for some time. $1\frac{1}{4}$" and $1\frac{1}{2}$" are
likely to be substantially different
when metric. At the moment there
is no "standard" at all for these
pipes which vary therefore from
make to make.

NOTE: Pipes of similar bore but o
different materials, doing a simila
job, may be called by different
names after metrication, e. g. , 1"
pipe is 28mm (copper) or 25mm
(iron).

*(conversion pieces needed between
$\frac{3}{4}$" and 22mm. The conversion is
only approximate)

2.09.00 JOINING PIPES

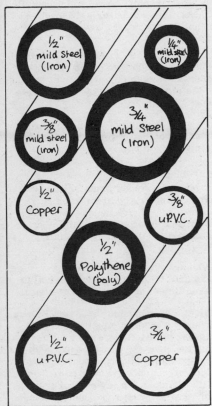

Approximate sizes of pipes

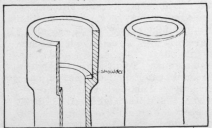

The socket or female end and spigot or male end.

2.09.01 Being able to make a leak-proof joint
between two pipes is the crux of plumbing. For this there are numerous
types and configurations of joints but
they all work by one of nine principles.
As well as having a range of functions
(e.g. elbow, tee, etc.), there is also
a range of connectors which combine
two of the principles of joining (and so
allow unlike materials to be connected -
e.g. copper to iron connectors, etc.).

2.09.02 A socket (female) is the recess in a
joint into which pipe is inserted. A
spigot (male) is that part of the pipe
or fitting which is inserted into the
socket.

2.09.03 Types of joints:

1) Wiped joint (lead)
2) Compression joint (copper, polythene)
3) Capillary joint (copper)
4) Threaded joint (BSP thread, mild
steel, taps, etc.)
5) Union coupling (BSP thread, taps,etc.)
6) Solvent weld joint (PVC or ABS plastic)
7) Corbyn joint (polythene)
8) Push-fit joint (PVC or Polypropylene
plastic)
9) Caulked joint (Asbestos, Ceramic,
Cast iron, etc.)

Making a taft joint... Cut a square end and bell out with a tampin

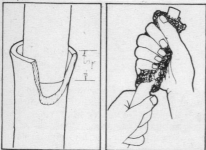

Check the fit between the copper and lead.   Clean copper with wire wool

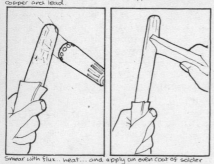

Smear with flux.. heat... and apply an even coat of solder

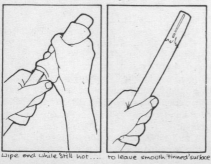

Wipe end while still hot....   to leave smooth 'tinned' surface

2.10.00 LEAD

2.10.01 Lead is a soft heavy metal, dull grey in appearance, but bright when freshly cut or scraped. It's easily worked with a hammer and will take a lot of flexing before it breaks. It doesn't easily corrode and lasts a long time.

2.10.02 It has been widely used in all aspects of plumbing - service pipes, cold and hot water supply, waste and even soil stacks. It's no longer used much except in repairing already existing pipe.

2.10.03 Lead needs a lot of skill to be used well; joints are made with brass or copper inserts, "sweated" ("wiped") or welded to the pipe, or simply by welding the pipes directly together.

2.10.04 It's very expensive - even for repairs. Lead is not easily repaired, but is still fairly easy to buy.

2.10.05 Taft joint ("sweated" joint) -
In general, welded joints should be avoided unless you are skilled at such work. There is one joint, however, that may be unavoidable - lead to copper. Fortunately it is fairly easy to do.

2.10.06 In most houses the service pipe will be lead and to join any other material to it you'll need to first join it to copper.

2.10.07 Select a short length (5" - 10"; 150mm - 250mm) of copper pipe that has a similar bore to that of the lead pipe. Cut a square end on the copper and on the lead (keep lead shavings out of the lead pipe). Clean off any burr on the copper. With a tampin, or any conical shaped object (a skipping rope handle, chisel handle, etc.) open the lead end by carefully hammering the tampin into the opening. It may be easier to do this if you bend the lead upwards - bend it carefully over three or four feet in a gentle curve. Support the lead while hammering. Test fit the copper tube, it should enter the lead where it has been opened but be too big to enter where it's at its original size. (If the copper is too small you can open one end of that, also using a tampin).

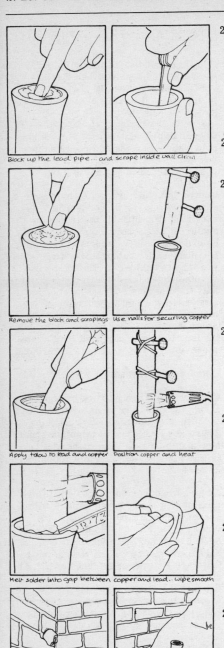

Block up the lead pipe... and scrape inside wall clean

Remove the block and scrapings Use nails for securing copper

Apply tallow to lead and copper Position copper and heat

Melt solder into gap between copper and lead.. wipe smooth

If lead is in difficult position... make joint from outside.

2. 10. 08 Clean about 4" (100mm) of the end of copper with wire wool and apply flux. Heat the copper and rub a bar of solder (known here as plumber's metal) along the heated pipe till there's a good coating all round. Keep it hot and with a wiping-cloth (or fluff-free leather or several folds of brown paper) wipe off excessive solder in one clean stroke.

2. 10. 09 Inspect and repeat if there isn't a smooth even film covering the last two inches of copper. (This is called 'tinning').

2. 10. 10 Clean the inside of the opened out lead - use a file, or scrape with a knife. Keep scrapings out of the pipe. Hammer a large nail into the wall, making sure no debris falls on the cleaned lead, and tie the lead pipe to it. Position the tinned copper in the mouth of the lead and hammer two more nails into the wall so that the copper can be tied to the nails and be held in line with the lead. Apply tallow (flux for lead) to the lead and copper and position the copper pipe.

2. 10. 11 Heat the lead and copper. Don't heat the lead too much for it will just melt away. Keep the heat on the copper and start melting solder into the mouth of the lead, slowly build up a ring of solder, pushing it in with the bar of solder and wiping cloth - leave to cool.

2. 10. 12 Release the nails and carefully bend the lead back into place. (Don't put any force onto the copper.) And secure them to the wall. Put an end stop or stop-cock on the copper and turn on at the mains if you want to test the joint. If it leaks saw off the bad joint and start again. Remember - any dirt or water will ruin your joint.

2. 10. 13 You will often find that the lead has been cut off flush with the wall - vandals are mean that way! You may have to dig a hole in the wall to get at the work, or even take the pipe out the other side of the wall, make your joint, and push it back through.

2. 10. 14 You may also have to do your joint horizontally or upside down. This is a more skilled operation as you can't rely on gravity to help you. You might consider getting an experienced plumber to do this for you, or practicing on some unwanted pipe before you start making a mess of the pipe you will need.

Compression joint

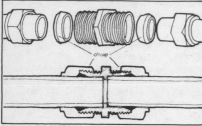
Compression joint (non manipulative)

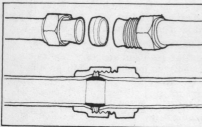
Compression joint (manipulative, not recommended)

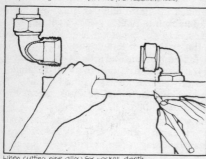
When cutting pipe allow for socket depth.

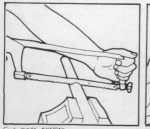
Cut pipes square

Clean off burr

2.11.00 <u>COPPER</u>

2.11.01 Copper is reddish-brown in colour,
having a bright lustre when clean. It's
very durable and easily worked (e. g.
malleable). It doesn't easily corrode
and has a long life.

2.11.02 Copper is now widely used for hot and
cold water services and to a lesser
extent for gas plumbing. It's
occasionally used for waste pipe.

2.11.03 Copper is easily available, but fairly
expensive - it can be recovered although
once bent it's difficult to straighten
again. It's probably too expensive to
be used for cold water systems in short-
life houses. If you have over five years
you might consider it. However, it's
recommended for hot water pipes and for
any gas pipework. Short lengths are
often needed as intermediaries or for
making corbyn joints (see 2. 13. 17).
Short lengths of copper waste pipe can
be used to repair damaged lead waste
pipes using a taft joint (see 2. 10. 05).

2.11.04 Compression fittings -

Compression fittings work by squeezing
a ring (or olive) between the fitting and
the pipe to ensure a leak-proof joint.
There are two types: manipulative and
non-manipulative. The manipulative
type needs special tools and should be
avoided.

2.11.05 Copper to copper compression fittings
consist of a heavy brass casting with a
socket for each pipe connection. A
copper olive (or ring) is held in the
socket by a nut. The inner edge of the
socket, the inner face of the nut and
olive are chamfered so that they fit into
each other. The long shallow chamfer
fits into the socket; the steeper chamfer
fits into the nut. When the nut is tightened the olive is squeezed between the
socket and nut onto the pipe.

2.11.06 Fitting a compression joint -
The pipe is cut to length - allow for the
depth it goes into the socket. The end
should be square and any roughness removed with a file. Dismantle the fitting,

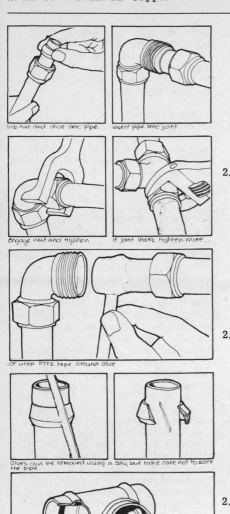

Slip nut and olive onto pipe.

Insert pipe into joint

engage nut and tighten

If joint leaks tighten more....

...or wrap P.T.F.E. tape around olive

Olives can be removed using a saw, but take care not to score the pipe

Capillary joint

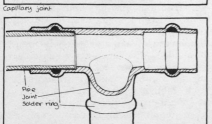

Pipe
Joint
Solder ring

Section through a capillary joint

slip the nut and olive onto the pipe -
make sure they are the correct way
round. Push the pipe up to the shoulder
of the socket, push the olive into place
and engage the nut. Tighten to finger
tightness. Fit pipes to other sockets
on the same fitting before tightening
with a spanner (a second spanner may
be needed to prevent the fitting from
turning). Do not over tighten; three or
four revolutions are enough.

2. 11. 07 If the joint leaks, give a few more turns
with the spanner. If the leak persists,
turn off mains and drain pipes, dismantle the fitting and check that the
olive is the correct way round and that
the pipe goes right into the end of the
socket. If the leak still persists, try a
little PTFE tape wound round the olive
or remove it and replace with a new
olive or complete new fitting. There
should be no need to use tape or Boss
White on the thread of a compression
fitting.

2. 11. 08 Fittings are easily disconnected by undoing the nut. Once the nut has been
tightened, the olive becomes crimped
into the pipe. It may become necessary
to remove the olive without damaging
the pipe. It can be sawn off using a
hack-saw, but extreme care must be
taken not to make a groove in the pipe
as this will cause the joint to leak when
reassembled with a new olive. You can
simply saw the end of the pipe off, but
only when it doesn't matter that the
pipe is shortened.

2. 11. 09 There are several makes of compression fittings· Prestex, Conex,
Kontite, Kuterlite, Jevco, etc. The olives
are interchangeable, but the nuts are not,
so try to stick to one make. The olives
can be bought separately.

2. 11. 10 Capillary joints -

Capillary joints use capillary action to
fill the small gap between socket and
spigot with molten solder.

2. 11. 11 They are light copper fittings with a
socket for each pipe connection. Inside
the socket there is enough solder held
in a groove to ensure a good joint.

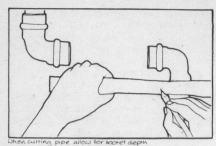
When cutting pipe allow for socket depth

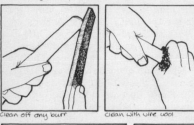
Clean off any burr   Clean with wire wool

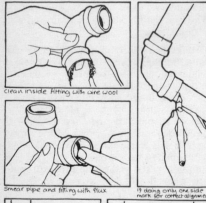
Clean inside fitting with wire wool

Smear pipe and fitting with flux   If doing only one side
                                        mark for correct alignment

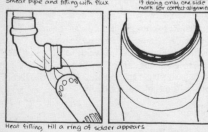
Heat fitting till a ring of solder appears

Insert length of copper and wrap with wet cloth to leave empty
socket

There are some capillary fittings in which the solder is added from the outside, but they are more difficult to use and are not recommended. Capillary fittings are relatively cheap but cannot easily be re-used.

2. 11. 12   Fitting a capillary joint -
Cut the pipe with allowance for the depth of its fit into the socket; cut it square and clean off any burr. Clean about 2" (50mm) of the end of the pipe and the inside of the socket with wire wool or fine sandpaper (don't use emery paper). Make sure the pipe will go right up to the shoulder inside the socket.
Test the fit between the socket and pipe. (If you're joining in only one pipe, then align the fitting so it will be correctly positioned and scratch across the socket to the pipe). Remove the fitting and coat the inside of the socket and the outside of the pipe end with flux, refit them, remove any excess flux and re-align. Heat the joint with a blow lamp, play the flame as evenly around the joint as you can. When the solder appears around the mouth of the fitting, heat for a few seconds longer and then let cool. Be careful not to underheat - it's almost impossible to overheat.

2. 11. 13   It's best to prepare and fit all the pipes entering the fitting at the same time. They can all be heated together. It ensures correct alignment of the fitting and that solder in an unused socket doesn't melt and run out into the pipe. If you have to leave a socket empty while heating the others, then insert a short length of uncleaned, unfluxed copper into the empty socket, and wrap a damp cloth around the socket.

2. 11. 14   When making a capillary joint (or any soldered joint) the pipe must be free of water. Even a slight drop of water will prevent the solder reaching the right temperature, and a proper joint won't be made. Slow drips can be held back (e.g. if the stop-cock doesn't fully cut off the water) by pushing bread into the pipe (Mother's Pride works a treat). It should give you enough time to do a good joint. The bread can then be blown out by turning on the water when the pipes are reassembled.

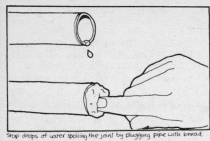

Stop drops of water spoiling the joint by plugging pipe with bread.

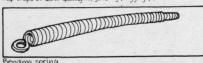

Bending spring

Inserting a bending spring

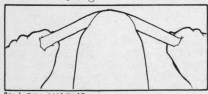

Bend pipe over knee

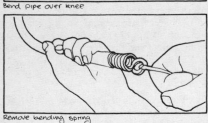

Remove bending spring

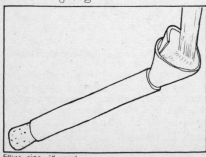

filling pipe with sand

2.11.15 Capillary joints are cheap and easy to use. They are almost 100% successful if you clean and flux well, make sure the pipe is inserted right up to the shoulder of the socket and heat well. A ring of solder around the mouth of the socket is a guarantee of a good joint.

2.11.16 The idea of using a blow lamp might put you off, but they are no harder to use than a camping gas fire (see 2.18.01).

2.11.17 Bending copper -
If copper is bent without precaution, the walls will flatten and constrict the flow of water. This flattening can be prevented by using a bending spring, by filling the tube with sand, or by buying a special annealed copper which is soft enough to make large radius bends by hand.

2.11.18 a) A bending spring is a heavy metal spiral which can be inserted into the pipe and prevents it distorting or collapsing when bent. They are fairly cheap and easy to use. You need one for each size pipe that you want to bend. Mark on the pipe the approximate centre of the bend to be made, insert the spring so it extends well past the centre on each side. It is possible to bend 15mm and 22mm copper pipe using your knee, but this is not recommended as it can injure the kneecap. Alternatively drill a hole in the end of a stout piece of wood, slip the pipe through the hole and bend it using the wood as a lever. If it's to be a sharp bend (90° or more) do it in two or three stages moving the pipe slightly each time. Bend slightly more than required then bend back, and the spring will come out more easily.

2.11.19 A strong cord should be attached to the spring for pulling it through the pipe. If the pipe is buckled in any way, the spring will not fit.

2.11.20 b) The pipe is plugged or sealed at one end (a wooden or cork plug) and filled with fine dry sand, packed fairly tight. Plug the other end and bend in the same way as for springs.
Release the plugs and clear out all the sand.

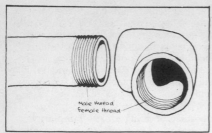

BSP threaded joint

Male thread
Female thread

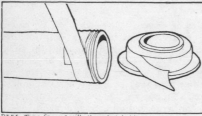

P.T.F.E. Tape for use with threaded joints

BOSS WHITE

Boss White, sometimes used with horse hair on threaded joints

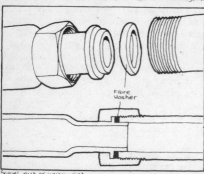

Fibre
Washer

Swivel nut or union joint

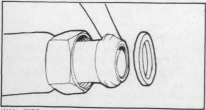

Using PTFE tape to repair a swivel joint

2.12.00 MILD STEEL PIPE (IRON OR GAS BARREL)

2.12.01 Cold blue grey, hard, heavy metal which has a ring when struck. It's not easily worked; it corrodes in certain circumstances but generally has a long life.

2.12.02 Mild steel is used mainly for gas plumbing but if galvanised can be used for water or (using large diameter pipe) for waste pipes. It's fairly difficult to use, needing thread-cutting tools to make the threaded joints it needs. It has to be bent with a bending machine (although it can be bent in a cast iron street drain grid, with care) and requires exact fitting. There are pre-threaded pipes available but these don't allow enough flexibility for more than minor repairs.

2.12.03 It's easily available, fairly expensive and can be easily recovered but cannot be unbent. It can be joined to most materials.

2.12.04 'British Standard Pipe' threaded joints · BSP threads are used for joining iron pipe (mild steel) and for most joints to fittings such as taps, ball valves, etc. The pipes or spigots have a male thread and the sockets a female thread. Just screwing a male thread into a female thread does not give a leak-proof fit, a seal is needed. This is usually provided by Boss White, a soft putty-like mixture. The Boss White is smeared into the threads of the male iron, the two screwed together, and the excess removed. Plumber's hemp is sometimes wound round the threads in combination with Boss White. PTFE tape, although more expensive, is much easier and cleaner to use.

2.12.05 Where there is a plastic male or female BSP thread, use PTFE tape. You shouldn't use Boss White on any plastic threads. Wrap the PTFE tape around the male iron (in a clockwise direction, i.e. the same direction in which the fitting is turned) two or three turns is enough. When tightening plastic threads be careful not to over tighten - this will only deform the plastic and won't make a good joint - finger tightness is really enough although a quarter of a turn with a spanner may be necessary for mains pressure.

2.12.06 There is another type of joint that uses BSP threads, the swivel (or union) nut.

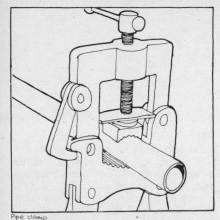

Pipe clamp

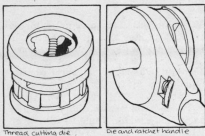

Thread cutting die

Die and ratchet handle

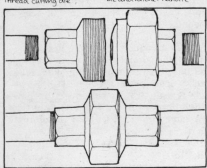

Union coupling

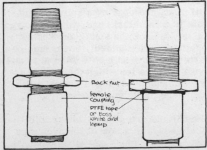

Back nut

Female coupling

PTFE tape or boss white and hemp

long thread connector

This is a loose captive nut with a flange onto which fits a fibre washer. It's this washer that seals the joint when the swivel nut is tightened against a male iron end. There should be no need for Boss White or tape, but if this joint leaks, a twist of PFTE tape round the washer seating, with the washer on top, may help. Swivel nut connectors are sometimes called tap connectors or spigot and washer joints.

2. 12. 07 For cutting threads on mild steel pipe you need a good vice and a set of thread-cutting "dies". The dies come in various sizes, but the ones in most common use would be BSP $\frac{3}{4}$", $\frac{1}{2}$" and 3/8". They cut a tapered thread which gives a good water-tight joint. The dies are fitted into a ratchet handle which gives the leverage necessary to cut the metal. Cut the pipe square and clean off any burr. Allow for the length of the thread at each end. Secure the pipe in the vice and put the appropriate size die in the handle. Slip the die's guide over the pipe and engage the cutters. Be careful to get the die cutting squarely with the pipe. If it goes on at even a slight angle, it may jam and you will have to start on a fresh pipe. A little cutting oil helps to keep the dies cutting smoothly and making a quarter of a turn back helps to clear cut metal and keeps the die from jamming.

2. 12. 08 One problem you meet in using iron pipe is when bridging between two fixed ends. If you simply screwed in one end of the pipe and then the other, the first end would unscrew! Therefore, use a union connector which consists of two sections. These are screwed onto each pipe and a large nut is tightened to pull the two halves together. It has the advantage of being easily disconnected. A cheaper method is to use a long-thread connector. This is a connector with a long-threaded piece on one end which has a back-nut and female coupling on it. The short-thread end is screwed in first and then the female coupling is screwed out over the other piece of pipe. Then the back-nut is tightened against the coupling with PTFE tape or hemp and Boss White between the back-nut and the coupling.

2.13.00 PLASTIC

2.13.01 There is a range of different plastics used for piping - each one having different properties and therefore different uses. Plastic has a moderately long life, no corrosion, but is more susceptible to physical damage. Most plastics are affected by heat.

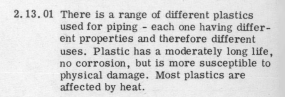

Solvent weld joint

2.13.02 PVC - Unplasticised polyvinyl chloride (uP. V. C.) Class E (e. g. Polyorc) - is used for cold water plumbing, although it isn't widely accepted by the trade. It shouldn't be used for hot water or gas plumbing.

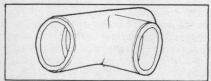

2.13.03 PVC uses a solvent weld joint which is easy to use and the slight flexibility of the pipe allows it to be fitted together more easily. It can be bent but care is needed.

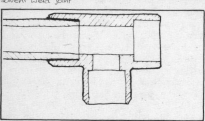

Section of a solvent weld joint

2.13.04 PVC is not widely available but it's cheap, though not easily recovered. It can be joined to most other materials except lead (see 2. 16. 00). Don't confuse it with PVC or poly overflow pipes which have a thin wall and will not take pressure. (See 3. 10. 07 for suppliers.)

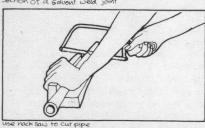

Use hack saw to cut pipe

2.13.05 Solvent joints (PVC, ABS) Plastic to Plastic -
Joints between PVC for cold water systems and for some overflow, waste and soil pipes are done by a solvent weld. This is a chemical bond, using a solvent ('glue') to bond the spigot and socket together. Once joined, they cannot be parted. You should only attempt to weld those plastics for which the solvent is recommended - it doesn't work with Polythene or Polypropylene.

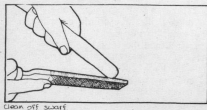

Clean off swarf

2.13.06 The fittings are simple, cheap injection mouldings with a socket for each pipe connection. (Pipes can also be bought

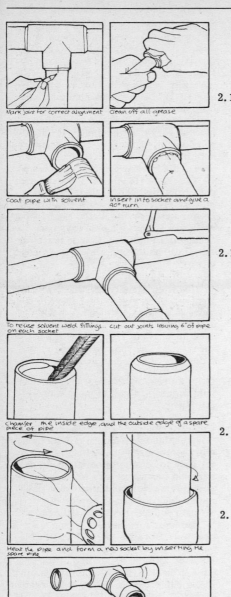

Mark joint for correct alignment

Clean off all grease

Coat pipe with solvent

Insert into socket and give a 90° turn

To re-use solvent weld fittings... cut out joints leaving 6" of pipe on each socket

Chamfer the inside edge, and the outside edge of a spare piece of pipe

Heat the pipe and form a new socket by inserting the spare pipe

Reform sockets on each arm.

Bending uPVC pipe

with a socket end). Methods of making solvent welds vary slightly between manufacturers, so it's always worth consulting their instructions which you can get when you buy the pipe.

2. 13. 07 This is a typical solvent weld:
Cut the pipe square, clean off burr and fit into socket to check alignment. Mark the position, clean the socket and spigot ends with cleaning fluid. Coat both surfaces with a liberal coat of solvent and fit together immediately. Give fitting a 90° turn to ensure even covering of solvent and remove excess solvent squeezed out of the joint. Leave three to four minutes before handling - 12 hours before applying working pressure.

2. 13. 08 If you want to re-use salvaged pipe you can reform socket connections. When removing fittings leave 6" (150mm) of pipe in each socket. Chamfer the inner edge of each of these pipes and the outer edge of a spare piece of the same diameter pipe. Carefully heat the pipe that's attached to the fitting - using a slow gentle heat - insert the chamfered end of the spare pipe into the heated pipe till a socket $\frac{3}{4}$" (20mm) deep is formed - cool with a damp cloth and remove the spare pipe leaving a re-formed socket end.

2. 13. 09 Solvent joints are cheap and fairly easy to do, but require care as a leak is difficult to repair, and will most likely require the whole joint to be replaced with anything up to a 12 hour wait before the joint can be used at full pressure.

2. 13. 10 Bending PVC cold water pipe -
Changes in direction are best dealt with by using elbows, but if these are not appropriate, i. e. where a slight bend is required, then it's possible to bend PVC pipe by using heat.

2. 13. 11 Heat the pipe on a slow flame. A stroking action avoids charring the pipe. For slight bends plugging both ends keeps the pipe from deforming, for tighter bends fill with fine dry sand before heating. Once bent keep in position till cold, which can be hurried by applying a damp cloth.

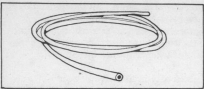

Polythene pipe

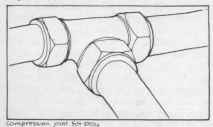

Compression joint for poly

Compression joint showing liner

liner   olive

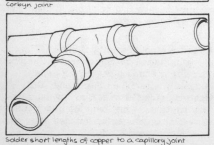

Corbyn joint

Poly

olive

Jubilee clip

Copper Capillary Joint

Solder short lengths of copper to a capillary joint

2.13.12 Polythene (or Poly BS 1972 - class 'C' or possibly 'D', e.g. Alkathene or Telcon) - is mainly used for farm and industrial water supply but can easily take normal cold water pressure. It's normally joined with a brass compression fitting but a cheaper method has been developed especially for short-life situations. Poly's not to be used for hot water or gas plumbing. It's flexible and so easily fitted and recoverable and not affected by water freezing in the pipe. It's not easy to find supplies of poly (see 3.10.06) but it's extremely cheap, easily recovered and has a moderately long life. It's sometimes frowned upon by the Water Board - but so far as is known has always been accepted. Polythene is also made for overflows and waste - make sure you don't confuse them.

Note: BS 1972 is Low Density. There is also High Density (BS 3284) which is lighter, more rigid, thinner-walled and more expensive. If you are buying liners (see 2.13.14), make sure that they provide the right liners for the pipe - i.e. low density and the right class.

2.13.13 Poly is probably the best pipe to use for cold water services in most short-life situations.

2.13.14 Compression fittings for joining poly - The accepted way to join poly is by using a brass compression fitting. In order for poly to be able to stand mains pressure the walls are very thick, so $\frac{1}{2}$-inch poly (bore size) has an external diameter equal to $\frac{3}{4}$-inch copper pipe. This means you have to use $\frac{3}{4}$" fittings for $\frac{1}{2}$" diameter pipe, which becomes expensive. Because the poly is flexible and crushable, a copper liner has to be inserted into the spigot end of the pipe so that there is something for the olive in the compression fitting to be tightened against. Kuterlite 1700 series of fitting are specially made to fit poly. The liners can be bought with the fitting or separately. The liners are marked with a class letter (C or D): make sure the ones you buy are the same as the pipe you are using. You can use a stub of $\frac{1}{2}$" (15mm) copper instead of a liner for class 'C' poly.

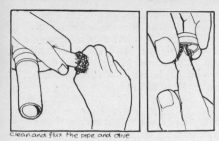

Clean and flux the pipe and olive

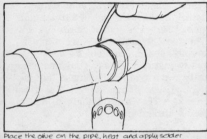

Place the olive on the pipe, heat and apply solder

Slip the jubilee clip over poly and insert copper pipe

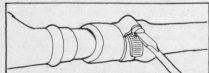

tighten the jubilee clip behind the olive

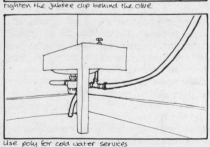

Use poly for cold water services

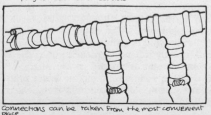

Connections can be taken from the most convenient place

2.13.15 Old $\frac{3}{4}$" compression fittings also fit poly but the new metricated size - 22mm doesn't. By changing the olive to a 'Polyring' you can use 22mm fittings with $\frac{1}{2}$" poly. Conex manufacture these 'Polyrings'.

2.13.16 The compression fittings are fitted in the same way as for copper pipe except that the liner is inserted into the pipe. Using this fitting allows easy connection to copper pipe and means most copper fittings can be used with poly. This method of joining poly tends to be expensive and somewhat reduces the advantage of the cheapness of the pipe, but makes an extremely flexible easily demountable system.

2.13.17 Corbyn joint - poly to poly, poly to copper

The corbyn joint has been specially developed as a cheap alternative to the compression fitting for use with poly in short-life situations. Fittings are made up using 15mm ($\frac{1}{2}$") capillary joints and short pieces of 15mm copper pipe. These can be manufactured over the kitchen stove if you don't have a blow lamp. A copper olive is soldered to each of the copper pipe about $1\frac{1}{2}$" (40mm) from the end.

2.13.18 Clean and flux the pipe and olive as for capillary joints. Place the olive on the pipe and heat, using grade A wire solder, touch the solder to the edge of the olive letting the solder run into the gap between the olive and pipe. Wipe any excess solder off with a wiping cloth while still molten. The shallow chamfer of the olive should be away from the spigot end of the pipe. Let it cool, slip a jubilee clip over the pipe, and push the polythene pipe over the end of the copper and well past the olive. Place the jubilee clip just behind the olive and tighten with a screwdriver. Take care not to get solder over the top of the olive, it may result in a leak.

2.13.19 This gives an effective method of joining poly to copper, and, therefore, to any material that joins easily to copper. It allows the use of 'ends' of copper and cheap capillary joints. Because of the cheapness of polythene pipe, one can afford to use longer runs than with more expensive pipe. It's better for instance to let the poly take a large bend than to

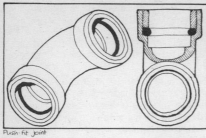

Push-fit joint

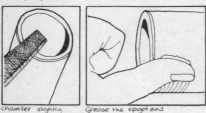

Saw pipe square

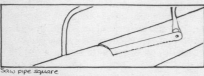

chamfer slightly   Grease the spigot end

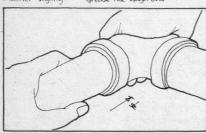

Push pipe into socket.

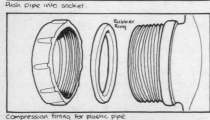

Rubber Ring

Compression fitting for plastic pipe

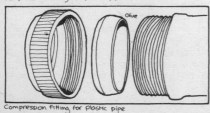

Olive

Compression fitting for plastic pipe

cut it and insert an elbow. In a key place like the bathroom a series of capillary tees can be soldered together and all the branches taken from that one spot. If you use 22mm ($\frac{3}{4}$") tees with 15mm ($\frac{1}{2}$") branches it gives slightly better flow of water.

2.13.20 ABS, PVC, Polypropylene are used for waste pipes and soil stacks. These are now widely used by the trade. There are several manufacturers, each with a slightly different range of fittings and pipes. They are joined easily by solvent or push-fit joints. They are slightly flexible but can't as such be bent - you have to insert elbows. They are cheap, easily recoverable (if you use the push-fit joint), easily available and unaffected by frost. They are difficult to join to other materials.

2.13.21 Push-fit joints - Push-fit joints are exclusively used for waste systems, overflows and expansion joints for soil pipes. A rubber ring fitted in the socket end of the fitting forms a seal when the pipe is inserted.

2.13.22 Cut the pipe square and slightly chamfer the outer edge. Lubricate the pipe end with soap or grease or just water. Push the pipe into the socket. Make sure it goes in past the ring up to the socket shoulder - withdraw it $\frac{1}{4}$" (5mm) to allow for expansion.

2.13.23 This joint is extremely easy to use, it's easily recoverable and easily available. It's slightly more expensive than solvent joints but probably worth the little extra. There is danger that the joint can be pulled apart inadvertently so make sure the pipe is well supported.

2.13.24 PVC to PVC There are two slightly different designs of compression joints. One uses a nylon olive which is used in a similar way to the copper olive. The nut is only hand tightened. The other uses a rubber 'O' ring which again is squeezed round the pipe by a hand tightened nut. These types of joint are found on the W.C. flush pipe connection and on waste pipe connections. They are relatively cheap and easy to use.

2.14.00 <u>HOSE PIPE</u>

Hose joint using brass fitting and jubilee clip

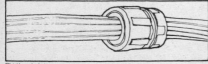
Corbyn joint

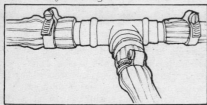
Plastic joint

2.14.01 Hose pipe is normally used for gardening and washing the car. It's flexible, fairly resilient, but has a short life (3 to 6 months) when used under constant pressure. It's fairly cheap and very easily available. Hose pipe is hard to join to other materials and fittings such as taps, etc. It's not known if the Water Board would accept it. The joints in hose plumbing usually start leaking first.

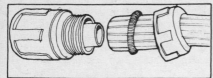
Plastic joint using a ring and screw cap

2.14.02 There are no hard and fast rules - do what you can, what you find works. You can use a corbyn joint as used for poly (2.13.17 to 2.13.19) or there are special brass connections with ridge sides for use with jubilee clips. There are patented plastic connections such as 'Gardena' but they tend to work out a bit expensive. They do have the advantage of being easy to use and available at gardening or DIY shops and even department stores.

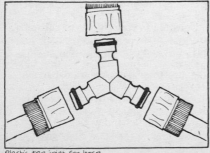
Plastic tee joint for hose

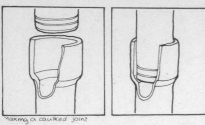

Making a caulked joint

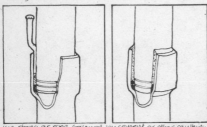

Use string or rope followed by cement or other caulking material

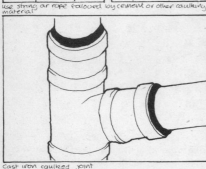

Cast iron caulked joint

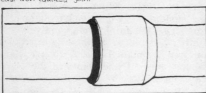

Asbestos joint

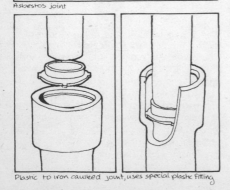

Plastic to iron caulked joint, uses special plastic fitting

2. 15. 00 CAST IRON, ASBESTOS, CERAMIC

2. 15. 01 Cast iron is a very hard, heavy metal - its used for rainwater pipes and soil stacks. It rusts easily and is therefore painted for protection. Although still available, cast iron has been largely superseded by plastic.

2. 15. 02 Asbestos is used as flues for gas water heaters and some types of central heating boilers. Its also been used for rainwater pipes.

2. 15. 03 Ceramic is used for underground drains. It is salt-glazed with spigots and sockets.

2. 15. 04 All three of these materials use caulked joints.

2. 15. 05 Caulked joints -
Caulked joints are the traditional non-pressure joints which are used to join many different types of material. Rather than being a separate joint fitting which is used with lengths of pipe, there is a socket and a spigot on each pipe.

2. 15. 06 There is usually a clearance of $\frac{1}{4}$" - $\frac{1}{2}$" (5 - 15mm) between the socket and spigot sides. This gap is filled with various materials and rammed home with a blunt chisel (caulking chisel). But any blunt instrument that fits between the socket and spigot will do. The spigot should always face towards the direction of flow in the pipes.

2. 15. 07 It's important when making a caulked joint not to let the caulking material get into the pipe as it may cause a blockage. Usually some sort of seal is rammed in first - yarn, string, rope, or even soaked brown paper - the caulking compound is then rammed down over this (cement, prompt cement, fire cement, Mastic, etc.).

2. 15. 08 a) Iron to iron (soil stack, rain-water down pipes) - yarn or rope followed by cement.
b) Ceramic to iron (W.C. to soil pipe, soil pipe to drain) - brown paper soaked until soft and cement (prompt cement).
c) Ceramic to plastic (W.C. to soil pipe, soil pipe to drain) - brown paper and prompt cement or Farocaulk.
d) Plastic to iron (soil stack to soil stack) - use method recommended by the plastic pipe manufacturers.
e) Asbestos to asbestos (flue pipe) - asbestos rope and fire cement.

2.16.00 RANGE OF JOINT FITTINGS

2.16.01 Various types of joints are made to cover a wide range of purposes.

Plastic (PVC) Female Iron Male Iron Copper (comp.) Copper (Cap)

Straight connectors (or couplings)

2.16.02 Pipe connectors or couplings: for connecting two lengths of pipe.

Copper (Capillary)   Plastic (P.V.C)   Reduction Insert replaces Olive

Iron   Copper Compression

Reduction Joints

2.16.03 Reduction joint, connector or coupling: for joining two different sizes of pipe.

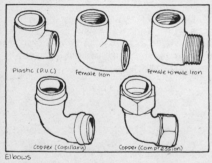

Plastic (P.V.C)   Female Iron   Female to male Iron

Copper (Capillary)   Copper (Compression)

Elbows

2.16.04 Elbow or bend: for making a 90-degree or 45-degree bend between two pipes.

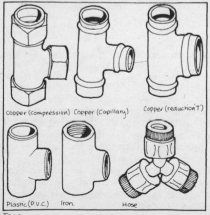

Copper (compression) Copper (Capillary)   Copper (reduction 'T')

Plastic (P.V.C.)   Iron   Hose

Tees

2.16.05 Tee, or three-way connector: for connecting three pipes together. These can have various configurations of sockets, T-shaped or corner-tee and have one or more of the sockets to take a smaller pipe (reduction tee).

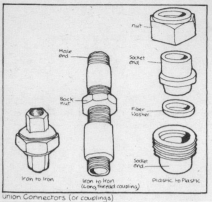

Union Connectors (or couplings)

2. 16. 06 Union connector: for making a discon-
nectable joint between two pipes (or in
the case of threaded joints, to allow a
joint between two existing pipes to be
made).

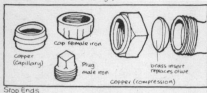

Stop Ends

2. 16. 07 Stop end or cap (female); plug (male):
for capping off an unwanted pipe.

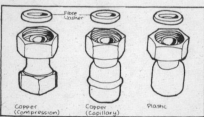

Swivel Connectors (or tap or washer connectors)

2. 16. 08 Tap or swivel connector (or washer
joint): for connecting taps or other fittings with a BSP thread so they can be
disconnected. These can be straight or
bent, or one or more branch of a tee,
or be a reduction piece.

Iron to Copper Connectors

2. 16. 09 Iron to copper connector : for connecting
a male or female iron thread to copper -
can be bent or straight or reducing.

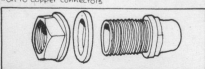

Tank connector

2. 16. 10 Tank connector: for connecting pipe to
a tank - can be straight or bent.

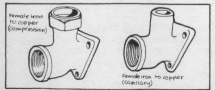

Back plate Elbows

2. 16. 11 Back plate elbow ('bib-cock wall-flange'
or 'wall plate elbow'): for connecting a
bib tap to a pipe and the wall. Bent with
a female iron thread for the tap.

2. 16. 12 If you get a catalogue of the pipe fittings
you're using it will include a description
of all the basic and special fittings that
are available.

2.17.00 PIPE FIXING

2.17.01 There are several types of fixing brackets for use with all types of walls and partitions. The spacing between each bracket varies with the material it is supporting and whether the pipe is running vertically or horizontally. Brackets should never be tightened so much that they prevent pipes moving with expansion and contractions.

2.17.02 Saddle brackets are probably the most versatile; they can be fixed to most surfaces by screws after the pipe has been fitted.

2.17.03 Plastic pipe clips have to be fitted before the pipe is in place - most plastic pipes use this type of fitting - they have the advantage or disadvantage of only having one screw hole. This is convenient for good surfaces, but difficult to get a good fixing on loose surfaces.

2.17.04 Spacing of brackets:

	Vertical	Horizontal
Copper and PVC (cold supply):	48" (1200mm)	24" (600mm)
Poly:	24" (600mm)	12" (300mm)
Polypropylene and ABC, PVC waste :	48" (1200mm)	36" (900mm)
Iron:	6'-9' (2-3m)	6' (2m)

2.17.05 Water Board regulations say that pipes should be 'adequately supported'. This means that it should be well secured to the wall, and not taking any stress from its own weight. The above distances are a rough guide to the spacing of brackets.

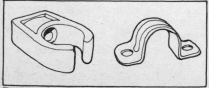

Plastic pipe clip and saddle bracket

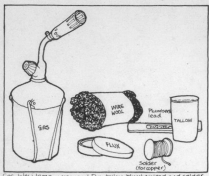

Gas blow lamp, wire wool, Flux, tallow, plumbers lead and solder

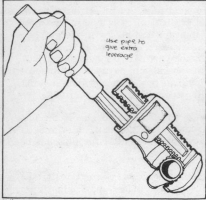

Stillson

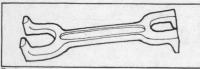

Basin wrench

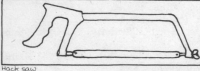

Hack saw

Metal file

Tampin

2.18.00 <u>TOOLS</u>

2.18.01 Blowlamp - The easiest and cheapest blowlamps work off butane gas canisters that are similar to those used for camping fires and lights. The blowlamp attachment can be bought separately and replacement gas containers are easily available. There are different makes, so make sure you get the correct refill. Solder can be bought as wire or bars. Flux and wire wool.

2.18.02 Stillson - is a special spanner or wrench used for iron pipe work. They come in various sizes depending on the range of pipe sizes you are working with. The jaw is adjustable and is designed to grip the smooth pipe as you exert force to turn it. It's useful if you are working with gas fittings (iron pipe).

2.18.03 Mole Grips - Unless they are hefty or you are working on small pipe they are not as good as a Stillson. They are a good general purpose tool though. The jaws are adjustable and have a vice action which clips them onto the nut or pipe.

2.18.04 Basin wrench - a tool designed to fit two sizes of BSP nuts ($\frac{1}{2}$" and $\frac{3}{4}$" are most convenient). They are very helpful for getting at nuts in tight corners, and are cheap.

2.18.05 Adjustable spanners, box spanners, etc. any kind of spanner may come in handy.

2.18.06 Hack saw - metal saw with replaceable blades, used for cutting all types of pipe (including plastic). There are pipe cutters available, which are not worth buying unless you plan to do a lot of plumbing.

2.18.07 Metal file - for smoothing the cut ends of pipes.

2.18.08 Tampin, Mandril - boxwood conical tool for opening out the mouths of lead pipe.

2.18.09 Steel rule - get one which has metric measurements on one side and feet and inches on the other.

2.18.10 Hammer, screwdriver, rawl plugging tools (see 3.07.00) - Floorboard lifting tools (see 3.05.00) - Electric drill or hand drill - Stanley knife.

2. 19. 00 PLANNING A NEW PLUMBING INSTALLATION

2. 19. 01 In planning a new installation for a short-life house, there are some points to remember. In most houses the bathroom and kitchen are next to each other, either side by side, or one on top of the other. Keeping together all those functions which require water and waste services cuts down on the materials needed. It enables the use of a single soil stack and drain, and minimises the runs of pipe, etc. If you're making changes or additions, you should keep this in mind. The position of the soil stack is particularly important.

2. 19. 02 It's cheaper and simpler to install a water system without a tank. There should be no danger of contamination if you use modern non-return stop-cocks, anti-syphon cistern valves and keep taps well above the highest possible level of water in the sink or bath. If there hasn't previously been a tank, then you should have no trouble with the Water Board (See 2. 03. 00).

2. 19. 03 It is fairly unlikely that they will inspect your plumbing unless you have had to have the supply reconnected in the road. If there is a tank already installed, then it may be worth connecting into the system as it does have advantages - or you may want to install one.

2. 19. 04 The safest rule is to put things back from where they came. This will almost always be simpler than installing an entirely new system in a different place than the old one. Keep the installation as simple as possible. Do a section at a time if you feel it may be a big job: connect up a cold tap and W. C. ; then add hot water and baths later. Don't worry about the pipes showing. Always take them directly to where you want them to go - even if it is diagonally across a wall. But do not put them in a position where they are vulnerable (where they could be walked on or banged by a door for instance).

2. 19. 05 The W. C. has to be connected to the soil stack but other waste can normally be run into ground floor gully traps.

2. 19. 06 For long-term installations consult the Local Authority district surveyor.

End of existing rising main

Make a taft joint between copper and lead

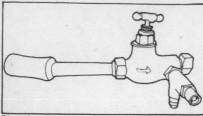

Fit combined stop and drain cock

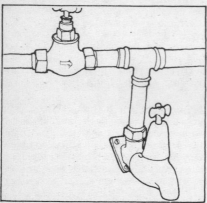

or a stop cock and bib tap.

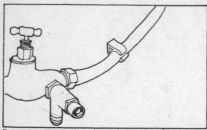

Run rest of rising main in pipe you've decided to use

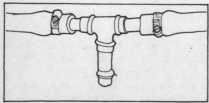

Provide tees for any connection from the main.

2. 20. 00 FITTING A RISING MAIN

2. 20. 01 For use with a tank -
You need to prepare a path (or follow one taken by the old pipe) to the tank, in such a position that a connection to the kitchen cold tap (and possibly to a gas water heater, see 2.31.00) can be easily made. It's better to keep the pipe on an inside wall to avoid freezing.

2. 20. 02 The pipe should have an internal diameter of $\frac{1}{2}$" (outside diameter of 15mm if copper) - $\frac{3}{4}$" can be used but as the water is under high pressure, the smaller bore will be sufficient.

2. 20. 03 It is almost certain that the incoming service pipe will be of lead ($\frac{1}{2}$" or $\frac{3}{4}$"). Make a taft joint between this and a length of copper pipe (see 2.10.05).

2. 20. 04 If the original internal stop-cock was removed with the lead, a new one should be fitted. It can be joined easily to copper on the incoming side, and to whatever material the rising main is being run in on the outgoing side. It's wise to fit a drain-cock; this is sometimes combined with the stop-cock, or a normal bib tap, on a branch a few inches from the stop-cock will do. The drain-cock allows the rising main to be emptied for repair and to prevent frost damage.

2. 20. 05 Stop-cocks often use an unpinned valve which can stop water flowing backwards. An arrow indicates direction of flow.

2. 20. 06 Run the pipe to the tank. Insert a tee for the pipe connection to the sink cold water tap. The connection to the ball valve in the tank is usually made with a female iron connector (BSP thread).

2. 20. 07 For use without a tank -
This is not strictly a rising main, but requires the same procedure for fitting to the incoming lead service pipe, and connection of the stop and drain cocks. The path of this pipe should be such as to enable easy short connections to be made to each fitting that requires cold water. In larger houses the facilities may be split with kitchens on one side of the house and bathrooms on the other. In a case like this it is probably best to split the pipe into two separate branches. If you want to get the water working quickly, run the pipe to essential services (cold tap and a loo) but insert the tees for all future connections. These can be capped off until needed.

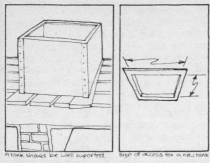

A tank should be well suported.   Size of access for a new tank

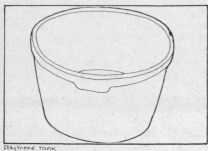

Polythene tank

Avoid uneven support for polythene tanks

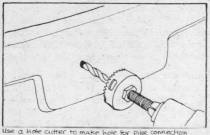

Use a hole cutter to make hole for pipe connection

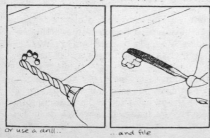

or use a drill..   .. and file

2. 21. 00 <u>FITTING A TANK</u>

2. 21. 01 The tank should be situated in the loft or well above the highest tap which it has to serve. It should be near enough to an outside wall for an overflow to be easily fitted. Water is heavy so the tank needs well supporting in the loft. It should be rested on planks running at right angles to the joists (preferably not in the centre of the joist span), or over a stud or partition wall that ends at loft height.

2. 21. 02 There are second hand galvanized tanks easily available, or a new polythene tank is quite cheap. You have to get the tank through the access hole, so measure it and the clearance in the loft before you buy a tank. Polythene tanks, being flexible, can fit through quite small holes, but they also need a flat base on which to rest. If they are not well supported, the weight of the water may crack them.

It is best to do as much work on the tank as you can before installing it into its final position. You need three holes, which can be cut by a special tool or with an electric drill by drilling around the circumference of the hole and finishing it with a file.

2. 21. 03 Its size depends on the outside size of the ball valve threads, i. e. 11/8" (28mm) for a $\frac{3}{4}$" valve, 7/8" (22mm) for a $\frac{1}{2}$" valve; $\frac{1}{2}$" is sufficient.

overflow should project 12" from the wall

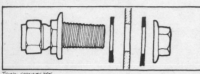

Tank connector

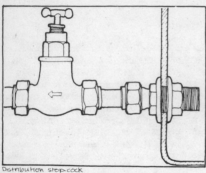

Distribution stop-cock

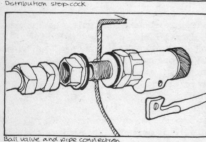

Ball valve and pipe connection

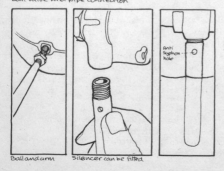

Ball and arm   Silencer can be fitted

2. 21. 04 The overflow hole should be 4"-6" (100 -150mm) from the top. The size of the overflow should be one size up from the size of the rising main. If the rising main is $\frac{1}{2}$" (15mm) then the over-flow should be $\frac{3}{4}$" (22mm). The hole for th ball valve should be as high as possible, well above the height of the overflow.

2. 21. 05 The distribution hole is 2" (50mm) from the bottom of the tank. Normally the distribution pipe is $\frac{3}{4}$" (22mm) with $\frac{1}{2}$" (15mm) connection to various fittings, except for $\frac{3}{4}$" (22mm) pipe to bath taps. This ensures a good supply of water, compensating for the reduced water pressure in the distribution system. However, if you're not too fussy, $\frac{1}{2}$" (15mm) pipe is sufficient throughout. (It means if one person is using a tap others won't work or will give a weak flow). Cut the size of hole to fit the appropriate tank connector.

2. 21. 06 Fit the two tank connectors (using Boss White or PTFE tape on the threads) and fit the ball valve. The ball valve should be a high (mains) pressure type. The arm of the ball valve attaches to the valve with a split pin, and the ball screws onto the arm. There should be a lock nut to secure the ball arm connection.

2. 21. 07 Install the tank and make the connections to the rising main, overflow and distribution. The level of the water in the tank can be adjusted by bending the ball valve arm. The level of the water should be an inch or so lower than the overflow.

2. 21. 08 A silencer can be put on the ball valve. It consists of a plastic tube which extends from the valve outlet to below the water level. A small hole in the top of the tube acts as anti syphon device, it must be above the level of the water in the tank

2. 21. 09 From the tank, through a stop-cock, the distribution pipe is run to the fittings needing a supply of cold-water, W. C., cistern, basin, bath, gas water heater, etc. The pipe can be $\frac{1}{2}$" (15mm) bore throughout. Run the pipes so connections can be easily made using a minimum of pipe. If you want to do the plumbing in stages, then insert tees where they'll be needed in the future and cap them off.

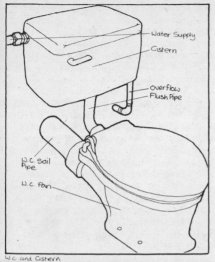

Water Supply
Cistern

Overflow
Flush Pipe

W.C. Soil Pipe

W.C. Pan

W.c. and Cistern

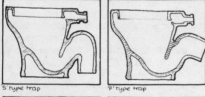

S' type trap

'P' type trap

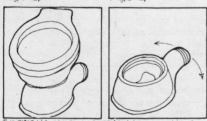

Two piece W.C. pan, can be swivelled to take a connection at any angle

Cone connector on flush pipe

Push back

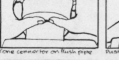
and pull, to disconnect.

Remove screw from Pan base

2.22.00 FITTING A WATER CLOSET SYSTEM

2. 22. 01 There are two designs for W.C. pans, the most common (wash down) uses the force of the flushed water to wash out the contents of the pan, cleaning it and replacing fresh water in the trap at the same time. In the other type (the syphon pan) the flushed water causes a drop in pressure behind the water seal, so sucking the contents into the soil pipe. The flushed water cleans and refills the pan.

2. 22. 02 The pans themselves vary - one-piece or two-piece with 'P' or 'S' traps. Always try and get a similar pan to the one that was installed before. If the soil pipe leaves the room straight down through the floor you'll need an 'S' type. If it leaves through the wall you need a 'P' type trap. If you have a 'P' type W.C. pan and an 'S' type soil pipe, a curved extension pipe can be used to connect them.

2. 22. 03 There are other variations with the soil pipe leaving at an angle and through a side wall or floor. This type needs a two-piece pan. The bottom piece of the pan is joined to the soil pipe in the normal way. The top part can be swivelled round to face in the right direction and then cemented to the bottom section with 'prompt' cement.

2. 22. 04 There are three common materials used for soil pipes: ceramic, cast iron and plastic. In each case, before removing an old or damaged pan, disconnect and empty the cistern and pan and disconnect the flush pipe. Push back the rubber cone and pull the flush pipe from the pan.

2. 22. 05 Plastic Soil Pipe -

Remove any screws securing the base of the pan, or break away any of the remains of the pan. The spigot end of the pan should pull straight out from the soil pipe

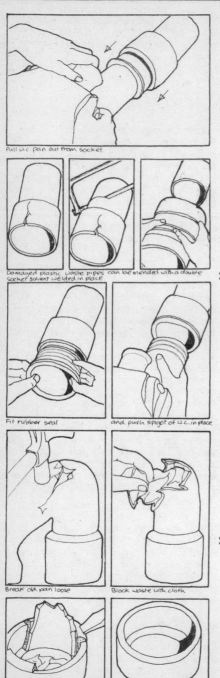

Pull W.C. pan out from socket.

Damaged plastic waste pipes can be mended with a double socket solvent welded in place

Fit rubber seal

and push spigot of W.C. in place

Break old pan loose

Block waste with cloth

and chisel away remaining ceramic.

and rubber sealing ring. Inspect the soil pipe and socket end. If they are damaged, cracked or broken you may have to remove the damaged part of the pipe and solvent weld a double socket onto the cut back pipe. If the new pan is similar to the old one you should be able to slip it straight onto the socket end. If not then pack the pan until it is the right height - the pan should put no strain on the pipe. Remove the rubber ring from the socket and place it over the spigot end of the pan, then push the spigot end and ring into the socket. There are several different types of plastic pipes, so, if you can, identify the make of the pipe (series 10, Terrain, Osma, etc.) and get hold of fitting instructions from their local dealer. Secure the pan to the floor with brass screws (they won't rust!).

2. 22. 06 Ceramic or Cast Iron -

Remove most of the old pan, being extremely careful not to damage the soil pipe. When you can, push a rag into the soil pipe to prevent bits falling into the soil stack, carefully chisel out the ceramic spigot end and cement from the soil pipe socket. Should you damage the socket (or if it is already damaged) you can buy double end sockets, which, once the damaged socket is removed, can be fixed onto the soil pipe giving a new socket for the pan. Test that the new pan fits into the socket; it should leave a $\frac{1}{4}$" to $\frac{1}{2}$" (5mm - 13mm) gap all round. Secure the pan to the floor, packing it if it does not fit. Make a caulked joint using wet brown paper followed by a quick drying cement (prompt cement). The same cement can be used for joining two-piece pans.

2. 22. 07 Alternatively you can use a patented connector called a Multikwik. These come in several designs and sizes to cope with most possible combinations of pan and pipe sizes. They fit most types of pipe and pan, using a rubber seal. A Multikwik doesn't need any cement so it's immediately ready for use and also removable on leaving a house. You need to get the correct dimensions of the pan spigot and internal diameter of the socket when buying a connector. Ask at your local builders' merchants for a leaflet.

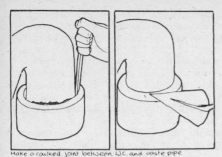

Make a caulked joint between W.C. and waste pipe

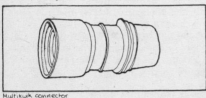

Multikwik connector

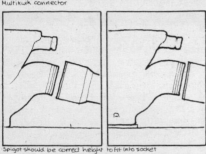

Spigot should be correct height to fit into socket

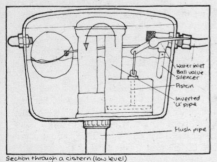

Section through a cistern (low level)

Water inlet
Ball valve
Silencer
Piston
Inverted 'U' pipe
Flush pipe

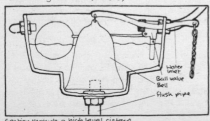

Section through a high level cistern

Water inlet
Ball valve
Bell
Flush pipe

2.22.08 The W.C. Cistern (also known as 'waste-water-preventor' or w.w.p. by some plumbers) -

The cistern supplies the water to flush out the pan. It is connected to the pan by the flush pipe and joined to a cold water supply from the tank (or direct from the mains).

2.22.09 There are two types, the high level and the low level, but they both work on the same principle. The level of water is controlled by a low pressure ball valve (if water is coming from a tank) or a high pressure one for a mains connection. In a modern cistern, the flush lever is connected to a plunger in a plastic cylinder. By operating the lever the plunger is raised in the cylinder and water is lifted over the edge of an inverted 'U' tube and flows down into the flush pipe. Once water has been pulled over the edge of the 'U' tube, the rest of the water in the cistern is sucked after it.

2.22.10 The old high level cisterns have a bell over the end of a pipe, which extends just above the water level in the cistern. When the bell is lifted by pulling the chain, and released, water is forced over the top of the pipe, sucking the rest with it.

2.22.11 High level cisterns are placed about 6' 6" (2m) from the ground and low level about 6" to 13" above the top of the pan. If you have one already installed then it will probably work quite well if it is cleaned out. But if you are installing a new one, it is probably better to use the same type as was there before.

2.22.12 You can reconnect the water supply using a female iron connector and if the overflow pipe is missing, replace it with plastic overflow.

2.22.13 Flush pipes are now plastic and come in one, two, or three pieces. Which one you need depends on the position of the pan and cistern. If it is directly above the pan, then a one or two piece will do; only use a one-piece if you can put the cistern at whatever height the flush pipe comes to - if the cistern is already fixed in place, you can cut a two piece

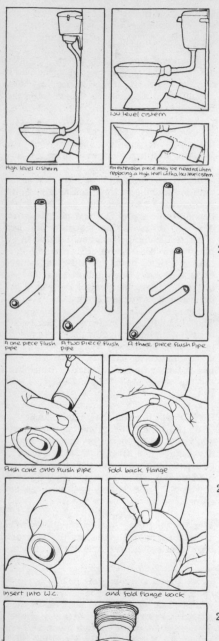

High level cistern

low level cistern

An extension piece may be needed when replacing a high level with a low level cistern

A one piece flush pipe

A two piece flush pipe

A three piece flush pipe

Push cone onto flush pipe

fold back flange

Insert into W.C.

and fold flange back

Connection to cistern uses a compression joint

pipe to fit it. If the cistern is on a side wall you will need a three piece flush pipe. Or you can make a pipe yourself from $1\frac{1}{4}$" and $1\frac{1}{2}$" plastic waste pipe if you have difficulty in getting a three piece one - just avoid having sharp bends which will impede the flow of water to the pan. The pipe connects to the cistern via a special $1\frac{1}{2}$" nut (its actual diameter is to fit the 1 7/8" - 45mm - spigot from the cistern). Although the threads are the same size as a nut for a $1\frac{1}{2}$" waste system, the hole in the nut is only big enough for a $1\frac{1}{4}$" pipe. If you are using a second-hand cistern, try and get the nut with it as it will be difficult to buy one in a shop. You may be able to get the nut from an old $1\frac{1}{2}$" waste trap to fit it with some bodging.

2. 22. 14 The connection to the W.C. pan uses a rubber cone - either $1\frac{1}{2}$" or $1\frac{1}{4}$" depending on the size of the pipe where it goes into the pan. There are two types of cone. One type is pushed onto the flush pipe and the outer cover bent back, the pipe and cone are inserted into the pan spigot and the cover pulled back over the spigot. The other type fits simply over the pipe and over the spigot (push the pipe well into the spigot). If there is little room between the back of the pan and the wall you may sometimes have to chip a little hole in the wall to give the flush pipe room to fit. Alternatively you can use a right-angle flush pipe cone which you have to seal tightly with wire, but which fits into a much smaller space.

2. 22. 15 The low level cistern is fixed to the wall using brackets and/or screwed through the back of the cistern wall. It should be placed on the wall at the back of the pan, 6 - 13" (150 - 320mm) above the top of the pan. Check that the ball valve is the right type: low pressure valves, tank feed, have a 13mm aperture; high pressure for mains have a 3mm aperture.

2. 22. 16 Fit a plastic overflow, run it to the outside through the wall, projecting about 12". The connection to the pan is the same as for the high level cistern but only a short one-piece flush pipe is needed.

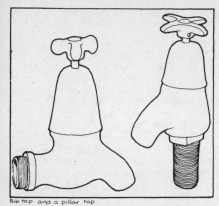
Bib tap and a pillar tap.

Back plate elbow.

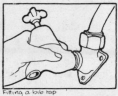
Fitting a bib tap.

Clean around hole.

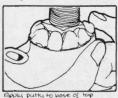
Apply putty to base of tap.

Place tap in hole.

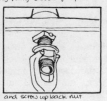
and screw up back nut.

Clean off excess putty.

Make pipe connection.

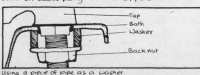
Using a piece of pipe as a washer.

2. 23. 00 FITTING A TAP

2. 23. 01 There are two main types of taps : the pillar tap and the bib tap (apart from fancy Supataps, etc.). Their sizes correspond to pipe sizes - $\frac{1}{2}$" and $\frac{3}{4}$" - but they can be fitted to either size pipe by using reducing fittings.

2. 23. 02 Bib taps are used with ceramic sinks or anywhere the tap is secured to the wall by a back plate elbow. This has a female BSP thread into which the tap is screwed, and a compression or capillary pipe connection. Three holes in the back plate enable it to be secured to the wall. You may need to convert to copper if using PVC pipe, as back plate elbows may be difficult to buy for plastic.

2. 23. 03 The pillar tap is for use with baths, basins, and pressed steel sinks. They have a long tap thread, with a back nut and a washer, which can go through the thickness of ceramic baths and basins. If you can, fit taps before the fitting is secured to the wall or moved into position.

2. 23. 04 Remove the old or damaged tap, and/or clean round the holes on the fitting. Remove all the old putty. Remove the back nut and washer from the new tap and apply putty round the shoulder of the tap. Place the tap into the hole and screw on the back nut and washer until the tap is secure. Remove excess putty. The tap thread sometimes ends $\frac{1}{2}$" (15mm) or so from the tap shoulder, so when securing it to a pressed steel sink, the nut can't be screwed up far enough. There are special washers, cap washers, which add 3/8" (10mm) to the thickness of the sink. If this is not enough, find a piece of old lead pipe (or any other pipe) which fits over the pipe thread, cut off an inch or so and use it as packing between the sink and the back nut.

2. 23. 05 Pipes are joined to taps using a tap or swivel connector. If compression joints are used, a copper to female iron coupling can be used with PTFE tape.

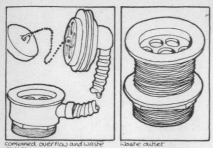

combined overflow and waste outlet.

Waste outlet.

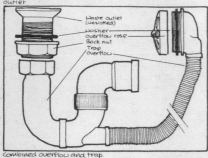

Waste outlet (unslotted)
Washer
overflow rose
Back nut
Trap
overflow

Combined overflow and trap.

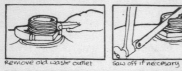

Remove old waste outlet   Saw off if necesary

clean around hole

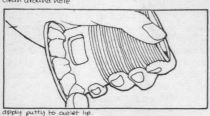

apply putty to outlet lip.

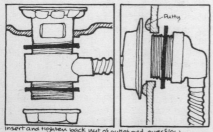

Putty

Insert and tighten back nut of outlet and overflow

2. 24. 00 FITTING A WASTE OUTLET

2. 24. 01 The waste outlet on baths requires a $1\frac{1}{2}$" or $1\frac{1}{4}$" waste pipe; on sinks, $1\frac{1}{2}$" or $1\frac{1}{4}$"; on basins $1\frac{1}{4}$" or 1". The internal measurement across the bottom (threaded end) of the outlet is about $1\,7/8$" (45mm) for $1\frac{1}{2}$" wastes, $1\,5/8$" (42mm) for $1\frac{1}{4}$" wastes, and $1\,3/8$" (35mm) for 1" wastes - not the same measurement as the pipe that will run from it. Apart from putting a new outlet into a new fitting, it is often necessary with old baths that have had lead waste and overflow, to change them into a combined outlet/overflow that can be run into plastic waste.

2. 24. 02 If your existing bath waste is plumbed-in lead and develops a leak it may be extremely difficult to repair. As a last resort, one may have to call a plumber or install a new plastic waste. The second-hand value of lead could finance new materials.

2. 24. 03 Most old baths have the overflow running straight outside, but now there are available combined outlet/overflows, and combined trap/overflows which simplify installing a bath waste. Sinks and basins have the overflow combined into the bowl and these need a slotted waste outlet.

2. 24. 04 Fitting a new outlet -

Remove the old outlet, cut it in half if the back nut is stuck, but be careful not to damage the enamel finish of the bath. Clean off the old putty. Remove the overflow rose and clean.

2. 24. 05 Dismantle the outlet overflow. Apply putty around the flange of the outlet and place it into position. Slip on the washer, the overflow collar, a second washer, and the back nut. Tighten until the outlet is secure. Place the overflow into the overflow hole and screw down the rose. Use washers if provided. If not use putty around the edge of the rose.

2. 24. 06 Before fitting an outlet, make sure it is the correct size for the trap you intend to use. Remember you cannot use a slotted waste outlet where there is not a combined overflow.

2.25.00 FITTING WASTE PIPES

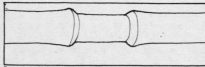

Repair lead with copper insert.

capillary joint for copper waste pipes

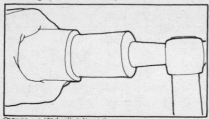

lead   copper   Push fit joint

Converting from lead to plastic

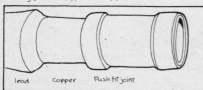

Opening up lead with a Mandril

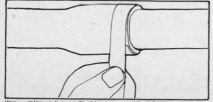

Using waterproof tape on a lead to plastic joint

2.25.01 The existing waste pipes may be run in lead, copper, or iron, or if the installation is more recent, in plastic (Polypropylene, ABS or PVC).

Some minor repairs to copper or iron can be attempted - lead is more difficult - but for major repairs, alteration or addition in these materials is made almost impossible by their expense and difficulty to work with.

2.25.02 Leaks in lead waste can be repaired by taft-jointing to copper (or calling a plumber). In copper, damaged sections can be replaced with a new piece joined by capillary fittings but this again is not recommended. Iron pipe can only be mended if you get the right length pipes already threaded, or have thread cutting tools.

2.25.03 Difficulties arise in joining plastic waste pipes to copper, lead or iron, although it can be done. There are certain makes of plastic waste pipes (Bartol or Coppertone) which have push-fit joints that are designed to fit exactly over $1\frac{1}{4}$" or $1\frac{1}{2}$" copper waste pipe. The best thing to do is cut off two or three inches of your copper waste, take it to the builders' merchants and go through the various makes to find one that fits. If you want to join plastic to lead, you can make a taft joint (see   2.10.05) with a piece of copper that you know will fit a plastic push-fit joint. If there is a good slope to the lead waste, you can try opening the mouth of the lead with a mandril (or any conical object that fits) and push the plastic pipe directly into the lead. Seal this with waterproof tape.

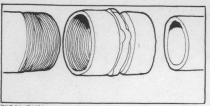

Iron to plastic

2. 25. 04 Plastics to iron

There are threaded plastic joints which fit the male threaded end of the iron pipe. You also get compression joints in plastic which use a nylon ring. Again, this might be adapted to fit over iron, copper or lead waste pipes.

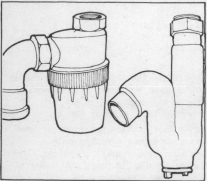

Plastic bottle trap (⅓'outlet) and copper trap

2. 25. 05 It is relatively easy and cheap to run plastic waste with push-fit (or solvent joints) so that, unless there is only a minimum of connections between plastic and other materials, it seems justified to pull out the damaged existing pipe and use plastic throughout.

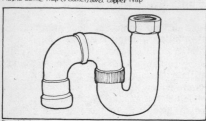

Plastic 'S' trap

2. 25. 06 Traps are available in lead, copper and plastic; lead and copper traps should only be used where there is no alternative. Plastic traps come in several designs - 'P' traps, 'S' traps, Bottle traps, traps with combined overflows, etc. They are connected to the waste outlet by a swivel nut with a fibre or rubber washer to seal the joint. Bottle traps are mainly used with sinks but it doesn't make much difference. You may need a shallow trap to fit under a bath. Alternatively you can cut a hole in the floorboards in the right place.

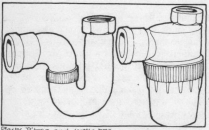

Plastic 'P' trap and bottle trap.

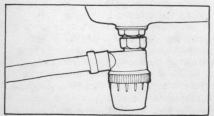

Bottle trap

2. 25. 07 If you can, re-run the waste pipe in the same place as the old; if not, then there are certain things to avoid.

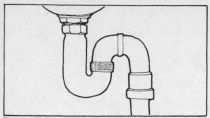

S'trap in place

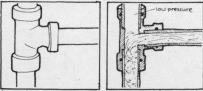

low pressure

Joining two waste pipes may cause syphoning of the water seal

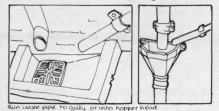

Run waste pipe to gully or into hopper head.

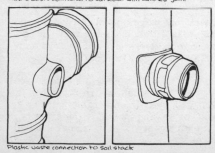

Plastic waste connected to soil stack with caulked joint

Plastic waste connection to soil stack

2. 25. 08 Once the pipe has left the trap, it should always be on the incline. If at any point it dips and traps water it is likely to collect debris and eventually block. In slow draining fittings like a bath it does not matter at what angle the waste pipe leaves the trap - it can be straight down if that is convenient. But in fittings that empty quickly like a basin or sink, if the waste pipe runs away at a steep angle the rush of emptying water plugs the pipe and syphons the water seal out of the trap. Although this may happen with the bath the last of the water runs out slowly enough to refill the trap. So with sinks and basins run the waste away at a very slight angle. The maximum length for a basin waste to avoid syphoning of the trap is 5'6".

2. 25. 09 It is also unwise to join two waste pipes together, although it can be done. If water runs rapidly down one pipe, when it passes the connection to the other fitting it may syphon the water out of the other fitting's trap. It is best always to run separate wastes for each fitting, running them out through a wall to discharge into a Hopper head, into the soil pipe, or into an open drain. Keep waste pipes as short as possible.

2. 25. 10 Connecting waste pipes into the soil stack -

Most soil stacks are made of cast iron and connecting waste pipes into them is done by means of a branch with a socket end, using a caulked joint. If there isn't a branch already in the soil pipe and this is the only way to discharge waste water it will be necessary to seek the help of a plumber.

2. 25. 11 If the soil pipe is plastic, waste pipes are run in by means of an incorporated socket end (Boss adaptor) or by fitting a Boss anywhere in the pipe (see 2. 27. 00).

2. 26. 00 INSTALLING A BATH, BASIN AND SINK

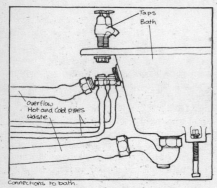

Connections to bath.

2. 26. 01 If the bath is not being put into the same position as the previous one, then position it so it's easy to run out the waste and make water connections.

2. 26. 02 The positioning will have to be considered in conjunction with the positioning of the basin and W. C. , hot water heater, or whatever else you are fitting.

2. 26. 03 Leave enough room to enable you to make pipe connections once the bath is installed. You could fit it so the business end is away from any walls. Fit the tap outlets and overflow before positioning the bath.

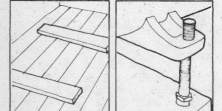

Use boards to spread the load.   Adjust feet to level bath

2. 26. 04 It is best to spread the weight of the bath by putting two planks under the bath feet (old floorboards are ideal). Level the bath allowing a slight incline for the water to run out, and make sure it does not rock by packing or adjusting the feet.

2. 26. 05 Check that there is enough room for the trap to be fitted under the bath. If not, raise it on blocks of wood or bricks or cut a hole in the floorboards.

2. 26. 06 Connect up water and waste pipes. Seal the edge of the bath where it touches the wall with putty (metal frame putty is best) or sealing mastic. The sides of the bath can be covered in, but it is not necessary.

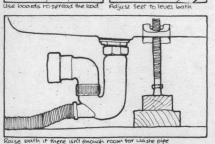

Raise bath if there isn't enough room for waste pipe

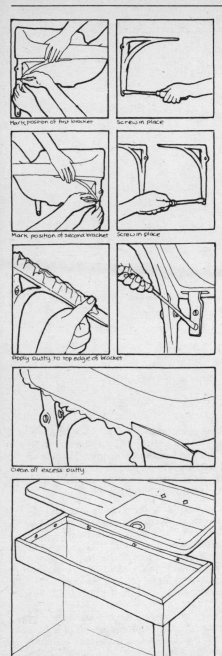

Mark position of first bracket   Screw in place

Mark position of second bracket   Screw in place

Apply putty to top edge of bracket

Clean off excess putty

Kitchen sink unit

2. 26. 07 Basins are held by brackets or stand on a pedestal. The brackets should be well secured to the wall. If there are no brackets with the basin you can buy new or second-hand ones.

2. 26. 08 Make sure they are the same height and correctly spaced. Apply putty to the brackets and place the basin on them. There may be holes in the back of the basin or slits for small brackets to hold the basin against the wall. Fit the taps and outlet before positioning the basin. Seal the gaps between the basin and wall with putty or plumbers mate.

2. 26. 09 Pedestal basins are simply rested on the pedestal, possibly with a nut to secure the two together. Again, there should be provision for fixing the basin back to the wall. Connect up taps and waste.

2. 26. 10 Pressed metal sinks need a special sink unit or a simple wooden structure on which to rest. Keep the structure simple with just one or two legs to the floor. The less you have touching the floor, the easier it is to keep the area under the sink dry and clean.

2. 27. 00 FITTING A SOIL STACK

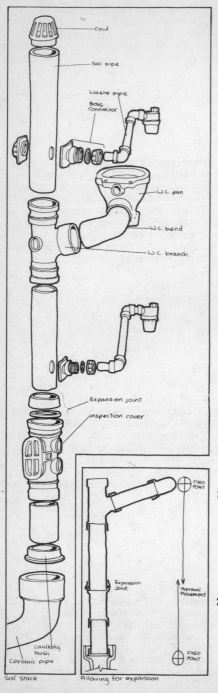

cowl

soil pipe

waste pipe

Boss connector

W.C. pan

W.C. bend

W.C. branch

Expansion joint

Inspection cover

caulking bush
Ceramic pipe

Soil stack

FIXED POINT

Expansion Joint

Thermal Movement

FIXED POINT

Allowing for expansion

2. 27. 01   It is most unlikely that you will need to replace a soil stack. If you do, make sure the house has plenty of life to justify the expense. For new work building regulations require the soil pipe to be inside the building.

2. 27. 02   The easiest and cheapest material is plastic. There are several manufacturers and each has slightly different methods and fittings, so ask for a brochure or fixing instructions from the dealer. Most makes provide special caulked joints between plastic and ceramic drain pipes.

2. 27. 03   There is sometimes an anti-syphon pipe. This is a small pipe running side by side with the soil stack. It is sometimes needed where more than one W. C. is connected into the soil stack and prevents water seal being syphoned out of one W. C. when another is flushed.

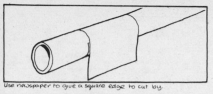
Use newspaper to give a square edge to cut by.

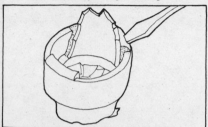
Clean existing socket of drain

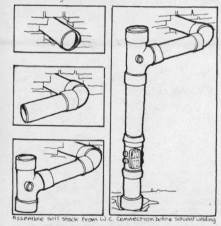
Assemble soil stack from W.C. connection before solvent welding

Make caulked joint and solvent weld soil stack together

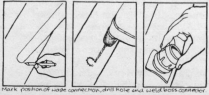
Mark position of waste connection, drill hole and weld boss connector.

2. 27. 04 The pipe comes in 3" (80mm), 4" (110mm) and 6" (160mm) diameters. The 4" (110mm) is normal for domestic soil pipes. There is a range of fittings joined by using a solvent weld :

2. 27. 05 W. C. branch - a 4" (110mm) branch to take a connection from the W. C.

Pipe connector - Inspection pipe connector (for connecting two pieces of pipe together) allows for clearing blockage.

Expansion joints - When the soil pipe is fixed at two ends, to the drain and to the W. C., allowance has to be made for expansion. This is achieved by having one joint that can move. It is sealed with a rubber seal and is similar to a push-fit joint.

Caulking ring to allow caulked joints to ceramic and cast iron pipe.

Boss connector for connecting waste pipes.

Vent cowl, etc.

2. 27. 06 Clear away the remains of the old soil stack. Clear and clean the socket end of the drain pipe (test drain if you have not already done so). Prepare a hole in the wall for the W. C. connection. It is probably easier to fit the W. C. pan first with the soil pipe connected to it, and assemble the soil pipe to fit this pipe. Cut and assemble the soil pipe and take care to get the W. C. branch at the right height for connection to the W. C.   Mark the position of the boss connectors for waste pipe and dismantle the pipe, fix bosses to the pipe, and fix the bracket to the wall. Solvent weld the caulking ring to the first piece of pipe. Convert one of the joints of the inspection cover pipe connectors to an expansion joint. Caulk in the soil pipe to the drain, use prompt cement, and solvent weld the inspection pipe connector to this. Insert the next section of pipe into the expansion joint and remove it $\frac{1}{2}$" (10mm) to allow for expansion. Weld on the W. C. branch and W. C. pipe. Secure brackets as you go. Extend the pipe above the roof level about 3' (1m) above the highest windows. Top the pipe with a vent cowl. Make the waste connections to the bosses.

2. 28. 00 <u>GAS PLUMBING</u>

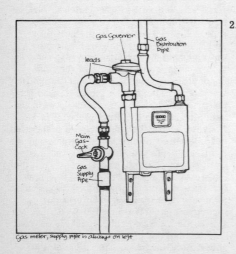

Gas Governor

Gas
Distribution
Pipe

leads

Main
Gas-
Cock

Gas
Supply
Pipe

Gas meter, supply pipe is always on left

2. 28. 01 In principle, gas plumbing is similar
to water plumbing. Many of the
materials and fittings used, and the
techniques employed, are the same
as those already described (2. 07. 00
to 2. 18. 00). However, the risks from
faults, bad workmanship or accidents
are much greater - some potentially
fatal. These dangers are present
whether you have done your own gas
fitting or not. Short-life houses are
especially hazardous, as installations
are often substandard and do not comply
with more recent regulations. It is the
aim of this section to point out these
dangers, to advise on how to make
installations safer, and to give specific
information on making reconnections,
minor changes and improvements.

2. 28. 02 The Gas Safety Regulations (1972) -
the relevant passages of which are

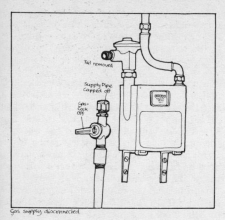

Tail removed

Supply Pipe
Capped off

Gas-
Cock
Off

Gas supply disconnected

reproduced in the Appendix (pp. 226-29)
- lay down the basic rules for maintaining the safety of gas installations.
Only persons employed with the local
Area Gas Board may work on the service pipe (the incoming supply pipe),
the meter or the main gas-cock. The
main gas-cock, which controls the
supply to the house, may be operated
by anyone in an emergency (see 2. 28. 05).
Only 'competent' persons may make
alterations to the gas installations (the
pipes and appliances on the consumer
side of the meter), and these must be
done in sound materials, in a workmanlike manner and in accordance with the
other provisions of the act.

2. 28. 03 We strongly recommend that anyone
attempting gas installations should
have had some practical experience
with domestic water plumbing and be
familiar with the basic techniques
described in 2. 11. 00 and 2. 12. 00
(copper and iron pipework). Also that
only the minor changes and alterations
described in this manual should be
attempted, and that the Gas Board be
asked to check the installation before
it is brought into permanent use.

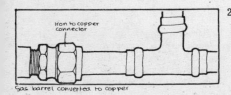

Iron to copper
connector

Gas barrel converted to copper

2. 28. 04 Only copper or iron pipe (gas barrel)
should be used for gas installations.
Where an appliance cannot be connected
directly to an existing pipe, use copper
pipe, connected to the iron with an iron
to copper connector. Pipes should be
well secured to the wall with pipe
brackets (2. 17. 00) and laid so that
they are not easily damaged. They
should also be electrically bonded (see
1. 13. 15).

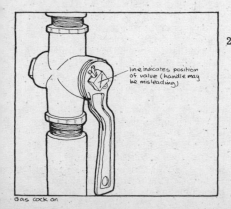

line indicates position
of valve (handle may
be misleading)

Gas cock on

2. 28. 05 The main gas-cock is situated on the
left or incoming (service pipe) side of
the meter, and is operated by an attached lever. If this handle is missing, the
shank can be turned using a stilson or
adjustable wrench. This method should
not be used frequently, as the wrench
may tear the end of the shank - so ask
the Gas Board to fit a new handle. A
line stamped into the end of the shank
indicates 'on' or 'off' positions: across
the pipe for 'off', in line for 'on'. If
the meter is missing, or if the tails or
'leads' (lead connectors between the

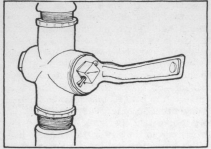
Gas Cock off

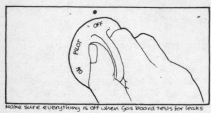
Make sure everything is off when Gas board tests for leaks

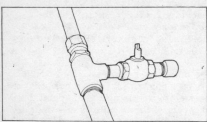
Always cap off disused branches

Smelling for gas leak

pipes and the meter) have been removed, these will be replaced by the Gas Board. From the meter, distribution pipes run to the various appliances where there may be secondary gas-cocks.

2. 28. 06　Always turn off at the main gas-cock and any secondary cocks before starting any repair work. Remember to turn off all appliances, especially pilot lights: if you don't, the pilots will go out when the gas is off and will leak gas when it is turned on again. (All appliances must also be off when testing for leaks.) If there are any redundant pipes, they should be disconnected and the branches capped off - even if they are controlled by stop-cocks. If there is a gas-lighting installation which you are not going to use, disconnect it and cap it off. In general, stick to existing pipework (unless damaged), adding only the minimum of extensions. Don't use damaged, buckled or suspect pipe, and ensure that all fittings are sound and properly installed. Always reseal any BSP threaded joints that you have dismantled and want to reassemble with new PFTE tape or Boss White. Under no circumstances should you use PVC or polythene or any other plastic pipes for gas.

2. 28. 07　Testing for leaks can be done if you already have a metered supply connected up. Ensure that all new joints are properly made, that redundant branches have been capped, that all the appliances and pilots are off and that there are no naked flames near any of the gas installations. Turn the gas back on and watch the large dial on the meter. If the needle moves - even very slowly - there is a leak (or you have left a pilot on somewhere). Use your nose: gas is made to smell so that leaks will be noticed. Using a 50-50 mixture of water and washing-up liquid squirt it onto any suspect joints. If the liquid forms bubbles, then the joint is leaking. (It's worth testing all new joints in this way.) Turn off the gas, re-do the joint and re-test (see 2. 11. 07, 2. 12. 06). Ask the Gas Board to check and test the installation before bringing it into permanent use.

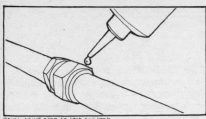

Using liquid soap to test for leak.

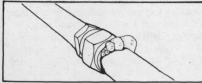

escaping gas will form bubbles

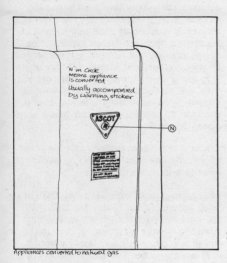

'N' in circle means appliance is converted
Usually accompanied by warning sticker

Appliances converted to natural gas

Town gas pilot

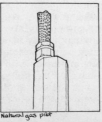

Natural gas pilot

2. 28. 08 'Purging' is the clearing of air from newly laid pipes or from existing pipes that have been opened to the air. In small domestic installations this is generally done by simply opening all the doors and windows, and then running gas through each branch separately. You stand by each branch and appliance being purged until you can smell gas coming through. Then you turn off the appliance at its controls. Purging should be done by the Gas Board when they come to check the installation and before it is brought into use.

2. 28. 09 Natural Gas -
Most of England and Scotland have now been converted to natural gas. It is safer than town gas, since it doesn't form an explosive mixture with air so easily as the old 'town' gas, though it explodes more violently when it does. Natural gas is also less dangerous if breathed. If you're buying a second-hand appliance, always check that it has been converted. Don't always believe the salesman; he may not know. It is dangerous to run an unconverted appliance on natural gas, so, if it hasn't been converted, arrange for the Gas Board to do so. Gas water heaters have a small silver 'N' and a warning label stuck on the cover when they have been converted. But the surest way of telling is to look at the pilot light. The old town gas pilots are small ceramic tips, while the natural gas pilots are small tubes of metal gauze. Appliances run on the wrong gas give low heat and yellow, sooty flames.

2. 28. 10 The regulations require that 'competent persons' instal gas installations and appliances. If, after studying this and the following section, you still feel in doubt as to your competence, you should seek further advice or assistance.

2. 28. 11 The Gas Board is responsible for ensuring that a service is safe and sometimes disconnect it if they think there is any danger. They also check gas water heater flues. They operate a 24-hour service, and should you suddenly find yourself with a big leak, turn off at the main gas-cock and call them. They charge for finding and repairing leaks.

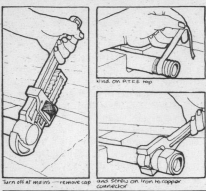

Wind on P.T.F.E tap

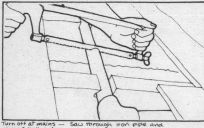

Turn off at mains —remove cap and screw on iron to copper connector

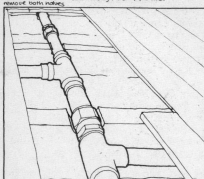

Turn off at mains — Saw through iron pipe and remove both halves

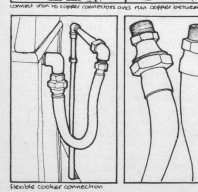

connect iron to copper connectors and run copper between them

flexible cooker connection

2. 29. 00 INSTALLING A GAS COOKER

2. 29. 01 When the previous cooker was moved, the gas supply should have been capped off. There are available cooker connectors ('cooker flexes') which make connection much easier and allow for the cooker to be moved for cleaning. The gas inlet is usually situated to one side at the back of the cooker, and usually takes $\frac{1}{2}$" BSP female iron connectors. Do not connect to a smaller diameter pipe than on the appliance.

2. 29. 02 Turn off the gas and remove the cap. Connect the necessary elbows and pipe to bring the supply pipe directly in front of the cooker inlet. Use a union joint to connect the supply and inlet pipes together (see 2. 12. 08). If you are using a flexible connector, the supply and inlet should be fitted with elbows facing downwards so the flexible connector can loop easily without strain. There is already a union joint on flexible connectors. If you are running the supply in copper, you don't need a union joint if the iron to copper connector has a compression joint.

2. 29. 03 If there is no convenient gas pipe from which you can take a supply, you may need to run new pipework.

2. 29. 04 Trace the supply pipes leaving the meter (they normally run under the floor) till you find the one that goes nearest the intended cooker position. If this is the end of a pipe, you can simply convert to copper and run the extension in copper. If you need to break into a run of gas pipe, then you will have to cut the pipe, remove the two cut pieces at the nearest joint, and connect a copper to iron connector at each end using copper between with a tee from which to take the new supply. Do not lay pipes where they can easily become damaged. Avoid using capillary joints on copper when they are made with the pipe already connected to existing gas piping - even though the gas is off. Take care with compression joints: make sure they are exactly aligned before tightening.

2.30.00 <u>INSTALLING A GAS FIRE</u>

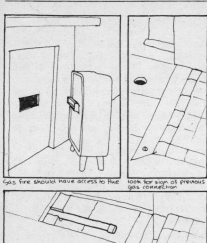

Gas fire should have access to flue   look for sign of previous gas connection

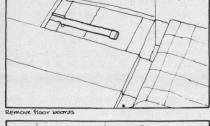

Remove floor boards

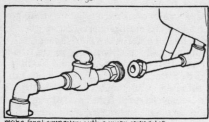

Connect appropriate fittings

2.30.01 Gas fires must have access to a flue; the best place for them is in front of a disused fireplace. You can seal the fireplace off with a board, but cut a slot for the gas fire's flue. Test that the chimney is unblocked before installing the gas fire. Light a piece of newspaper and hold it in the chimney. If the smoke is drawn up, the chimney is clear (don't let the flaming paper fly up the chimney).

2.30.02 There are quite often gas points under the floorboards by the side of a fire. If not, lay on a new supply (see 2.29.00). You should fit a stop-cock between the supply and the fire. Most fires use a 3/8" or a $\frac{1}{4}$" supply pipe.

2.30.03 Turn off the gas and remove the cap. Convert to 3/8" or $\frac{1}{4}$" BSP and connect gas-cock. Use a union joint connector and pre-threaded iron pipe to connect to the gas fire inlet, or else use copper pipe and compression joints.

2.30.04 There is a special, easily bent, $\frac{1}{4}$" (7mm) copper gas fire pipe which can be used for more difficult installations. It uses standard copper fittings.

make final connection with a union connector

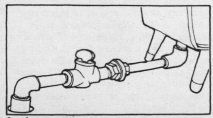

Gas fire connection

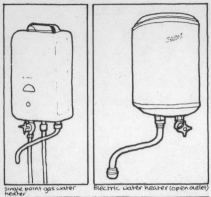

Single point gas water heater

Electric water heater (open outlet)

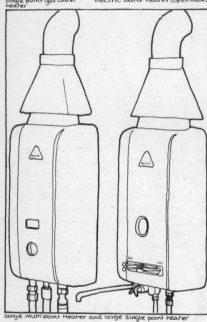

Large multi point Heater and large single point heater

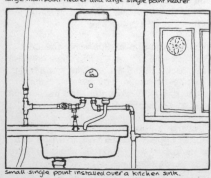

Small single point installed over a kitchen sink.

2.31.00 HOT WATER SUPPLY

2.31.01 The most convenient source of hot water, especially in short-life houses, is from self-contained heaters like Ascots and Mains (gas water heaters) or Sadias (electric immersion and storage heaters). Both are easily available second-hand, can be fairly easily installed and removed, and are cheap to run.

2.31.02 Gas Water Heaters -
Installing a gas water heater is probably the most exacting task needed to be undertaken in short-life domestic plumbing. They require careful positioning, an efficient flue, cold, hot and gas plumbing.

2.31.03 Badly installed gas water heaters in badly ventilated small bathrooms can be lethal. If the flue is not working efficiently carbon monoxide (a colourless, odourless gas) will get back into the room; even a small amount can cause unconsciousness and death. First symptoms are dizziness, loss of coordination (making it difficult to undo the door latch) and ringing in the ears. There are regulations governing the installation of gas water heaters. It is the one thing the gas board is likely to get upset about.

2.31.04 There are two sizes of heaters. The large heater consumes 150-180 cubic feet of town gas per hour (75-90 cu.ft. of natural gas) and the small sink heater uses almost 80 cubic feet per hour (40 cu.ft. natural gas).

2.31.05 There are two distinct types: the single point and the multipoint. The single point heaters deliver water through a swing arm which supplies a single fitting (or two fittings - e.g. bath and basin - that are close together). The 'hot' tap is situated on the heater. The multipoint can supply several fittings, serving them through pipe work, and operated by a separate tap on each of the fittings.

2.31.06 There are several makes of gas water heaters: Ascot, Main, Ewart, etc., each with several models, so there's quite a range to choose from. On the whole, small heaters are single point (there is one small model, a 525 which is a multipoint) and don't need flues. Large heaters can be either multipoint or single point and always require a 4" or 5" flue.

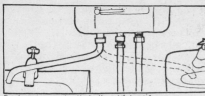

Single point used with bath and basin.

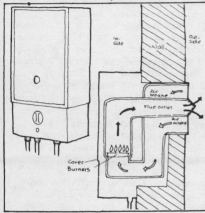

Balanced flue gas water heater.

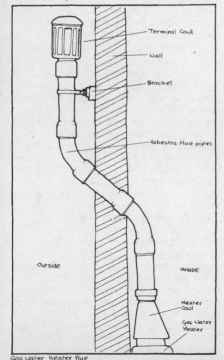

Gas water heater flue.

2.31.07 Positioning a Water Heater –
Small heaters can be positioned above
the sink in the kitchen. A cold water
supply can come from the mains or
from a tank, providing there is more
than a 7' (2.1m) head, i.e., the level
of the water in the tank is more than 7'
above the heater. A gas supply can
come from the nearest gas point,
probably the cooker gaspipe.

2.31.08 Small heaters don't need a flue but should
not be run for more than 10 minutes
Never use a small heater for a bath.
It will take so long for the bath to fill
that the water will get cold before it is
ready. It will also take longer than ten
minutes, and in a small room without a
flue it will be dangerous.

2.31.09 If you use a large single point heater,
it can be situated so that it can serve the
bath and the basin by swinging the arm
across. It can be fed by the mains or
the tank. A tank may need as much as
14' (4.2m) head to operate a large heater,
which may be difficult to arrange. Check
makers' specifications, or connect the
heater to the water mains. Depending
on the model, it will need a 4" or 5"
flue (110 or 140mm).

2.31.10 Flues need to be installed correctly,
both for safety's sake and because the
Gas Board may disconnect the gas
supply if they think a flue is dangerous.
They can be consulted (free of charge)
about positioning and installing flues
but they tend to be conservative, often
recommending a balanced flue heater
(difficult to get second-hand) when they
are not strictly necessary.

2.31.11 The flue should conform to these regulations:
It must be the correct diameter (4" or
5").
It should rise for at least 18" vertically
after leaving the heater cowl.
There should be as few bends as possible
(90 degree bends should be avoided,
45 degree are preferable).
Horizontal runs should be avoided, or
be as short as possible (e.g. through

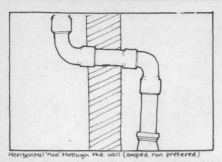

Horizontal 'run' through the wall (angled run prefered)

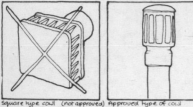

Square type cowl (not approved)   Approved type of cowl

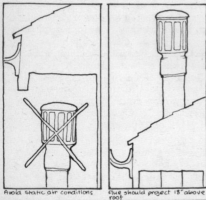

Avoid static air conditions   Flue should project 18" above roof

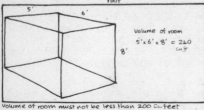

Volume of room
$5' \times 6' \times 8' = 240$ cu.ft

Volume of room must not be less than 200 cu. feet

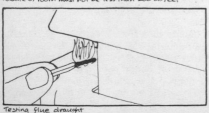

Testing flue draught

the thickness of the wall). As a general rule, the flue should rise vertically 4' for every horizontal foot.

The flue should terminate outside the house with an approved terminal cowl (i. e. the round type; the square type is no longer accepted).

It should terminate in moving air; avoid static air conditions - e. g. under roof, eaves, or balconies, etc.

If it terminates against a wall, it should be 9" off the wall and not be close to or below any windows.

If it terminates above the roof it should project at least 18", or, if above a flat roof, 2' above any parapet wall.

2. 31. 12 The room in which the heater is fixed should be adequately ventilated and be over 200 cu. ft. for large heaters. Ventilation should be on the same wall as the heater flue - by means of an airbrick and a ventilator in the window. Holes bored in the door may be useful. Adequate permanent ventilation and flues are extremely important to prevent the risk of carbon monoxide poisoning.

Heaters should not be fixed in cupboards and should not be close to combustible materials (e. g. wooden shelves).

2. 31. 13 There are many existing installations which would not conform to the above. If you inherit one by moving into a house, try to improve it, or be very careful in using it (e. g. don't run the heater while in the bath, etc.). If you are improving or replacing an existing installation, it should comply with the above. If it's a completely new installation, you are advised by the Gas Board to fit a balanced flue heater. The building regulations are being amended so that only balanced flue heaters may be installed in bathrooms and in other rooms under a certain size (not yet specified). These regulations should not affect existing installations.

2. 31. 14 A flue can be tested by holding a smoking paper or match under the cowl while the heater is working. If the flames are extinguished, there may be carbon monoxide escaping into the room. Although this gives some indication of the efficiency of the flue, this is likely to change under different weather conditions.

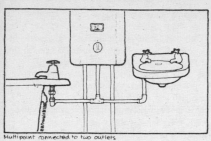

Multipoint connected to two outlets

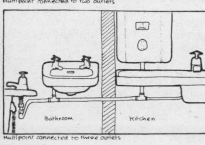

Bathroom   Kitchen

Multipoint connected to three outlets

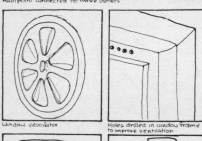

Window Ventilator   Holes drilled in window frame to improve ventilation

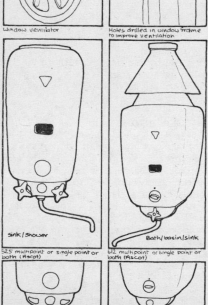

sink/shower

525 multipoint or single point or both (Ascot)

Bath/basin/sink

612 multipoint or single point or both (Ascot)

525 as multipoint (Ascot)   612 as multipoint (Ascot)

2. 31. 15 If you plan to use a large multipoint to serve a bath or basin in a bath room, then the same applies for flues as for a large single point. The hot water is fed to each appliance through pipes from the heater to run-off points on each fitting.

2. 31. 16 If you want to use the multipoint to supply a bath, basin and a kitchen sink, the gas water heater should be installed in the kitchen. The kitchen and bathroom should be next to each other (side by side or one above the other), or the runs of hot water pipe will be too long. The longer the run, the more water you have to run off before the hot water comes through, the more pipe there is for heat loss, and the more hot water you have to leave in the pipe when you turn the water off. So group the fittings together as closely as possible, have the heater between them, and keep the pipe runs as short as possible.

2. 31. 17 Never run a hot water supply from a multipoint in a bathroom to a run-off point out of the room. There's danger of fumes collecting in the room while someone is in the bath and the heater is being used from outside the room. Occasionally, heaters go wrong and when you turn the water off the gas keeps burning. Unless you turn the gas supply off quickly, the heater will start to melt. If you were operating it from another room, you might not notice that anything had gone wrong.

2. 31. 18 Whatever the room, the heater in that room must be well ventilated. You can put a vent into the windows (which is one of the things North Sea conversion units do) or you can drill a series of holes along the top of a window frame and an internal door frame to give cross ventilation.

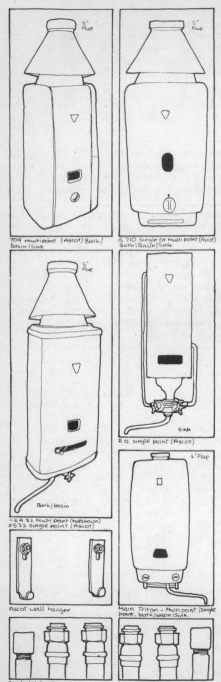

709 multipoint (Ascot) Bath/
Basin/Sink

G 710 Single or multi point (Ascot)
Bath/Basin/Sink

6"
Flue

Sink

R 12 single point (Ascot)

4"Flue

Bath/basin

N.E.A 32 Multi point (Notshown)
SG32 single point (Ascot)

Main Triton - Multi point/Single
point, bath/basin/Sink.

Ascot Wall hanger

Gas/inlet/outlet

Inlet/outlet/gas

2.31.19   Types of Ascots -

If there was a heater installed previously, then it is easiest to install one in the
same position, using the existing flue
and pipe connections. It is even better
if you can install the same model. However, if the old heater did not comply
with the regulations, then improve it to
comply with them. There are several
ways of finding out the model of the previous heater, and it is worth going to
some trouble to identify it and buy the
same model. For identification you
should check:

2.31.20   The size of the flue -
Main Triton and Ascot 612 need a four-
inch flue; Ascots 709, 709b, NEA 32/6,
SG 32/1 use a five-inch flue.

2.31.21   Shadow -
Heaters tend to leave a patch of clean
wall when removed, leaving a distinctive shape. All large Ascots leave a
distinctive cowl shape. The Main
Triton is more rectangular and straight
sided. Small Ascots, except the 525
and 526, have a gap between them and
the wall, leaving an indistinct shadow,
while small Mains leave a sharp
shadow.

2.31.22   Type of hanger -
Large Mains are fixed directly to the
wall by large screws or nails. Large
Ascots usually have special hangers
which are often left behind.

2.31.23   Position of pipes -
All single point heaters will have only a
water and gas pipe. Multipoints have
three pipes. On Ascots the gas pipe can
be either on the right or left, Mains on
the left. The water outlet is in the
middle on Mains and on the right of the
inlets on Ascots. Small Ascots usually
have two female iron backplate elbows,
one above the other, the bottom one for
water, the top one for gas. Small Mains
usually have vertical connections for the
services and not horizontal ones as in
Ascots.

**2.31.24   Sometimes parts are left behind and may
be a guide to the identity of the heater.**

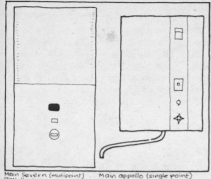

Main Severn (mutipoint)   Main appollo (single point)
Bath/basin   Sink

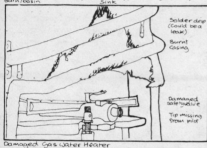

Solder drip (Could be a leak)

Burnt casing

Damaged safety valve

Tip missing from pilot

Damaged Gas Water Heater

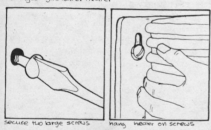

Secure two large screws   hang heater on screws

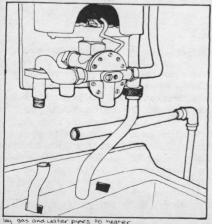

lay gas and water pipes to heater

2. 31. 25 In choosing a water heater, you will of course be constrained by what's available and how much you have to spend. The scrap value of a heater is about three pounds, and you can buy them second-hand from £7 to £20 or £30 depending on the model and age, and whether they are reconditioned and guaranteed. You will know whether you need a large or a small, single or multipoint, but the more flexible your needs are, the better deal you might get. If you are after a specific model, then you may have to look around in several shops and pay whatever they ask. Lift the outer cover of the heater and look for scorching or damage to the pipes. It is not easy to tell if a water heater will work until it is connected up, so get an assurance from the seller that it does work, and make sure you can exchange it if it doesn't.
It is essential to check whether the appliance has been converted to natural gas, since most areas in England and Scotland now use it (see 2. 28. 08).

2. 31. 26 Installing a Gas Water Heater -

If you are simply replacing the same model heater there should be no difficulty. Follow any relevant suggestions below, otherwise it's simply a matter of reconnecting pipes and flues.

2. 31. 27 Small single point heaters - Position the heater above the sink, make sure that burnt gasses from the heater will not be directed onto inflamable material. If there is exposed wood on the wall or ceiling above the heater then it should be covered with asbestos sheeting. Remove the cover of the heater, there should be two holes in the back plate through which it can be screwed to the wall. Screw the heater firmly to the wall. Identify the pipes. The water heater inlet should have a tap attached; if not, you will need to connect a stop-cock to it. Both the water and gas supply can be run in $\frac{1}{2}$" bore pipe. A gas-cock can be attached to the gas inlet - this is useful but not absolutely necessary. Connect the water inlet to the water supply and the gas inlet to the gas supply.

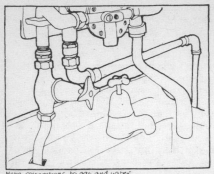

Make connections to gas and water.

2.31.28 Turn on the gas and the heater knob to 'pilot', light the pilot, leave for two minutes for the safety valve to open, and turn the heater to 'on'. Test that it works. It may be a bit sluggish if it hasn't been used for a while. Ensure adequate ventilation. If the heater is not working well, see 2.31.43.

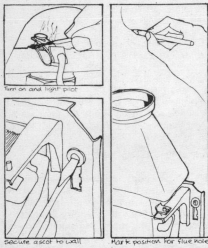

Turn on and light pilot

Secure ascot to wall   Mark position for flue hole

2.31.29 Large single point -
If you want to use the heater for more than one fitting, arrange them so that the arm can be swung from one to the other.

2.31.30 It is rare that second-hand heaters come with their hangers, so use two large screws with washers fixed through the hanger slots. Large heaters are heavy so secure them well. If necessary, drill more holes in the back plate.

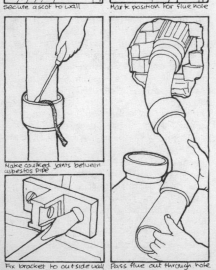

Make caulked joints between asbestos pipe

Fix bracket to outside wall   Pass flue out through hole

2.31.31 Replace the cover and the cowl and work out the position for the flue. Cover the heater and knock a hole through the wall in the appropriate place. If the flue is short it may be possible to assemble it inside before joining it to the heater cowl. Measure the distance from the cowl to the first bend, the distance to the wall, etc., and cut the pipes accordingly. Make the caulked joints between each piece, and between the pipe and the outside cowl, using asbestos string and fire cement. Leave the joints to dry. Secure a bracket on the outside wall.

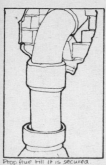
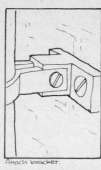

Prop flue till it is secured.   Attach bracket.

2.31.32 Pass the flue out through the hole; you may need someone on the outside to steady it. Slot the free end in the heater cowl and secure the bracket to the pipe. Make the caulked joint between the cowl and the flue and cement up the hole. Remember that asbestos pipes are not very strong, and care should be taken when handling them.

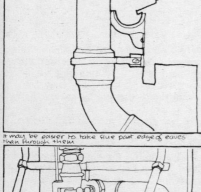

It may be easier to take flue past edge of eaves than through them.

2.31.33 If the flue needs to extend above the eaves of the roof, you can assemble the section of the flue that passes through the wall as above, but the rest will have to be fixed from the outside. It may be simpler to take the flue out past the side of the guttering rather than through the eaves. Make sure the flue is well secured to the wall. Don't use a smaller flue than is recommended for the type of heater you're using.

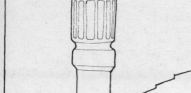

Make gas and water connections

gas inlet

Water inlet

2.31.34 The gas connection to the heater is best done in $\frac{3}{4}$" (22mm) pipe. If you use $\frac{1}{2}$" (15mm) you may find that not enough gas is delivered, especially when there are other gas appliances in use. It's no good running a $\frac{3}{4}$" pipe from a $\frac{1}{2}$" supply. If you can only get to a $\frac{1}{2}$" gas supply you can try using that; it may work. The water supply can be $\frac{1}{2}$" (15mm) or, if it is from a tank, $\frac{3}{4}$" (22mm).

Turn on and light pilot

2.31.35 The gas connection should be in copper or iron. Once all the connections are made, turn on the gas, light the pilot, and test the heater. Ensure adequate ventilation. See 2.31.43 for gas water heater faults.

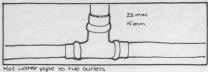

Hot water pipe to two outlets

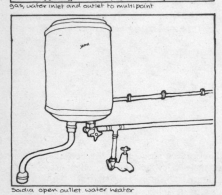

gas, water inlet and outlet to multipoint

2. 31. 36 Multipoint gas water heaters -
Secure the heater to the wall in the
optimum position for flue runs and pipe.
Fit the flue in the same way as for
single point heaters (see 2.31.10).
Connect the gas inlet to the supply.
Use $\frac{3}{4}$" (22mm) where possible.

2. 31. 37 Connect the water inlet to the supply,
$\frac{1}{2}$" (15mm) from mains or $\frac{3}{4}$" from tank.
The water outlet can be run in $\frac{1}{2}$"
(15mm) copper pipe or in $\frac{3}{4}$" (22mm)
branching into $\frac{1}{2}$" at each run-off point
- this gives a better flow of water when
two taps are operated at the same time.
Connect to the tap nearest the heater
for shortest runs (the "H" or "C" mark-
ings can be changed over).

2. 31. 38 If you can, put a stop-cock on the
gas and water inlets. This makes
maintenance of the heater easier.

2. 31. 39 Electric water heater

Electric water heaters are much easier
to install. They need no flue, and sink
ones can run off a 30 amp ring main
(see 1.10.00). However, they are
more difficult to come by second-hand.

2. 31. 40 There are several models and makes,
but only two main types: single point
(open outlet) and multipoint. Small ones
are only suitable for sinks or basins,
as they heat a tank of water which contains from 1 - 3 gallons (5 - 15 litres).
When the stored hot water has run off,
you have to wait for several minutes
for it to heat up again.

2. 31. 41 They are screwed to the wall as with
gas water heaters. A flex is stapled to
the nearest socket point where a 13 amp
fused outlet is installed (see 1.10.04);
don't try to run it off anything less than
a 13 or 15 amp socket. Water connections can be from the mains or from a
tank depending on the type. The multipoint must be fitted with a vent pipe which
discharges over the cold water tank from
which it is fed. On some large Sadias,
the cold water tank is built into the heater
and the expansion pipe discharges into
this. There should be an overflow from
the tank to the outside of the house.

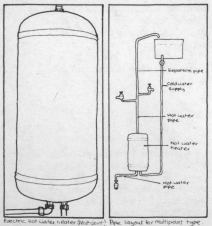

Electric hot water heater (Multipoint) Pipe layout for Multipoint type.

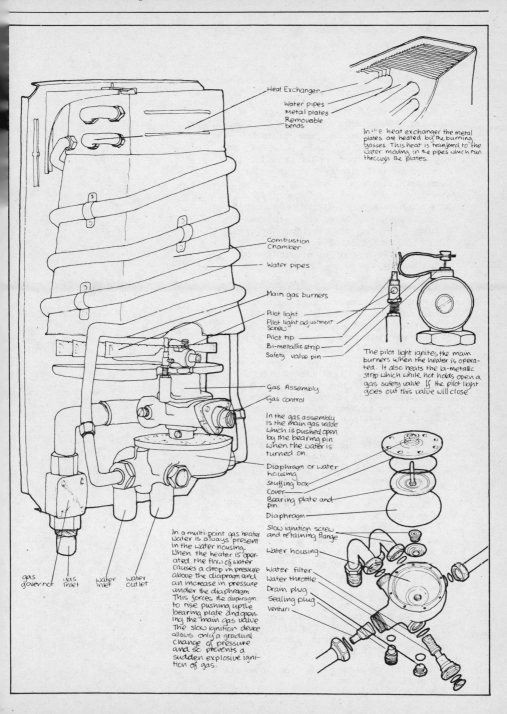

2.31.43 FAULT FINDING IN GAS WATER HEATERS

Most comments refer to Ascot gas
water heaters and especially to the 709,
probably the most common multipoint
model found second-hand. However, the
principles involved are the same for all
other makes and models of gas water
heaters.

If you have a particular difficulty which
is not dealt with here, or is still confusing, you can phone the manufacturers
and ask for technical enquiries. They
will usually answer any queries though
it's easier if you have some knowledge
of the terms that are used.

It may be necessary to find the specifications of the model you're repairing
(i.e. the amount of gas consumed and
the water delivered per minute). This
can be got from the manufacturers.

It's often easier to get spares directly
from the manufacturer. This can be done
if you know what you want, or better
still, if you can take the faulty item and
get an identical replacement.

If you're overhauling a heater then it's
often wise to get a new set of washers
which can be bought as a set for any
particular model.

It's often difficult to loosen screws and
nuts on the heater mechanism. It may
help to heat the metal over a gas flame
or to use penetrating oil. Sometimes it's
necessary to cut damaged parts to get
them off. Always be careful not to
damage the main body or housing of the
heater.

The two main manufacturers are:
Ascot Radiation Ltd. , Radiation House,
225 North Circular Road, London N. W. 10
(Phone: 01-459 1234)

Main Gas Appliances Ltd. , Gothic Works
Angel Road, London N. 18.
(Phone: 01-807 3030)

PILOT LIGHT WON'T WORK

PILOT LIGHT TOO LOW
(Flame should be $\frac{3}{4}$'')

PILOT LIGHT TOO HIGH
(causing waste of gas, noise and wear of bi-metallic strip)

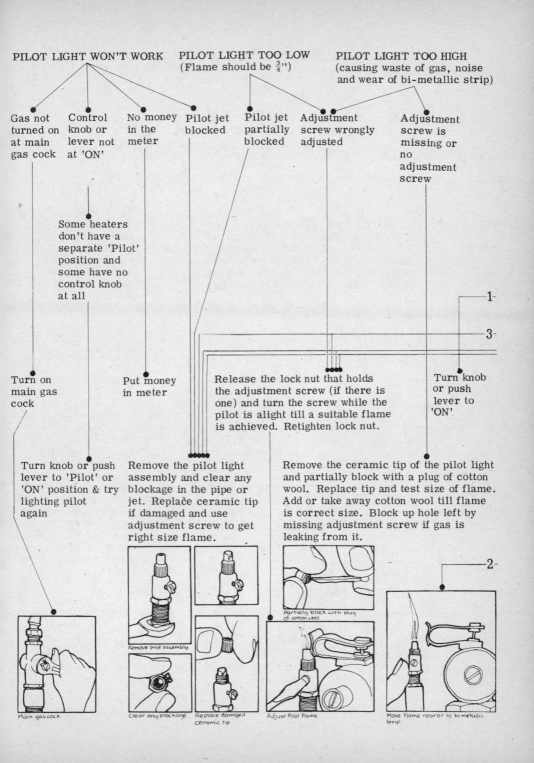

Gas not turned on at main gas cock

Control knob or lever not at 'ON'

No money in the meter

Pilot jet blocked

Pilot jet partially blocked

Adjustment screw wrongly adjusted

Adjustment screw is missing or no adjustment screw

Some heaters don't have a separate 'Pilot' position and some have no control knob at all

1-

3-

Turn on main gas cock

Put money in meter

Release the lock nut that holds the adjustment screw (if there is one) and turn the screw while the pilot is alight till a suitable flame is achieved. Retighten lock nut.

Turn knob or push lever to 'ON'

Turn knob or push lever to 'Pilot' or 'ON' position & try lighting pilot again

Remove the pilot light assembly and clear any blockage in the pipe or jet. Replace ceramic tip if damaged and use adjustment screw to get right size flame.

Remove the ceramic tip of the pilot light and partially block with a plug of cotton wool. Replace tip and test size of flame. Add or take away cotton wool till flame is correct size. Block up hole left by missing adjustment screw if gas is leaking from it.

2-

Partially block with plug of cotton wool

Remove pilot assembly

Main gas cock

Clear any blockage

Replace damaged ceramic tip

Adjust Pilot Flame

Move flame nearer to bi-metallic strip

PILOT LIGHT WORKS BUT NO GAS COMES FROM THE MAIN BURNERS WHEN THE HEATER IS OPERATED

4●

Control knob not at 'ON' position

Pilot light not been on long enough

Pilot light too low

Pilot light not near enough to bi-metallic strip

Bi-metallic strip worn or broken

Safety valve pin is sticking

Bi-metallic strip is not opening the gas safety valve. With pilot light lit push the end of the bi-metallic strip down using the end of a screwdriver. If the burners ignite, then the safety valve is not being opened. If not it is some other fault.

●If pin is already down but the main burner does not release gas it may be the main gas valve that is stuck.———5●

●1

●3

11

10
9

Leave for 5 minutes after lighting pilot before operating the heater

Bend pilot light back to a position where the flame touches the edge of the bi-metallic strip

Replace bi-metallic strip. Loosen the nut holding strip and slide it out from under the nut. Slide in new strip engaging the top slit in the safety valve pin. Re-tighten the nut and retest.

●Replacing a gas safety valve and pin - Remove main burner by loosening nut. Disengage the top of the safety valve pin from the bi-metallic strip and remove safety valve and pin. Clean, straighten, or replace. Lubricate pin and refit (Vaseline will do). Test that the valve and pin move freely up and down. Reassemble and retest.

Turn off gas and work the pin up and down a few times. This may loosen it. Relight pilot and retest.

●2

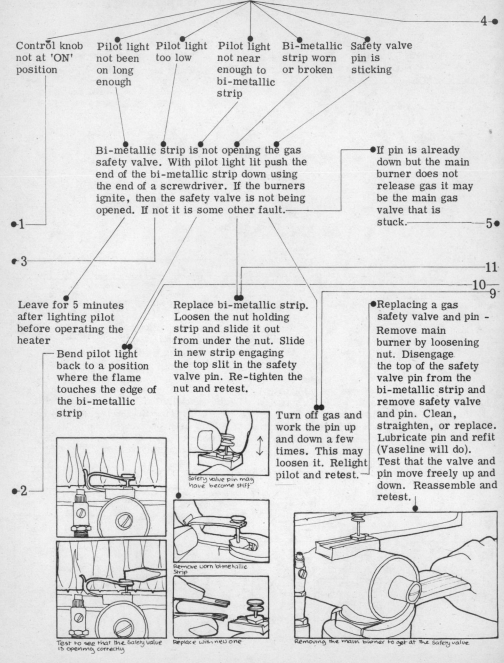

Safety valve pin may have become stiff

Test to see that the safety valve is opening correctly

Remove worn bi-metallic strip

Replace with new one

Removing the main burner to get at the safety valve

-4-

Water inlet
and outlet
connected
wrongly

-7-

● Testing the main gas valve - Turn off the water
but leave the gas and the pilot alight. Remove the
water section. Locate the hole under the gas section.
Insert a thin rod into this hole and push the gas valve
open. If the gas valve moves freely the main burner
should ignite - in which case the fault is in the water   ●If main gas
section. Don't keep the burners alight for more than   valve moves
a second as it may lead to overheating. If the pin is   freely it may
stiff or won't move then the gas valve is jammed.   be a fault
If the valve sticks open then turn the gas off at the   in the water
control knob to prevent overheating.   section —8●

-5-

Work pin up and down
a few times (with gas off)
as it may simply be disuse
that has caused the sticking.
If it begins to move freely
(against the spring) then it
may not need overhauling.
However, it's wise to test
water section before
reassembling. ————6●

Multipoints only -
switch pipes around.
The water inlet is
usually on the left
of the water housing.

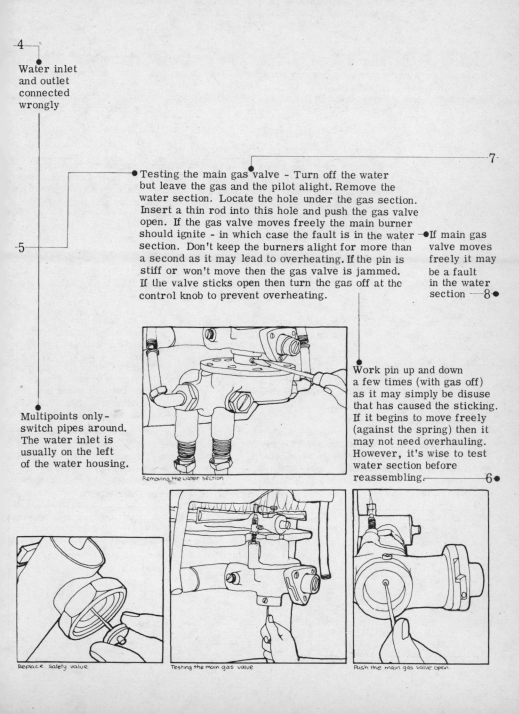

Removing the water section

Replace safety valve.

Testing the main gas valve

Push the main gas valve open.

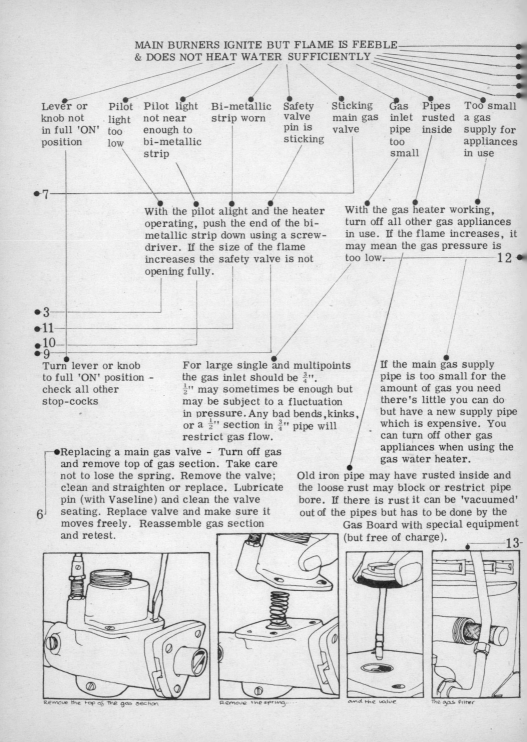

MAIN BURNERS IGNITE BUT FLAME IS FEEBLE
& DOES NOT HEAT WATER SUFFICIENTLY

Lever or knob not in full 'ON' position

Pilot light too low

Pilot light not near enough to bi-metallic strip

Bi-metallic strip worn

Safety valve pin is sticking

Sticking main gas valve

Gas inlet pipe too small

Pipes rusted inside

Too small a gas supply for appliances in use

● 7

With the pilot alight and the heater operating, push the end of the bi-metallic strip down using a screwdriver. If the size of the flame increases the safety valve is not opening fully.

With the gas heater working, turn off all other gas appliances in use. If the flame increases, it may mean the gas pressure is too low. ——— 12 ●

● 3
● 11
● 10
● 9

Turn lever or knob to full 'ON' position - check all other stop-cocks

For large single and multipoints the gas inlet should be $\frac{3}{4}$". $\frac{1}{2}$" may sometimes be enough but may be subject to a fluctuation in pressure. Any bad bends, kinks, or a $\frac{1}{2}$" section in $\frac{3}{4}$" pipe will restrict gas flow.

If the main gas supply pipe is too small for the amount of gas you need there's little you can do but have a new supply pipe which is expensive. You can turn off other gas appliances when using the gas water heater.

● Replacing a main gas valve - Turn off gas and remove top of gas section. Take care not to lose the spring. Remove the valve; clean and straighten or replace. Lubricate pin (with Vaseline) and clean the valve seating. Replace valve and make sure it moves freely. Reassemble gas section and retest.

6

Old iron pipe may have rusted inside and the loose rust may block or restrict pipe bore. If there is rust it can be 'vacuumed' out of the pipes but has to be done by the Gas Board with special equipment (but free of charge).

——— 13-

Remove the top of the gas section

Remove the spring.....

and the valve

The gas filter

MAIN BURNER GIVES GOOD FLAME BUT WATER DOES NOT HEAT SUFFICIENTLY

Gas filter needs a clean

Diaphragm split or damaged

Gas governor needs readjusting

Water throttle misadjusted

Water filter blocked

Pipes in heat exchanger furred or blocked

Pressure of water at inlet not enough

-12 Measuring gas pressure - This can be done by operating the heater for a set time (a minute) while someone notes the amount of gas consumed on the meter - make sure other gas appliances are off. Compare this with the heater specifications.

Make sure all stop-cocks are fully open. Try adjusting the water throttle before investigating other low water pressure faults. —14•

—15•
—16•
20—17•

The water throttle is usually on the water inlet pipe under a screw cap. On the 709 it is on the left hand side of the diaphragm housing under a screw cap. Remove the cap and with the heater working adjust the throttle till the flames of the main burners are at their highest.

Not all models have a water filter. On some 709s it is incorporated in the water throttle assembly and is removed by undoing the large nut around the screw cap.

The gas governor or regulator is on the gas inlet pipe. Remove the cover and adjust the screw till the gas pressure is better.

Cubic Feet

Measuring the rate of gas consumption

Not all models have a gas filter. Usually they -13 are in the gas inlet pipe. Remove cover, remove and clean filter and replace.

Tails Governor

The gas governor on the gas meter

If there is a governor on the gas meter then the one on the heater can be removed.

Removing the screw cap of the water throttle

Adjusting the water throttle

The water filter

Removing the water filter

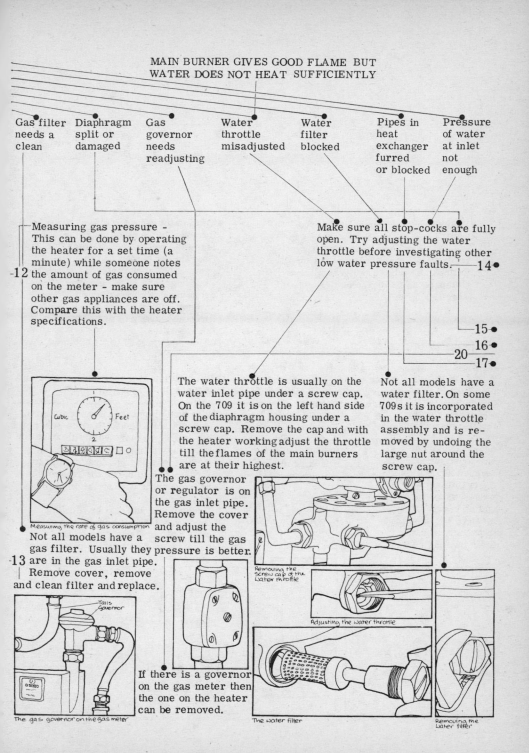

● Water pressure can be measured
by filling a container of known
volume; measuring the time it
-14 takes to fill it and working out the
gallons per minute delivered.
Compare this with the heater
specifications.

● Testing the water section -
Remove the gas section but
leave the water section intact.
Operate the heater and the
bearing pin should rise.
Test the force of the pin by
pressing it with your thumb
and comparing it with the
force necessary to push open
the gas valve.

18●

-15 ————————● Remove water section

-16 —— 8
-17 ⌐

19●

18●

If the water
pressure in the
mains seems
adequate, remove
the 'U' connections
on the heat excha-
nger. Clear out
any loose fur and
remove any solid
encrustations with
a de-scaler which
can be bought at
most D. I. Y shops.
They usually have
their own instruc-
tions.

If the heater is connected to the
rising main the water pressure
should be adequate. If connected
to a tank it should have $\frac{3}{4}$" supply
pipe and at least 7' of head,
(more for some models of
heater). Connect the heater to
mains if the tank head cannot be
improved.

Remove top of diaphragm housing and
inspect the diaphragm. Inspect it for
splits or holes or perishing. Replace
with new diaphragm if damaged or if
in doubt. Make sure that the bearing
pin is able to move easily through the
hole (or stuffing-box on multipoints)
in the top of the diaphragm housing.
Straighten and clean, or replace
bearing pin if it is sticking. Lubricate
with vaseline.
Reassemble and test by blowing
through inlet while partly covering
pipe that normally goes to heat
exchanger. The bearing pin should
rise.

Removing cover to diaphragm chamber

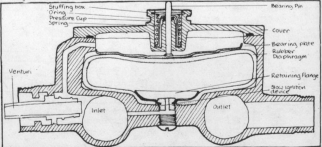

Removing the 'U' bends on the heat exchanger

Section through a 709 Ascot water heater diaphragm chamber (multi-point)

FLAMES DO NOT DIE DOWN IMMEDIATELY
WHEN THE HEATER IS TURNED OFF

Sticking main gas valve

Water and gas sections out of alignment

Tap on outlet of single point

Dirt on gas valve or valve seating

Split in diaphragm

Pilot light too low

Pilot light not close enough to main burner

• 7

18 •

Test for alignment between water section and gas section. Remove water section and dismantle. Replace top part of diaphragm chamber onto gas section and try to push bearing pin through the two holes to open gas valve.

This can be very dangerous and lead to a burn out of the heater. The heat exchanger may rupture, spilling boiling water. Turn off at the control knob or turn the tap back on till the gas can be turned off.

Allows build-up of gas before pilot ignites the main burners.

• 3

• 19

-18

If both the gas valve and the diaphragm are working it may be that the two sections are misaligned causing the bearing pin to stick between them.

NEVER instal a single point heater with any kind of tap on the outlet Remove tap and leave outlet open

Remove top of gas section - take care not to lose the spring. Clean the valve and valve seating or replace if permanently scored or damaged. Lubricate pin and replace. Make sure it seats properly and moves freely.

Try adjusting the two screws on the gas section till the water section is in alignment and allows the bearing pin to move freely. If this can't be done, try packing the joint between the two sections to bring them into line.

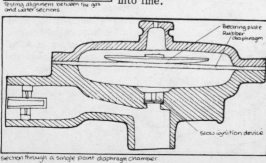

Testing alignment between the gas and water sections

Clean main gas valve

Bend pilot light pipe till it is closer to the main burners but don't move it too far from the bi-metallic strip.

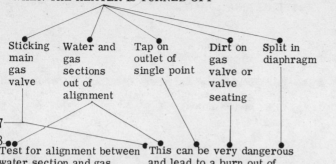

Bearing plate
Rubber diaphragm

Slow ignition device

Section through a single point diaphragm chamber

Clean gas valve seating

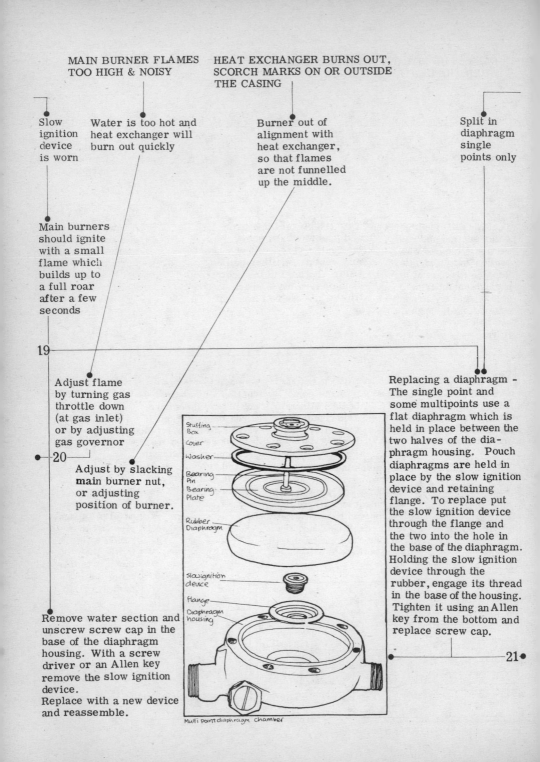

**MAIN BURNER FLAMES
TOO HIGH & NOISY**

**HEAT EXCHANGER BURNS OUT,
SCORCH MARKS ON OR OUTSIDE
THE CASING**

Slow
ignition
device
is worn

Water is too hot and
heat exchanger will
burn out quickly

Burner out of
alignment with
heat exchanger,
so that flames
are not funnelled
up the middle.

Split in
diaphragm
single
points only

Main burners
should ignite
with a small
flame which
builds up to
a full roar
after a few
seconds

19

Adjust flame
by turning gas
throttle down
(at gas inlet)
or by adjusting
gas governor

Adjust by slacking
main burner nut,
or adjusting
position of burner.

20

Replacing a diaphragm -
The single point and
some multipoints use a
flat diaphragm which is
held in place between the
two halves of the dia-
phragm housing. Pouch
diaphragms are held in
place by the slow ignition
device and retaining
flange. To replace put
the slow ignition device
through the flange and
the two into the hole in
the base of the diaphragm.
Holding the slow ignition
device through the
rubber, engage its thread
in the base of the housing.
Tighten it using an Allen
key from the bottom and
replace screw cap.

Stuffing
Box
Cover
Washer
Bearing
Pin
Bearing
Plate
Rubber
Diaphragm
Slow ignition
device
Flange
Diaphragm
housing

Remove water section and
unscrew screw cap in the
base of the diaphragm
housing. With a screw
driver or an Allen key
remove the slow ignition
device.
Replace with a new device
and reassemble.

21

Multi point diaphragm chamber

LEAKING FROM AROUND CONNECTION BETWEEN GAS SECTION AND WATER SECTION

Stuffing-box faulty

LEAKING FROM PIPE JOINTS, DIAPHRAGM HOUSING, ETC.

Loose nuts or screws

Missing or perished washers

Missing screw cap

Replacing the 'O' ring in a stuffing-box - Remove water section. Push and twist the retaining plate which will release the spring. Remove spring and pressure cup. Renew 'O' ring. Replace cup and spring and retaining plate. Test bearing pin to make sure it moves freely through stuffing-box.

Tighten, but not over-tight. If leak persists, renew washer.

Most adjustment screws leak and are normally covered by a screw cap. These must be replaced.

Be careful to keep all washers that are removed while doing repairs. If they become lost or broken, replace with a winding of PTFE tape. Or buy a complete set of washers for the particular model heater.

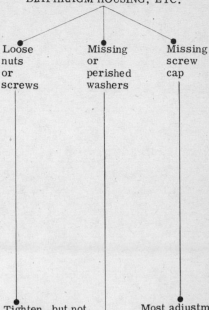

Push down and Twist

Remove spring and cap

Replace 'O' ring

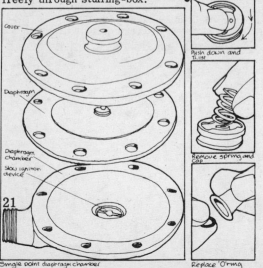

Cover

Diaphragm

Diaphragm chamber

Slow ignition device

21

Single point diaphragm chamber

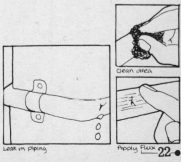

Leak in piping

Clean area

Apply flux

22

LEAKING FROM HEAT EXCHANGE UNIT

Damaged pipe work

Solder joints leaking

MAIN BURNER HAS HIGH YELLOW FLAME CAUSING SOOT, SMOKE AND LITTLE HEAT

Using unconverted town gas appliance on natural gas supply

It is possible to operate unconverted appliances with natural (North Sea) gas, but under no circumstances must this be done. As well as being unsatisfactory and giving off heavy soot, it is also dangerous due to the presence of carbon monoxide in the flue gasses (see 2.31.03).

Reheat solder joints adding new solder to edge of the joints. The solder should run into the joints by capillary action. Use wire solder with its own flux. Second-hand heat exchange units can occasionally be found.

Check with your local gas showrooms on type of gas used in the area. Natural gas appliances have larger jets as they have to mix the gas with air before it will burn properly. Conversion Kits are available and come with instructions but are very difficult to get hold of.

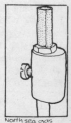

North sea gas
Pilot light

Solder over hole. Clean surrounding area with wire wool. Apply flux and heat with blow lamp. Apply solder and smooth down with wiping cloth.

-22-

Heat

Use grade 'A' solder

Main Burners for a converted, North sea Gas 709 Ascot

GENERAL REPAIRS

3. 01. 00　CARPENTRY AND JOINERY: INTRODUCTION

3. 01. 01　The repair of most short-life houses will require some carpentry - structural wood working (e. g. floors, walls, roofs) and joinery (e. g. stairs, doors, windows, etc.). Most of this can be done with a small number of tools but does require some degree of skill and experience of woodwork. If you don't have these skills, then expect a period of learning and practice before attempting more complex jobs.

3. 01. 02　The ability to work easily and well with wood cannot be acquired from instructions or books, but must be learnt directly from the wood. Advice does help, and, kept in mind while working, may help in understanding the experience. Most advice seems obvious and simple, but remember there's a difference between being told what's best, and actually 'knowing' it.

3. 01. 03　A major difficulty for beginners is having the right tools for the job, knowing the limits of those they have, and working within those limits. Much of the frustration beginners experience comes from trying to work out of the range of their tools. This results in bad workmanship, hours of remedial work and even damage to tools and hands. Obviously we can't all have every tool we need, especially if money is short, so when buying tools start with the most basic and versatile and only add specialised tools when necessary and if they can't be borrowed. More importantly, work within the range of your tools - for instance, cut mortices to the same width as the chisel you own (providing it's reasonable for the job you're doing) - and never push tools to a limit where they may be damaged or broken.

3. 01. 04　It took me a long time to discover the importance of keeping tools sharp and properly set. It seemed to me that tools could never be as good again as when they were new. In truth, if sharpened and set properly they will be much better; indeed, most new tools will need to be sharpened before use.

Having sharp tools not only means the work is easier and cleaner, but also that you work with more confidence and surety, never having to resort to brute force, or damaging wood and tools in an effort to 'make' things work.

3. 01. 05 Another important factor is careful measuring and marking. Where possible measuring should be done directly, by marking the work piece in situ. Check measurements twice before making cuts and always mark for orientation (i. e. which end fits which end).

3. 01. 06 Wood is an organic substance - no two pieces are ever exactly the same even from the same species - though certain qualities may be apparent. If you bear this in mind it allows you to respond to the wood as it demands, rather than as you think it should. It's no good to assume you can plane a piece of wood in both directions just because it worked once before. Wood is not uniform or homogeneous like glass or steel or sand, but has twists, knots and grain patterns that are characteristic of its species but unique to itself. The modern building industry has a great deal of difficulty in dealing with such a variable sub- stance and this partly explains the popularity of products such as block- board, chipboard, hardboard and veneer, which are attempts to 'standardise' wood.

3. 01. 07 Most of the above points aim at reducing the unnecessary hitches and drawbacks that lead so quickly to frustration and rage when working with as demanding a material as wood. Indeed, the 'secret' to working well with wood is to develop an attitude to the work that minimises the likelihood of snags and drawbacks and leaves you sensitive enough to follow what the wood wants to do, and thereby learn what it and the tools will do. It often seems that as soon as one thing goes wrong, and there is any undue tension, it leads to other mistakes and more tension, and escalates out of all proportion. While I'm not suggesting that this is inevitable, it's a situation that must be familiar to most people.

3.01.08 Think ahead, plan out what you intend to
do, make little drawings and talk it over
with someone - anyone - for the process
of thinking a thing through is as useful
as any suggestions you might receive.
Work slowly, carefully and tidily,
measure accurately, keep things well
marked, tools sharp and set, and
remain calm.

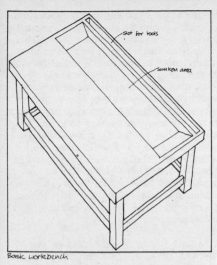
Basic workbench

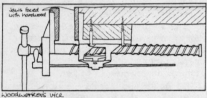
Woodworkers vice

3.02.00 BASIC TOOLS

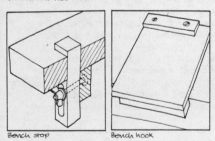
Bench stop   Bench hook

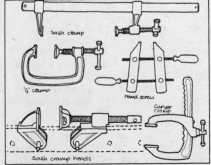
Some of the cramps available

3.02.01 For short-life house repairs and house repairs in general a combination of carpentry and joinery tools are needed. A major difficulty for beginners is knowing which tools are essential and which tools can be left out. There is no easy answer to this, as the choice always depends on circumstances and the particular needs of the work undertaken. Another problem is not knowing what tools there are and what they can do - often a very cheap tool can save a lot of time and effort. Buy tools that are the best you can afford; this will encourage you to look after them, and not just pop down to the local hardware shop whenever you can't find your chisel or screwdriver. Unlike most building tools, carpentry tools such as saws, planes, chisels and squares, etc., should not be lent out. All tools that can be easily damaged by wrong use should be considered personal tools. The following is a list of all the major tools, their use, most common abuse and hints on quality.

3.02.02 Workbench - It's not immediately obvious that a workbench is an essential tool - most of us make do with old tables, propped up planks, etc. You shouldn't necessarily rush out and spend £200 on a carpenter's bench, but

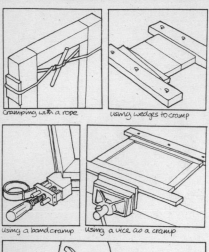

Cramping with a rope   using wedges to cramp

Using a band cramp   using a vice as a cramp

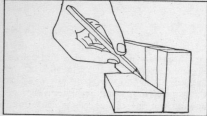

Using off-cut to make accurate measurements

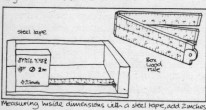

steel tape

Box
wood
rule

Measuring inside dimensions with a steel tape, add 2 inches

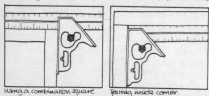

Using a combination square   Testing inside corner.

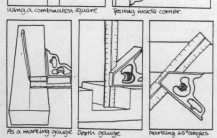

As a marking gauge   Depth gauge   Marking 45° angles

do try to provide yourself with as good a work surface as possible. Essential features: rigid flat surface (about 3' high or to suit); trough or sunken area where tools in use can be out of the way; if possible, a vice - a woodworker's vice must be fitted, but there are ones that are attached by a screw-on cramp. Always face the metal jaws with wooden blocks to prevent damage to work. Bench stops are useful for holding work while planning, and bench hooks as a sawing aid (easily made and extremely timesaving). There are a number of small work tables, like the Workmate, which are useful when you don't have a fixed workspace, or when working in different locations.

3. 02. 03 Cramp - It may be worth having one or two cramps, but again they are not essential, as you can use twisted rope or wedges (see illustrations). Occasionally a cramp will do in place of a vice. Sash cramps are generally used for cramping frames or panels made up of several pieces. The cheapest way of buying sash cramps is to get only the 'cramp heads' (about £4 - £50 a set) that are specially designed for using 1-inch thick timber. 'G' cramps are useful for cramping together work while glue dries or while it's still being worked on. Mitre cramps are specifically for holding mitred corners. Wooden hand screw cramps are for light work and deal easily with tapering surfaces. Particularly useful (and cheap) are the band or web cramps.

3. 02. 04 Measuring tools - Measurements can often be taken directly e. g. marked directly onto the wood while held in position - and this is often the most accurate method. A good measure remains invaluable, however. A 2 metre (6') or 3 metre (10') steel tape is best for larger dimensions; a folding boxwood (or plastic) rule (3' or 1m) is best for smaller measurements. Make sure it has both metric and Imperial measures.

3. 02. 05 Square - This is essential for accurate setting out, accurate cutting, and checking for squareness. A 'combination' square is probably the best for occasional

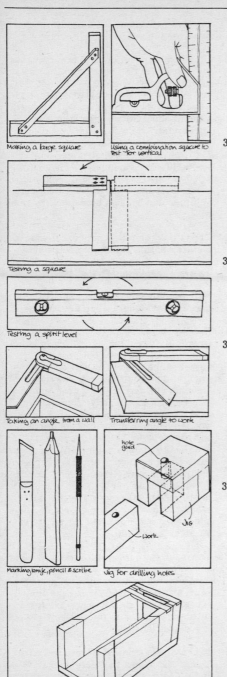

Making a large square

Using a combination square to test for vertical

Testing a square

Testing a spirit level

Taking an angle from a wall

Transferring angle to work

Marking knife, pencil & scribe

Jig for drilling holes

Mitre box

users but it tends never to be quite as accurate as separate tools that do the same jobs (squaring, 45-degree angles, measuring depths, drawing parallel lines and levelling). A carpenter's square is very useful for larger work but fairly expensive for most people; a large square can also be made, if needed.

3.02.06 Spirit level - Good spirit levels are expensive and are needed mainly for work that is being built onto or into existing structure - or for building itself. The longer the better - a 3' (1m) level is preferred. Check for accuracy occasionally by turning the level around. If the bubble returns to the same place, it's accurate.

3.02.07 Adjustable bevel - A surprisingly useful tool that is not too expensive. A bevel is simply an adjustable 'square'. Essential for any angled work - can be used for 'taking' angles off existing structures for transfer to work.

3.02.08 Scribe, marking knife and pencil - Scribes are used mainly for marking up metal, but give very accurate marking especially on hard woods. Marking knives are more generally used with wood, but are difficult to use properly - they tend to wander with the grain and care must be taken not to cut too deeply. If using a pencil, sharpen with a 'chisel' point - it lasts longer and is more accurate.

3.02.09 Template and jig - These are 'tools' that are made, not bought. That is, they are guides that can be made for a specific job where some repetition makes it worthwhile doing so. They increase accuracy and decrease the likelihood of mistakes. They can be simple - a batten cut to a specific length - or a complex frame on which the work can be assembled on a repetitive basis. Using an 'off-cut' to mark its depth on another piece of wood is a simple form of template. A mitre block or box is the most generally used jig, and invaluable for making mitred joints.

3.02.10 Marking gauge - Used for marking out mortise and tenons and other similar

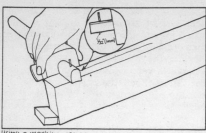

Using a marking gauge

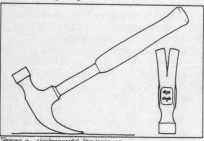

Testing a clawhammer for balance

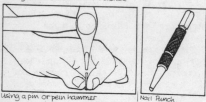

Using a pin or pein hammer   Nail Punch

Panel Saw

Blade

TOE   HEEL

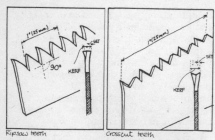

Ripsaw teeth   Crosscut teeth

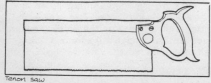

Tenon saw

work. Useful, but not essential; however, it's fairly cheap.

3. 02. 11   Clawhammer - A good clawhammer is very definitely a basic tool. Forged steel head, hickory or steel handle and finely cut 'V' for getting out the smallest nails. A well-balanced hammer will sit on its claw at about 30 degrees from the horizontal.

3. 02. 12   Mallet - A wooden mallet is useful with wood chisels, especially if they have wooden handles. Also, a mallet won't mark the surface of wood - but a claw-hammer and wooden block can do equally well.

3. 02. 13   Cross pein or pin hammer - Useful for smaller nails, panel pins, etc. The pein is used for starting pins while held between thumb and finger.

3. 02. 14   Nail punch - One of those small tools that are invaluable when needed.

3. 02. 15   Panel saw (10 teeth to 1 inch (25mm))- Originally used for the cutting of panels in furniture-making, but now the universal hand saw. It will do most work - cross cutting, rip sawing (sawing with the grain) - reasonably efficiently. The quality of a saw can best be judged by its price, but generally wooden handles are more comfortable and silver steel blades the best. Remember to check carefully for hidden nails when sawing re-used timber - it's the quickest way to ruin a saw. A recent development is to coat saws with teflon to stop rust and reduce friction while sawing. However, they cannot be file sharpened and I assume the teflon wears off after some use.

3. 02. 16   Crosscut and rip saws (8 teeth to 1 inch and 4 teeth to 1 inch) - The more teeth the finer the cut, but slower. Crosscut saws are for cutting large size timber across the grain. Rip saws are for cutting quickly with the grain. Neither are essential.

3. 02. 17   Tenon or back saw (14 teeth to 1 inch) - The 'back' keeps the blade more rigid, and therefore cuts more easily. It is used for cutting smaller timber to length

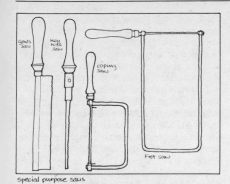

Special purpose saws

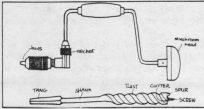

Brace and centre bit

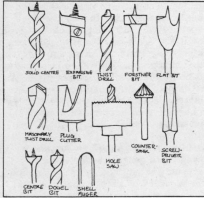

Some of the bits and drills available

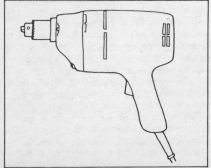

Electric drill

and for most joint-making. If smaller work is all you're doing (say up to 3 inch square timber) then you may get away without a panel saw.

3.02.18 Special saws - There are saws for finer work (more teeth per inch) - dovetail, bead saw or gents saw. For cutting internal shapes from a starting hole you need a keyhole saw. For cutting curves, a bow saw, fret saw and coping saw. If your budget doesn't run to such special saws a hack saw (normally for cutting metal) will give the fine clean cut in wood that's needed for smaller joint-making, though it won't deal with curved shapes.

3.02.19 Hand brace - While a hand brace is not as fast as an electric drill it is extremely versatile and a fraction of the cost. A good brace will take bits from 1/16" up to $\frac{1}{2}$", twist drills, wood bits, auger bits, expanding bits, masonry bits (which are best used at hand speeds), countersinks and, very useful, screwdriver bits. A brace with a ratchet attachment allows limited sweep to be used in restricted areas - also a good bearing, preferably a ball race, is needed on the mushroom head to ensure ease of operation and a long life.

3.02.20 Wheelbrace - I've always found wheelbraces awkward to use, so for smaller holes and where more control is required, I prefer the archimedean drill, which is cheaper, but more difficult to obtain.

3.02.21 Electric drill - It's best to buy a fairly good electric drill if you also intend to add sawing and sanding attachments. The capacity of the drill is indicated by the size of the chuck, $\frac{1}{4}$" (6mm) being the most common, though 5/16" (8mm) and $\frac{1}{2}$" (12mm) are also available on small drills. The chuck can be removed and replaced with a larger one, but the constant danger with small electric drills is of overloading and damage to the motor. A two-speed or variable-speed model, or one with an automatic cut-out, helps prevent this. But the golden rule remains: if the motor loses speed, or if there is a change in the 'note' of the motor, slacken pressure or remove

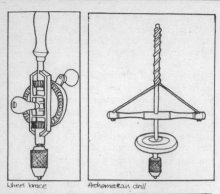

Wheel brace   Archomedean drill

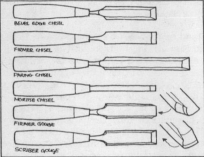

BEVEL EDGE CHISEL

FIRMER CHISEL

PARING CHISEL

MORTISE CHISEL

FIRMER GOUGE

SCRIBER GOUGE

Types of chisel and gouge

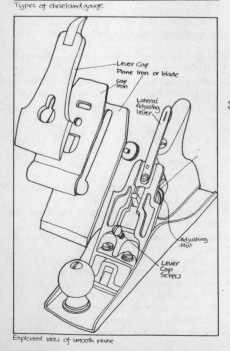

Lever Cap
Plane Iron or blade
cap
iron

Lateral
Adjusting
lever

Adjusting
Nut

Lever
Cap
Screw

Exploded view of smooth plane

the tool from the work, so the motor may recover its maximum speed; never start the motor while the tool is engaged in the work, and always work at a pace that allows the tool to cut at its own rate. Most attachments increase the danger of overloading the motor. This is especially true of circular saw attachments, where the flimsiness of guids allows the saw to wander and become jammed. Some people recommend using the jig saw attachment for its extra versatility, as it is less likely to jam and less dangerous than a circular saw. Other useful attachments are disc, drum and orbital sanders, but these should be used with restraint.

3. 02. 22 Wood chisel - If you can only afford one, $\frac{1}{2}$" (12mm) is the one to get. Otherwise, buy them as you need them, or buy a set of four: $\frac{1}{4}$" (6mm), $\frac{1}{2}$" (12mm), $\frac{3}{4}$" (18mm) and 1" (25mm). 'Firmer' chisels are for heavier work (carpentry) while bevelled chisels are more suited to finer joint-making. The modern plastic-handled ones are better than the wooden ones, especially if you're not the careful type and if you don't own a mallet. Sharpen chisels regularly and don't use them on other materials. Take care to remove all nails when working on old wood. An old chisel, one that can be chipped or blunted, is also very useful, and helps in keeping your good chisel for its proper use.

3. 02. 23 Wood plane - A plane may not seem essential to general house repair carpentry but it does extend the scope and accuracy of work that can be done. Many people are put off using planes because they need regular adjustment and sharpening. It's only when they are correctly set that you can get any pleasure from their use. However, it's worth the bother of mastering the finer points of planing. The basic 'jack plane' has remained the same since 1859, a testament to its versatility. You can do most general planing, shaping, sizing and smoothing with a jack plane. For cleaning larger areas, a 'jointer' plane is better, and for smoothing finer work a smoothing plane. A block plane is designed for planing end grain. A recent development has been the introduction

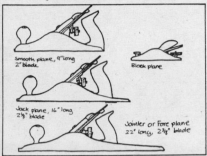

Section through metal plane

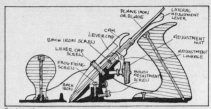

Smooth plane, 9"long, 2" blade

Block plane

Jack plane, 16" long, 2⅜" blade

Joiner or Fore plane 22" long, 2³⁄₈" blade

Planes

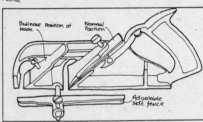

Bullnose Position of blade

Normal Position

Adjustable side fence

Rebate plane

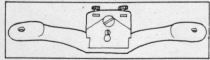

Open files or shaping tools (Surforms)

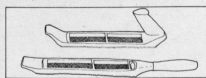

Metal spokeshave with adjustment screws

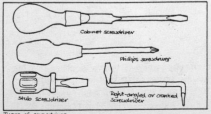

Cabinet screwdriver

Phillips screwdriver

Stubb screwdriver

Right-angled or cranked screwdriver

Types of screwdriver

of replaceable blade planes, which incorporate a rebating attachment. Blades can be resharpened, but the tendency is simply to throw them away. Always lay a plane on its side when not in use to protect the blade.

3.02.24 Special planes - Not necessary for general repair work, but it's worth noting that special planes can do rebating, grooving, moulding, concave and convex surfaces and are good for working close to edges and ends.

3.02.25 Surform, or open file cutter - These are cheaper and easier to master than planes and can do some of the shaping and sizing that a plane can do. They also cut and shape other materials, even mild steel! They are very useful for preliminary cleaning up of second-hand timber before planing.

3.02.26 Spokeshave - Another traditional instrument, intended for shaping and rounding, but sufficiently versatile to be used for a number of shaping, sizing and chamfering jobs. There are various types, some with flat, some with curved soles, for shaping curved surfaces.

3.02.27 Screwdriver - Two or three sizes of screwdriver will be needed for most jobs. A screwdriver bit for a brace is a useful addition, especially for driving large long screws. Some people swear by the Yankee ratchet screwdrivers, and these are useful when there is a lot of screwing to be done - but they are expensive.

3.02.28 Pliers - For general work, wire cutting, gripping and bending.

3.02.29 Countersink - For countersinking screwheads flush or below the surface. I prefer a countersink on a screwdriver-type handle, as this means you don't have to keep changing bits in your brace or drill.

3.02.30 Bradawl - Very cheap and useful for starting small screws and marking centres for drilling.

3.02.31 Oilstone - With fine and coarse sides (see sharpening, 03.04.00).

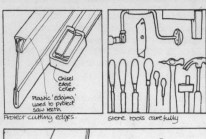

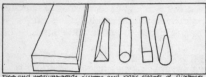

Protect cutting edges.

Store tools carefully.

3.03.00 TOOL CARE AND MAINTENANCE

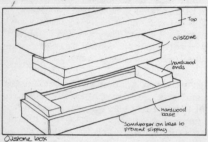

Fine and medium grade oilstone and basic shapes of slipstones

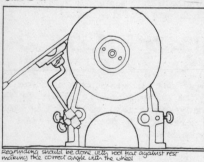

Oilstone box

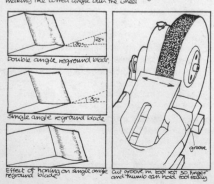

Regrinding should be done with tool flat against rest making the correct angle with the wheel

Double angle reground blade

Single angle reground blade

Effect of honing on single angle reground blade

Cut groove in tool rest so finger and thumb can hold tool easily

3.03.01 General care - Always protect cutting
        edges, especially if tools are kept
        loose in a bag. Take special care with
        squares, spirit levels and other measur-

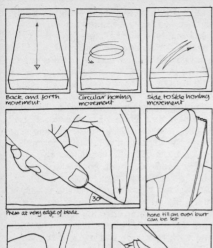

Back and forth movement.

Circular honing movement

Side to side honing movement

Press at very edge of blade

/30

hone till an even burr can be felt

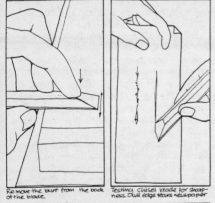

Remove the burr from the back of the blade.

Testing chisel blade for sharpness. Dull edge tears newspaper

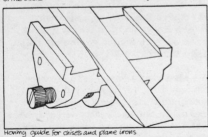

Honing guide for chisels and plane irons

Re-surfacing oilstone on glass with grinding powder.

ing tools. Store tools in a dry place and cover metal parts with a light oil if they are to be left for some time. Avoid using tools for jobs that they were not intended to do.

3. 03. 02 Sharpening - Sharpening chisels, plane irons and spokeshave blades is generally done with an oilstone; saw blades and some drill bits with a file. Slipstones - specially shaped oilstones - are used for sharpening less common tools such as gouges. There are other types of sharpening stone - wet stones (used with water) and Arkansas stones, etc. - but all do basically the same job.

3. 03. 03 As well as fine sharpening (or honing), blades may also need regrinding from time to time to remove chips and other damage or simply to resquare a blade. However, regrinding is a difficult skill to learn, and it may be best to have it done at a tool shop. Some of these faults can be corrected by careful honing on a coarse oilstone.

3. 03. 04 If you want to do your own grinding then it is best done on a hand wheel as these are much less intimidating than an electric wheel (and cheaper). They are also less likely to 'blue' or overheat the steel - which ruins its sharpening qualities. A small tool rest with a finger groove allows the tool to be held firmly at the correct angle (25 - 30 degrees) to the wheel and moved easily back and forth. Don't overheat the steel; if you do it will turn blue and this will have to be ground off before a suitable edge can be made.

3. 03. 05 Many people recommend a double angle for chisel and plane irons - a ground angle of 25 degrees and a honed angle of 30 degrees - and this seems more suitable if you cannot easily regrind the blade. Even if you do regrind the blade often, a single angle is still, as far as I know, just as good.

3. 03. 06 Honing - Start on the medium or coarse side and use thin oil to lubricate the stone. The important things when honing are to keep a constant angle - best done by pressing the blade at the

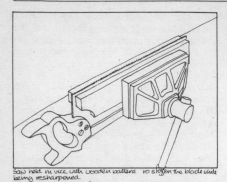

Saw held in vice with wooden battens   to stiffen the blade while being resharpened.

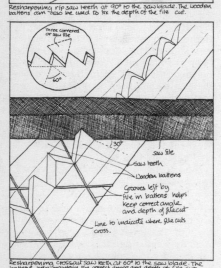

Resharpening rip saw teeth at 90° to the saw blade. The wooden battens can also be used to fix the depth of the file cut.

Resharpening crosscut saw teeth at 60° to the saw blade. The battens help maintain the correct angle and depth of file cut

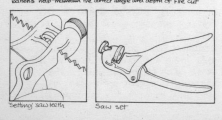

'Setting' saw teeth   Saw set

very end on to the stone - and to grind evenly across the blade to keep it reasonably square. There are several 'actions' that are recommended for sharpening: a full stroke from one end of the stone to the other, or a circular motion, or a crossways motion slightly curved. Use whichever you find easiest to control, and keep looking at the blade to make sure you're keeping a constant angle, and not taking more off one side. Hone the angled surface till you can feel a burr of metal when you run your finger along the back edge - this burr should run from edge to edge of the blade, and if it doesn't you're taking more off one side than the other. Turn the stone over to the fine side, oil, and, turning the blade onto its flat side and with this side flat against the stone, rub back and forwards for a few strokes. Turn the blade over and hone the angled face as before. Keep turning from one side to the other until the burr wears off to leave a sharp edge. Never lift the blade even the slightest angle while honing the back - this must always be done flat. A keener edge can be got from a leather strop - a piece of thick leather glued to a flat wooden block. A well-sharpened blade should cut a piece of newsprint held loosely, a blunt edge tends to tear the paper. Some people recommend removing the burr by making a cut in a piece of hardwood, and it's also said that it's better not to remove the burr on a spokeshave blade. If you find it difficult to get a good edge, a honing guide may help (see illustration).

3.03.07 It's also very important to keep the oilstone flat, for it's only if it's flat that blades can be kept square. It's inevitable that the centre is used more than the edges and so the stone itself must be squared from time to time. This can be done by using carborundum powder (or silver sand, e.g. sand used for canary cage bottoms) sprinkled on a sheet of glass with water, and rubbing the stone in a circular motion on it until the stone is reground flat.

3.03.08 Stones become clogged with oil after prolonged use and can be cleaned by setting in a tray and baking in a

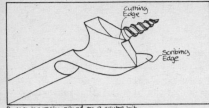

Parts to be resharpened on a centre bit

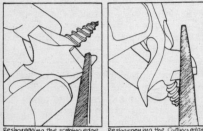

Resharpening the scribing edge with a file

Resharpening the cutting edge with a file

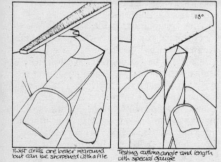

Twist drills are better reground but can be sharpened with a file

Testing cutting angle and length with special gauge

Critical angles and dimensions of a twist bit

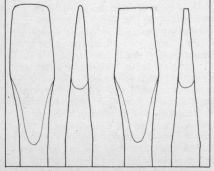

Badly rounded screwdriver can be reground or filed square

moderately hot oven for an hour or so. The lighter the oil used, the better - some people recommend paraffin, though this does smell quite strongly.

3.03.09 Saws are sharpened with a triangular file (or a saw file as it is sometimes called): though not difficult, it can be tedious. Again, saws can be sharpened at most good tool shops. The blade should be clamped between two stout battens to hold it rigid. Rip saws are sharpened at 90 degrees to the blade, each tooth being given a sharp point. If the teeth are very uneven in height, a flat file can be run along the top once or twice to even out the height before you start sharpening. Crosscut and panel saws are filed at about 60 degrees to the blade, each alternate tooth being sharpened one way, and the remainder the other. One tip is to set the two supporting battens with their top edge level with the bottom of the teeth. As you sharpen, a slight groove is also made in the wood, indicating which teeth have been done, helping to keep the angle constant and also the depth of the file cut.

3.03.10 All but the finer-toothed saws need to be given a 'set', usually done after sharpening, which consists of bending each alternate tooth slightly out, one way then the other. This can only really be done with a special tool, a 'saw set', which is fairly cheap. An adjustment allows for different size teeth to be set with the same tool.

3.03.11 In general many tools benefit from periodic maintenance. All bits and drills can be reground or filed to give a new edge. In most cases it's a matter of looking closely to see how the previous cutting edge was made, and grinding or filing at the same angle. There are also honing guides that can be bought for most tools, and which help in maintaining the correct angle and squareness. Other tools may also occasionally need regrinding, such as a screwdriver tip that has become rounded or the curls of metal on the end of a cold chisel. Don't be afraid of looking after tools, but do it with care and thought.

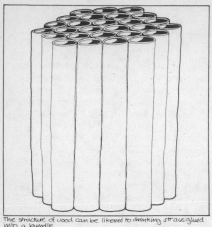

The structure of wood can be likened to drinking straws glued into a bundle.

Cracking of wood along the grain

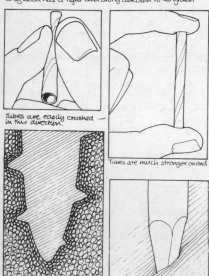

Why wood has a 'right' and 'wrong' direction to its grain

→ with the grain   ← against the grain

Tubes are easily crushed in this direction.

Tubes are much stronger on end

Wood screw compresses the fibres of the wood.

Nails part the fibres and crush them to make a path through wood

3. 04. 00 PROPERTIES OF WOOD

3. 04. 01 Weight for weight wood is stronger than most steels and must still be rated as one of the best building materials we know. Its one great difficulty is that, being a natural material, it's never quite as consistent as steel or glass, and because of this, and for other reasons, it's relatively difficult to work with.

3. 04. 02 The basic material of wood is cellulose, and the basic structures of cellulose are fibres wound spirally into tubes that contain the sap of living trees. This basic structure can best be visualised as a bundle of long drinking straws glued together. Wood's most obvious characteristic is its 'grain' and its tendency to split along the direction of the grain. With the drinking straws in mind you begin to see why this should be (especially if the glue binding the straws is weaker than the straws themselves, as is the case with lignin, the 'glue' that binds the cellulose). It also makes some of its other properties more explicable; for instance, imagine the bundle of straws cut down their length (with the 'grain'), but at a slight angle, so that you are cutting through straws but at a very oblique angle, and you can see why planing in one direction is fine, but simply 'raises the grain' in the other. Again, wood is much stronger end on than across the grain, just as straws are more easily crushed from the side than from the ends. Screws and nails work by forcing their way between bundles of fibres, and again you can see why screws hold much better than nails, and why nailing or screwing into end grain has almost no strength. Obviously, it is not altogether so simple, as there are great differences between the many types of woods - differences due to the variations in grain patterns, the length and direction of the fibres, and the number and type of transverse rays - and these differences are experienced as the working properties of different types of wood.

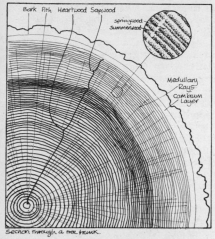

Section through a tree trunk.

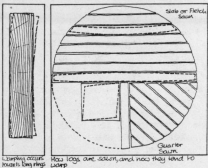

Warping occurs towards long rings

How logs are sawn, and how they tend to warp

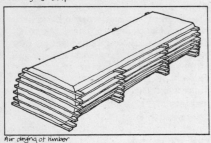

Air drying of timber

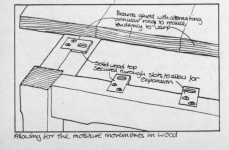

Allowing for the moisture movements in wood

3. 04. 03 There are two basic tree types, the coniferous - the softwoods, and broad-leaved trees - and the hardwoods. While in general softwoods are less dense (and weaker) than hardwoods, this is by no means true of all species. Yew, a softwood, is as hard as most hardwoods, while balsa, the least dense wood there is, is a hardwood. Hardwoods are also generally more expensive than softwoods and are used mainly for furniture, mouldings, edging and veneers. Almost all building timber is softwood, usually pine (construction) and cedar (cladding).

3. 04. 04 Growth in trees occurs in a thin layer - the cambium layer - under the bark. The rate of growth varies, being fast in spring (springwood), and slower and therefore denser in summer (summerwood). It is this change in density which gives wood it character-istic marking - seen in end grain as annual rings, or the familiar 'contoured' patterns of face grain. As the tree grows there is a gradual conversion of rings from sapwood to heartwood. Heartwood is preferred because it is less prone to rot or beetle attacks and is usually stronger than sapwood. Generally heartwood is darker than sapwood.

3. 04. 05 Seasoning - All wood has to be dried before it can be used, and this must be done carefully, as the moisture is locked into the sap channels throughout the wood - if drying is uneven the different rates of shrinkage cause crack-ing or checking especially on the ends, and this may ruin or reduce the amount of usable timber. Traditionally this drying was done by stacking cut timber in yards and leaving it for two, three or more years (air-dried), but now most timber is dried in special kilns (kiln-dried). Timber is never entirely dry, and its moisture content will fluctuate with the changes in the moisture content of the air. Thus, in England, a change of about 10 per cent in the moisture content will occur between a dry summer and a wet winter. Changes also occur if wood is moved to a different environment, from out-side to inside, or from an unheated room to a heated one, or to a centrally-

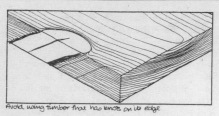

Avoid using timber that has knots on its edge

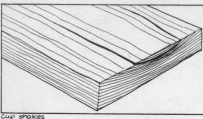

Live knots provide decoration but should be avoided for structural timber

Dead knots should be avoided or cut out

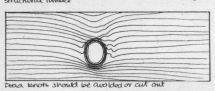

Cup shakes

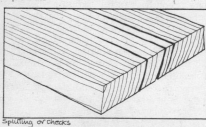

Splitting or checks

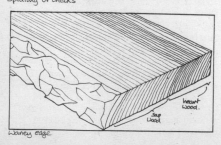

Waney edge

heated room. More importantly, these changes in moisture content cause shrinkage and expansion that must be allowed for in the design and use of wood. Much antique wooden furniture suffers, for instance, from being brought into centrally-heated rooms when it was intended for use in rooms with coal or wood fires. The movement is entirely across the grain - remembering the drinking straws, it is equivalent to them being 'rounded out' by moisture after being somewhat flattened. Their length remains unchanged - likewise, the length of timber remains the same.

3. 04. 06 Knots - Knots are a natural part of most woods and are the points at which branching occurred from the main stem. They get smaller towards the centre of the trunk. They add beauty and interest to grain patterns and give timber much of its decorative appeal. Knots also weaken timber, especially if they occur near or on the edge, and should be avoided when timber is used for heavy constructional purposes. (Pin knots - no bigger than 1/32" (0.8mm) can be disregarded). Avoid loose knots - knots that are not tightly held in place - and dead knots - knots that have a black surround and may later become loose.

3. 04. 07 Shakes and checks - These are caused by uneven or too rapid drying and are seen as cracks and splitting, often along the grain, and most often at the ends. Small splits (checks) can be cut off but if there are larger splits (shakes) then avoid buying or using altogether. Honeycombing, which consists of small but numerous checks throughout the wood, should also be avoided though it is not always apparent from the outside.

3. 04. 08 Waney edge - This consists of an area of bark and sapwood left on sawn timber (mainly hardwoods) and in general must be removed. The sapwood however can be kept if sound, and the change of colour between sap and heartwood is often used for decorative effect. If it is used it should be protected from rot and beetles. There is usually a great deal of wastage using waney edge timber.

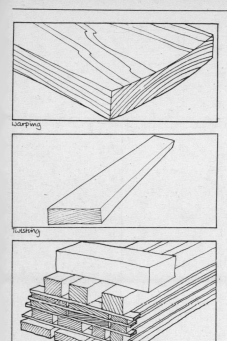

Warping

Twisting

Stacking cut timber while it is 'acclimatised'

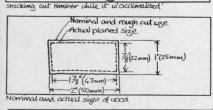

Nominal and rough cut size
Actual planed size

$\frac{7}{8}$"(22mm) 1"(25mm)

1$\frac{3}{8}$" (47mm)
2" (50mm)

Nominal and actual sizes of wood

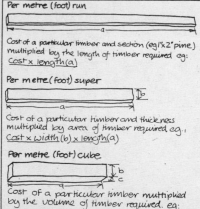

Per metre (foot) run

a

Cost of a particular timber and section (eg1"x2"pine)
multiplied by the length of timber required eg:
Cost x length(a)

Per metre (foot) super

a   b

Cost of a particular timber and thickness
multiplied by area of timber required eg:
Cost x width(b) x length(a)

Per metre (foot) cube

b
c

Cost of a particular timber multiplied
by the volume of timber required. eg:
Cost x thickness (c) x width(b) x length(a)

How wood is costed.

3. 04. 09 Warping and twisting - This occurs from a tendency of the wood to bend towards the longer rings, but can be increased by bad cutting, uneven drying and bad stacking. It consists of a slight curl across wide boards (warping) or a twisting along the length of the timber (twisting). Very slight twisting occurs in most long lengths, so select least twisted pieces when buying. Some warping and twisting can be corrected by stacking affected timber, or even by applying pressure against the twist over a period of weeks or months. If possible allow timber time to acclimatise after purchase, if from a wood yard, preferably in the same conditions as those in which it will later be kept and for at least three to four weeks. If timber is being resawn to smaller (cross-sectional) sizes, then again stack flat and allow to settle before use. Stacking timber should be done on a flat, even surface, with small battens ($\frac{1}{2}$" x $\frac{3}{4}$", 12mm x 19mm) put between each piece at about 3' (1m) intervals, so that air is free to circulate around the wood. The stack may also be weighted to further discourage twisting.

3. 04. 10 Timber sizes - The timber trade now officially operates in metric sizes, although Imperial sized woods are also still available. Wood is cut and machine-planed only to a limited number of sizes (see chart), less now in metric than in the old Imperial sizes. If you want wood that is a different size, then it must be specially machined, or cut from the next size.

In practice, therefore, it is better to work to the sizes available. It's also important to remember that with machine-planed wood its size is only a 'nominal' size and not its actual size. So, even though a piece may be sold as 2" x 1" (50mm x 25mm), its actual planed size will be about 1$\frac{3}{4}$" x 7/8" (45mm x 22mm).

3. 04. 11 Buying wood - Wood is much cheaper if bought from a timber yard than from a D. I. Y. shop - however, for small quantities, or if you want pieces precut and sized, then a D. I. Y. shop will be

Timber size chart

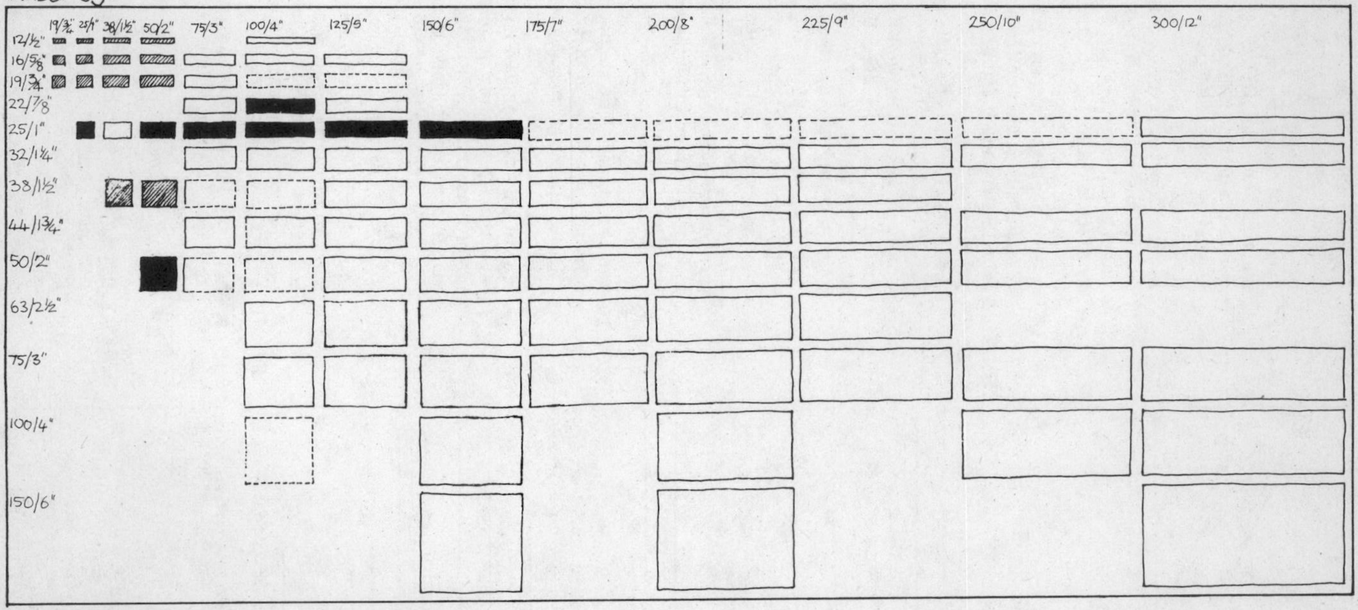

Top axis (widths): 19/¾" 24/1" 38/1½" 50/2" 75/3" 100/4" 125/5" 150/6" 175/7" 200/8" 225/9" 250/10" 300/12"

Left axis (thicknesses): 12/½" 16/⅝" 19/¾" 22/⅞" 25/1" 32/1¼" 38/1½" 44/1¾" 50/2" 63/2½" 75/3" 100/4" 150/6"

KEY

- Most comes only available planed from stock
- Frequently available planed from stock
- Sawn and rough sawn sizes
- Occasionally available

Note sizes are given first in metric (mm) and then to the nearest imperial size. For planed stock deduct 3mm or 1/8" from dimension given for actual size. The sizes given are the nominal sizes.

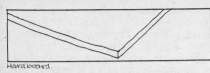

Hardboard.

Chipboard is also available faced with veneer.

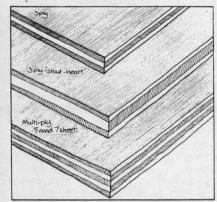

3ply

3 ply 'stout-heart'

Multi-ply,
5 and 7 sheet.

Types of plywood.

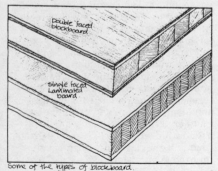

Double faced
blockboard

Single faced
Laminated
board

Some of the types of blockboard.

Top and bottom centre rails

Parting bead   stile

Bottom rails   Glazing bars   Stop   stile
                             bead

Mouldings: window frame profiles

Mouldings: hand rails

better. Make a list of all the different sizes of wood you need, and add together the lengths of those with the same width and height, e. g. 25' of 1" x 2" (10m of 25mm x 50mm), 10' of $\frac{3}{4}$" x $\frac{3}{4}$" (3m of 22mm x 22mm) and so on. You must keep in mind, however, the actual working lengths, for, if you need, say, 5 pieces 5' long, it's no good taking your 25' away as a 9' and two 8' lengths. Also add a few inches to allow for cutting of ends and similar wastage. Take your own tape measure and check sizes as you're buying them. Check each piece for splits, twisting, knots and general appearance, and, if possible, select your own pieces. If you're unfamiliar with buying wood then get a list of sizes and their price from the timber yard first. Price is usually given as pence per metre of the various sizes but it may also be given as pounds per 'metre super' (or metre square) and is found by multiplying length with width and multiplying this against the price for the particular thickness you need, or as pounds per cubic metre, which is found by multiplying all three measurements together (length, width, thickness).

3. 04. 12 Most constructional work is done in pine, and unless you specifically ask for some other wood this is what you'll be buying. If you need hardwood and do not specify, you'll probably be sold Ramin or Hoko. If you need a particular wood then you may have to shop around for it or be ready to accept an alternative. It's always worth getting prices from two or three places as they can vary tremendously.

3. 04. 13 Wood is least suited to covering a large flat area, or at least this is the most difficult job to do well. There are, however, several types of boards and sheets that are now generally used in place of solid wood. They are used both in general building work and in furniture and fittings.

Fibre building boards - Made up of various materials - wood, cane straw, etc. and made in a number of thicknesses and densities, ranging from insulation board (density 25 lb/ cu. ft.) and wall board (30 lb/ cu. ft.) to hardboard (50 lb/ cu. ft.)

Chipboards are made from wood chippings set in a casin (not suitable for

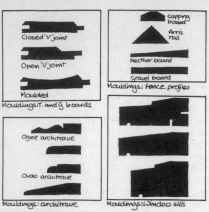

Mouldings:T. and g boards

Closed 'V'joint

Open 'V'joint

Moulded

Mouldings: fence profiles

capping board

Arris rail

Feather board

Gravel board

Mouldings: architrave

Ogee architrave

Ovolo architrave

Mouldings: Window sills

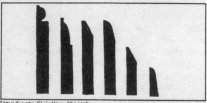

Mouldings: Skirting boards

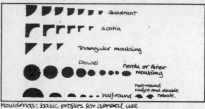

Mouldings: basic profiles for general use

Quadrant

Scotia

Triangular moulding

Dowel

Pencil or Arter moulding

half-round single and double rebate.

half-round

Mouldings: some special purpose mouldings

grooved moulding

Grooved moulding single

Double

Rebate moulding

Sliding door track

Flat corner moulding

Tray moulding

Handles

Picture framing

Cable cover

Ogee Panel Moulding

Weather moulding (for under Sills)

Base moulding

Double Astragal

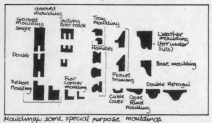

Some of the defects encountered in second-hand timber.

Avoid using timber that has been notched for structural work.

Look out for woodworm exit holes

Old brads are often broken off just below the surface

damp conditions) or resin glue. Plywoods which are made from wood veneers are again glued with either casin or resin (exterior quality) and come in various thicknesses depending on the number of layers of veneer used (three, five or more). By combining three layers of wood with their grains running at 90 degrees to each other most of the problems of shrinkage and expansion are solved. Blockboards consist of an inner core of glued timber battens covered with a single or double layer of veneer on the top and bottom.

3. 04. 14 Wood mouldings - There are dozens of different 'profiles' or 'sections' which timber is cut into and which are available as standard 'mouldings'. These are often intended for specific purposes, like skirting boards or glazing bars, etc. Others are for more general purposes, like dowels and half-rounds. More complex mouldings can also be made by combining two or more standard mouldings.

3. 04. 15 Second-hand timber - When doing carpentry, and some joinery for that matter, it may be as well to buy second-hand timber, which is very much cheaper than new, as well as often being of better quality (slower grown) and well-seasoned. There are problems, however; you must be careful of buying infected timber, timber with woodworm (look for holes) or with dry rot (see 3. 23. 00). Dry rot spores are constantly in the air, so only wood that is actually attacked must be avoided; if the wood has been in contact with rot it makes little difference. Also, look out for damage or notching, for nails and other ironware. Another difficulty is that many local authorities will not pass second-hand timber if they are supplying house improvement grants, so check first if this is the case. For short-life housing, second-hand timber should present no problem. Second-hand timber can be cleaned up, recut and planed (again, avoid nails!)

3. 04. 16 Timber treatments for wood pests - If buying new timber, especially if intended for structural work, then get pretreated wood. You can buy wood preservatives to be applied by brush or by hand pump (hired) for covering large areas. Treat second-hand timbers.

3. 05. 00 <u>BASIC WOODWORKING TECHNIQUES</u>

3. 05. 01 Wood needs to be cut and shaped with
as much accuracy as possible in order
to make full use of its structural
properties, and for it to look attractive and workmanlike. Accuracy also
saves time by reducing remedial and
repeated work - with wood it's worth
getting it right first time. Always
make allowance for the width of the
saw cuts by cutting on the waste side
of any line - if you want the wood on
both sides, then add the saw cut width
to the measurements when starting off.
If you're unsure of how a tool cuts,
test it on an off-cut and make adjustments for any discrepancies the tool
might naturally induce. Wood should
be checked for 'trueness' before
measuring - that is, you should make
sure that the faces are at 90 degrees
to each other, and that the surfaces
are flat. Using a plane, eliminate
winding (or twisting) with winding
sticks and get surfaces parallel and
flat.

3. 05. 02 Measuring out - Always work in either
Imperial or metric units - never in
both - it doesn't matter which; if you
buy wood in metric sizes, simply
measure it with an Imperial measure
and work from there - never try to
convert on paper, or in your head. I
prefer working in Imperial - it makes
more sense, not just because I'm used
to it, but because it works by propor-
tion, by halving, $\frac{1}{2}, \frac{1}{4}, 1/8, 1/16$, which
is easier for the mind's eye to grasp
and visualise.

3. 05. 03 When marking lengths always get
directly behind the line you're marking -
if you try to mark while looking from

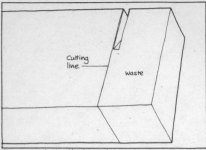

Always cut to the side of your line

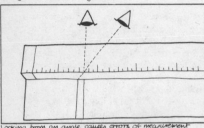

Looking from an angle causes errors of measurement

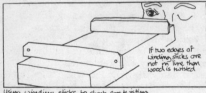

If two edges of
winding sticks are
not in line then
wood is twisted

Using winding sticks to check for twisting

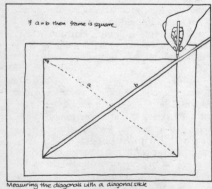

If a = b then frame is square

Measuring the diagonals with a diagonal stick

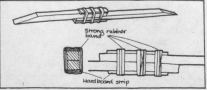

Strong rubber
band

Hardboard strip

Making an adjustable diagonal stick

an angle you may introduce small errors due to parallax.

3. 05. 04 If you're starting with new wood always cut or mark a square end an inch or so from the actual end (or in as far as you need to), to get rid of splits or damage, and then measure from there. On large sheets work from a base line or edge. Never assume that edges are square (e. g. at 90 degrees to each other) or parallel until you've checked.

3. 05. 05 Check for squareness in frames by measuring the diagonals - if they are the same then the surface is square, if not, then push or cramp the frame to reduce the longer measure (which will automatically increase the shorter length) until both diagonals are the same. You can make a measuring stick for measuring diagonals (see illustration)

3. 05. 06 Use a marking knife, or a scribe, or a pencil sharpened to a chisel point to give thin clear lines.

3. 05. 07 Where possible transfer measurements directly from already cut pieces, or from off-cuts that are the correct dimensions, or from the structure or space (e. g. an alcove or doorway, etc.) you're working to.

3. 05. 08 Use a square to mark planks and boards, etc. for cutting; mark on at least two edges, if not all round. Use a bevel for taking other than 90 degree angles from the structure or already cut piece and mark directly onto the wood. If a particular angle is needed over and over again, consider making a jig or template, but check its accuracy with a test piece.

3. 05. 09 Ensuring a structure is absolutely vertical or horizontal is best done with a spirit level. A 3' spirit level is best when dealing with carpentry and building, as it isn't so affected by local unevenness or rough surfaces and gives a better overall reading. Make sure the surface you're trueing and the edge of the level are free from debris, lumps, etc. A vertical or horizontal line can easily be made on an existing structure by simply holding the level against the

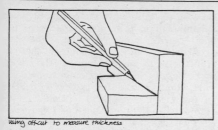

using offcut to measure thickness

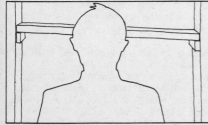

When levelling by eye, get directly infront of piece to be levelled

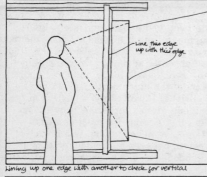

Line this edge up with this edge

Lining up one edge with another to check for vertical

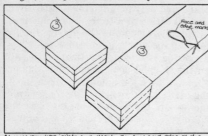

Face and edge marks

Always number joints and mark the face and edge of the work

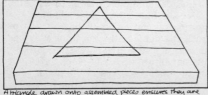

A triangle drawn onto assembled pieces ensures they are reassembled in correct order

structure, adjusting it until the bubble sits evenly across the line, and making a line. This may then act as the base line.

It's also possible to 'true up' a structure by eye. This can be done by lining up the work with an already vertical structure (e.g. a wall) or, for horizontals, by standing directly in front of the work and having someone else adjust it until it looks level; it's important to be directly in front of the structure and to have a clear view, without obstructions; and the helper must move out of the way while the sighting is done.

3. 05. 10 It's important to mark pieces of work. If it's important how the finished structure looks, then, when pieces are cut to length, inspect each piece and mark the best face and edge so they can be kept to the front. Also number each corner or junction so that joints can be tailored specifically to that place.

3. 05. 11 Hammering and nailing - A hammer is most efficient when held at the end of the handle and not near the middle, as many people seem to do. Use a nail punch for sinking nails below the surface. Never hammer directly on a wooden surface - use a scrap of wood held against the work to protect it from damage. When removing nails with the claw, make sure the nail goes as far as it can into the 'V', and slip a piece of scrap wood under the hammer head to prevent marking of the surface, and to increase leverage.

3. 05. 12 Sawing - Always mark a line on which to cut. Start the cut by drawing the saw backwards once or twice while guiding the saw with your thumb. Saw on the waste side of the line, and, as the cut comes to an end, support the waste so it does not break and splinter the piece you need. If the saw is sharp and well-set you should be able to make steady relaxed movements without jamming or using too much force. If the saw does jam it may be because the teeth have lost their set (see 3. 03. 10) or because the method of supporting the piece you're cutting is bending the saw groove closed and this is gripping the saw blade.

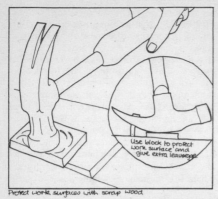

Protect work surfaces with scrap wood

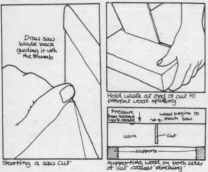

Starting a saw cut

Supporting wood on both sides of cut coolses 'pinching'

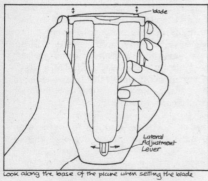

Look along the base of the plane when setting the blade

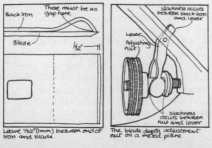

Leave 1/32"(1mm) between end of iron and blade

The blade depth adjustment nut on a metal plane

On long rip cuts (with the grain, or when cutting sheets, e. g. ply) use a wedge to open the cut, moving it along as the cut progresses. Rubbing a candle on the blade helps to make it move in the wood more easily. It's not possible to hold work steady enough for cutting without having adequate support, so find a comfortable table or bench or trestle with an edge that the work can be held against. Work can be cramped but remember to protect surfaces with a piece of scrap.

3.05.13 Planing - Planing is the most difficult technique to get a feel for. Don't expect it to come straight away, and to give yourself a fair chance, make sure the blade is sharp (see 3. 03. 02) and the back iron is on correctly - there should be 1/32" of blade protruding over its end. There should be no gaps between the back iron's leading edge and the blade, as shavings will become jammed between the two. If this happens, clean both surfaces, and if necessary hone the back iron edge flat. Make sure that the blade is correctly adjusted. On some planes (the replaceable blade and most special planes) the blade depth adjustment is positively linked to the adjusting nut, and one simply turns one way for out, the other for in. On most common planes, however, there is a linkage system between nut and blade that introduces a 'slack' area when adjusting the nut. This means in effect that the blade can only be adjusted positively in one direction at a time. When making large adjustments of the blade, simply take up the slack and move it in the direction you want, but final setting for cutting is best done in one direction only. Firstly, turn the adjusting screw until the blade can be seen while looking along the sole of the plane (from the back and against a light background), and adjust the lateral adjustment lever so the cutting edge is parallel to the sole. Retract the blade, and then, taking up the slack, move the blade out again, periodically testing the cut on a scrap piece of wood until the desired thickness of shaving is got. If you go too far, simply loosen the nut into its area of slack, give one or two more strokes of the plane - which will push the blade back in -

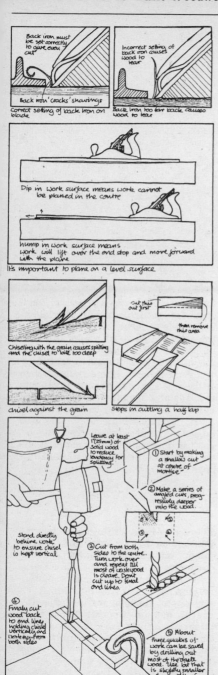

Back iron must be set correctly to give even cut

Correct setting of back iron on blade   Back iron 'cracks' shavings

Incorrect setting of back iron causes wood to tear

Back iron too far back causes wood to tear

Dip in work surface means work cannot be planed in the centre

hump in work surface means work will lift over the end stop and move forward with the plane

It's important to plane on a level surface

Chiseling with the grain causes splitting and the chisel to 'bite' too deep

Cut this out first

then remove this area

chisel against the grain   Steps in cutting a half lap

Leave at least 1"(25mm) of solid wood to reduce tendency for splitting.

① Start by making a shallow cut at centre of mortise

② Make a series of angled cuts, progressively deeper into the wood.

Stand directly behind work to ensure chisel is kept vertical

③ Cut from both sides to the centre. Turn work over and repeat till most of waste wood is clear. Don't cut up to final end lines.

④ Finally cut wood back to end line, holding chisel vertically and working from both sides

⑤ About three quarters of work can be saved by drilling out most of the waste wood. Use bit that is slightly smaller than width of mortise, and finish with a chisel.

Cutting a mortise

re-engage the nut and push the blade slightly out again, testing the cut as you go. Make sure that the work is held so a proper two-handed planing stroke can be made. On fairly large pieces of wood a small protrusion at the end of the work surface will be enough to stop the work from moving forward as you plane. Make sure it's thinner than the thickness of the piece you're planing and that the blade is in no danger of striking a nail head. Most woods can be planed in one direction only, and if this is the case, planing in the wrong direction will leave a rough torn look to the surface - like stroking a cat's fur backwards. Some woods (depending also on how they are cut from the tree) can be planed almost as well in both directions, and with some the direction changes over the area of the wood. Start the stroke with the front end of the plane's sole pressed flat against the wood, with most of the weight on the knob (toe); end the stroke when the blade is disengaged and with most weight on the handle (heel). You shouldn't have to lean too heavily on the plane; most force should be in moving it forwards.

3. 05. 14 Chiseling - Again it's important to keep your chisel sharp. Always chisel against the grain or across it, never with the grain as there is too much likelihood of the wood splitting and the chisel being deflected along the grain rather than keeping to a line. Always start a cut inside the line you eventually intend to cut to. If you start on the line the chisel may be forced back into the work or bite too deeply and without chance of correction. Never chisel towards a hand or limb; never hold work in such a way that if the chisel slips the first thing it hits is you!

3. 05. 15 In general keep tools sharp, well set and true. Work slowly and deliberately. If you have a doubt or are covering new ground then do a test piece. Use a piece of waste or off-cut of the same wood and do the test piece thoroughly, as if it were needed. Don't get over-confident, the best joints are often the second or third; the first you're learning, the fourth you're yearning to finish - so, make every joint like the second one.

3.06.00 <u>JOINTS</u>

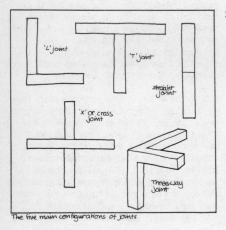

The five main configurations of joints

3. 06. 01 There are many types of joints, but about five basic ones, all others being variations of these five. The most important thing about a joint is that it facilitates the joining of two or more pieces of wood in a manner that keeps, or even enhances, the structural nature of the wood. Thus, certain joints are traditionally used for certain jobs; the mortise and tenon for joining rails to a leg, or the dovetail for joining drawer fronts to the drawer carcase. If you don't understand these principles, then use joints as they have traditionally been used.

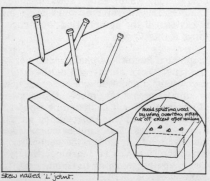

skew nailed 'L' joint.

3. 06. 02 There is a large difference between joints made in carpentry and those for joinery and cabinet-making. In general carpentry or structural timber work uses much less sophisticated joints, relying much more on the overall strength of timbers and the general overall method of construction. In joinery and finer work the size of the timbers is reduced to a minimum and the joint therefore becomes all-important The wooden kitchen or dining chair illustrates this in the extreme; in the finer examples the joints have been refined over many years to withstand the weight

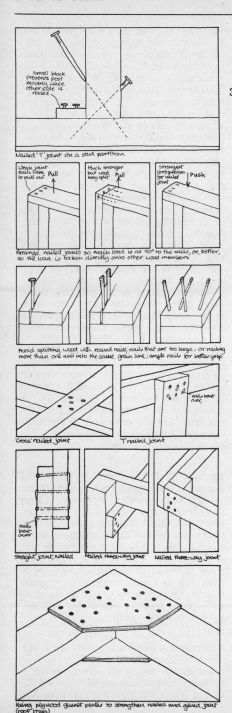

Small block prevents post moving while other side is nailed

Nailed 'T' joint on a stud partition

Weak joint nails liable to pull out   Pull

Much stronger but wood may split   Pull

Strongest configuration for nailed joint   Push

Arrange nailed joints so main load is at 90° to the nails, or, better, so the load is taken directly onto other wood members

Avoid splitting wood with round nails, nails that are too large, or nailing more than one nail into the same grain line; angle nails for better grip

'Cross' nailed joint   'T' nailed joint

nails bent over,

nail bent over

straight joint, nailed   Nailed three-way joint   Nailed three-way joint

Using plywood gusset plates to strengthen nailed and glued joint (roof truss)

of the heaviest person (rocking back on two legs!) on wooden rails and legs a square inch or less in cross-section.

3. 06. 03   Nailed joints - These are generally carpentry joints and may be used for making frames or partitions that will be covered with sheet material. In general nailed joints are butt joints, that is, where one piece of wood is offered straight onto a second piece, without tongues or grooves, etc. It's important that ends are cut square and pieces to the exact length. Nails tend to be very strong only in one direction, at 90 degrees to the direction they were driven in. If any force is exerted in the same direction they will easily pull free (just as easy as removing a bent nail with a claw hammer). Skew nailing helps prevent this - that is, nailing several nails all at different angles to the vertical. There are also special nails that are slightly grooved around their shank - annular nails - which resist direct forces more than ordinary nails do. Roof trusses are often nailed using gusset plates of plywood. These are triangular pieces cut to fit over the joint, one on each side, and give an easy large area for nailing into. The nailing is done at 90 degrees to the direction of the major forces, and spreads the area over which the nails can hold. Nailed plywood gusset plates generally make a very rigid joint. Another problem with nails is their tendency to split wood. Generally use nails only with softwoods such as pine; don't nail near the edge and use oval nails where possible. Nailing joints is often done as a temporary measure, keeping the framework together until it is positioned and a sheet covering applied. Used together, a structural framework and a non-structural sheet covering (e. g. hardboard, ply, or even weatherboarding) make an extremely strong and long-lasting structure. The sheet covering acts, in effect, like an overall gusset plate. Nailed butt joints are not normally glued, though ones that incorporate a gusset or fish plate can be glued. If a nailed frame is covered with a sheet material, this is normally not glued.

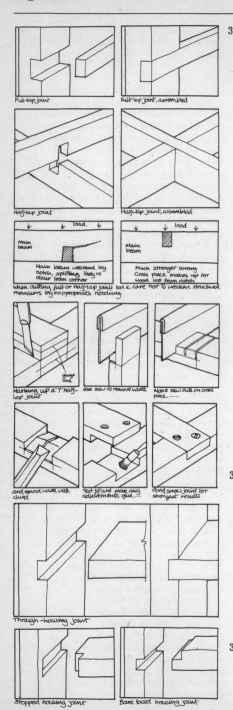

Full-lap joint

Full lap joint, assembled

Half-lap joint

Half-lap joint, assembled

load.

main beam

Main beam weakend by notch, splitting likely to occur from corner

load

Main beam

Much stronger arrang Cross piece makes up for wood lost from notch

when cutting full or half-lap joints take care not to weaken structural members by inappropriate notching.

gauge line

Marking up a 'T' half-lap joint

Use saw to remove waste

Make saw cuts on cross piece......

and remove waste with chisel

Test jt and make any adjustments, glue....

and screw joint for strongest results

Through-housing joint

Stopped housing joint

Bare faced housing joint

3. 06. 04 Full lap, half lap joint - A full-lap joint is made by cutting a notch into the edge or end of one piece, of a size sufficient to house a second piece. Generally this is used when the first piece is larger in cross-section than the second. A half lap is made by cutting similar notches into both pieces, and is used when both pieces are the same size. Cutting a notch weakens the wood considerably - the effective strength of the piece becomes equal to the thickness of the wood at the notch; for instance, a 2" x 1" (50mm x 25mm) piece would have the same strength as a 1" x 1" (25mm x 25mm) piece if it were notched to its centre. Indeed, it may be even less than this, depending on the type of wood, as such a notch encourages splitting along the grain from the inner corner. For full laps the depth of the notch will be equal to the thickness of the second piece. In the half lap, the depth of the notch will be half the depth of the wood. Take these measurements directly off the pieces themselves whenever possible. It is easier to cut the notch slightly smaller and plane down the piece going into it. Half laps may be glued or not - they are often used where the structure is made to take apart or where there is little or no structural work required from the piece; however, glueing does help to strengthen the joint, and reduces some of the strength lost by notching.

3. 06. 05 Housing joint - This is similar to a full lap joint, but refers more generally to joining wide boards to uprights. A long groove the same width as the board's thickness is cut into the upright and the board slotted in. The notching of the wood is much less weakening when done in an upright. As with most materials, wood is very much stronger as a leg or post than as a rail or beam. A stopped housing joint is used where the appearance of the front is important, and the joint needs to be hidden.

3. 06. 06 The mortise and tenon joint - This is the most important joint for general framing and making of structures. It is much less weakening to the wood than a lap joint. Its simplest form is

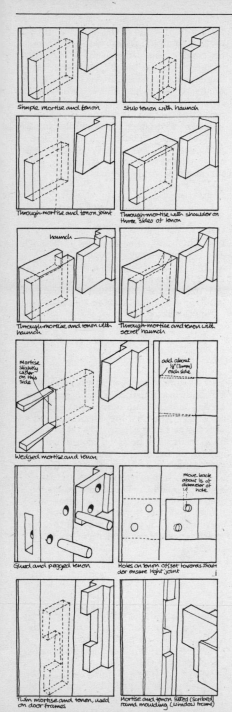

Simple mortise and tenon

Stub tenon with haunch

Through-mortise and tenon joint

Through-mortise with shoulder on three sides of tenon

haunch

Through-mortise and tenon with haunch

Through-mortise and tenon with secret haunch

Mortise slightly bigger on this side

add about ⅛″ (3mm) each side

Wedged mortise and tenon

Glued and pegged tenon

move back about ½ of diameter of ¼″ hole

Holes on tenon offset towards shoulder ensure tight joint

Twin mortise and tenon, used on door frames

Mortise and tenon fitted (scribed) round moulding (window frame)

when a hole (or mortise) is cut into one piece (usually the upright) of sufficient size for the second piece (usually the rail) to slot into. The mortise may go right through the wood (through mortise) or stop inside the wood (stub or stopped mortise). If the mortise is a through mortise then the second piece (the tenon) will need a shoulder, or stop, so that it cannot push through more than is required. This shoulder may be cut onto one edge, two, three, or all the way round, depending mostly on the relative sizes of the upright and rail. If the rail is smaller than the upright then the shoulder need only be at the top; if they are similar in size then the shoulder is cut in both sides and the top. If a shoulder is required on the bottom of a rail, or if the rail joins the upright at its bottom, or at its top, then a 'haunch' is cut into the tenon. This is to ensure the rail is not weakened by cutting into its base and also means that the mortise remains enclosed. In practice at least one shoulder is made on the tenon, even if it's a stopped mortise, as it's easier to control the depth the tenon goes into the mortise by a shoulder than it is to cut a mortise to a specific and accurate depth. The mortise is usually made slightly deeper than required. Mortise and tenons are glued, but they can also be glued and wedged or glued and pegged. Wedging is also done on through mortise, and consists of two wedges driven into the gap between the tenon and the mortise at top and bottom. The mortise is cut slightly wider than normal. Pegging is done when extremely tight joints are required. The secret is to drill the holes through the side of the mortise with the tenon out, push the tenon home, mark the hole positions and withdraw. Offset the position of the holes drilled in the tenon towards the shoulder by about a quarter of the diameter of the pegs you are using (less with harder woods). This ensures that the joint is pulled together when the pegs are inserted. There are many more variations of this joint, some illustrated here; if more detailed descriptions of these specialised joints are required, refer to books on cabinet-making.

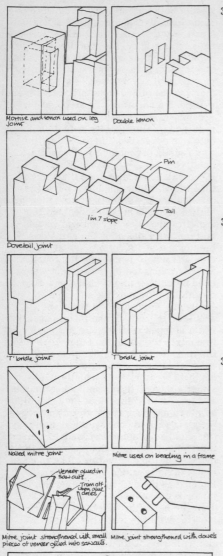

Mortise and tenon used on leg joint

Double tenon

Dovetail joint

Pin

Tail

1 in 7 slope

'T' bridle joint

'T' bridle joint

Nailed mitre joint

Mitre used on beading in a frame

Veneer glued in saw cuts

Trim off when glue dries

Mitre joint strengthened with small pieces of veneer glued into sawcuts.

Mitre joint strengthened with dowels

Mitre blocks

3. 06. 07 Bridle joint - This falls roughly between the lap joint and the mortise and tenon. On corner joints the 'mortise' is open to the end of the piece, while the 'tenon' has shoulders on each side. The 'T' bridle or through bridle is more like the half lap but using a third of the wood thickness to enable an 'open mortise' to be used. The bridle joints are very easy to cut, though they need to be accurate, are fairly strong, can be glued and pegged and are often ideal for more exacting carpentry.

3. 06. 08 Dovetail joint - The dovetail is specifically a cabinet-maker's joint. It is designed for joining wide boards, specifically where most of the 'pull' is from one direction (as for drawer fronts). For details refer to books on cabinet-making.

3. 06. 09 Mitred joints - Mitred joints have little strength in comparison to the wood or a good mortise and tenon joint, and are used mainly where the decorative effect of a mitre is required. It's often used on skirtings, door jamb mouldings, and where beading or moulding is being run within a main frame. The simplest method is to use a mitre box (home-made or bought). There are several methods of strengthening a mitre, as illustrated, but this is not usually necessary as it's best to avoid these joints where structural strength is required.

3. 06. 10 Lengthening joints - These are strictly a rag bag of joints, but as they perform a function that is often called on in house repairs, they are worth mentioning in detail.
Lapped joint - As for half lap, but with the pieces end on end. The joint should be half the thickness of the timber and

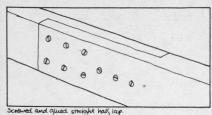

Screwed and glued straight half lap.

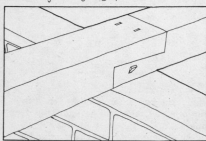

Splayed lap

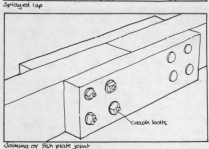

Coach bolts

Joining or fish plate joint

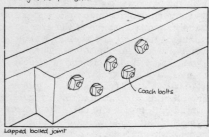

Coach bolts

Lapped bolted joint

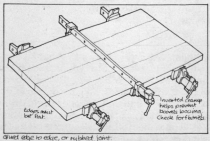

Edges must be flat.

Inverted cramp helps prevent boards bowing. Check for flatness.

Glued edge to edge, or rubbed joint.

the length of the joint about four times the thickness of the timber used. Both shoulders must meet exactly or the joint will be seriously weakened.

Screw and glue - Suitable for medium weight carrying (e. g. light roof structures).

Splayed lap joint - This is similar to the lapped joint but cut across the timber rather than down it, and with a slight angle. Suitable only when the joint is supported directly underneath - e. g. by a floor plate, joist or supporting wall, and when the timber needs to run on in a straight line.

Jointing or fish plates - For joining timbers end to end. Fish plates should be half the thickness of timber being joined, the same depth and about four times as long as it is thick. They should be glued and screwed, or glued and bolted. For heavier work - floor joists and flat roofs.

Scarfe joint - For experienced woodworkers only, but if you can do it, the best to use.

Bolted joint - Use with special timber connecting washers. Use coach bolts and washers to spread the 'pinch' of the bolts. Useful, but not as good as the fish plate method.

3. 06. 11 Edge to edge joint - The classic method of making up large solid areas of wood (e. g. for table tops) is to carefully edge plane several matched planks until each edge fits exactly with its neighbour, then glue along the whole length and cramp together with several sash cramps. In general house repairs this exactness is not usually necessary. For joining floorboards you rely entirely on exerting enough pressure to push the boards together until they are nailed (see 3. 18. 00). For external wallboarding a board with a special precut section - shiplap - is used. This section slots into each preceding board, thus giving a weatherproof joint, but allowing for expansion and shrinkage of the wood. A simpler method is to use weatherboarding, which is boarding cut thinner at one end. This thinner end is overlapped on the board beneath, giving a reasonably good weather seal. There are various types of tongue and grooved boards that are used for floors and walls.

3.07.00 WINDOWS: INTRODUCTION

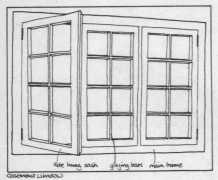

side hung sash   glazing bars   main frame

Casement window

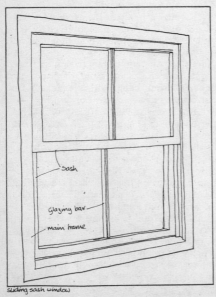

Sash

Glazing bar

main frame

sliding sash window

3.07.01 There are two basic window types in common use, the sliding sash, or double-hung sash - commoner in older houses - and casement windows, which can be made of wood, steel or aluminium. The opening part of the window is called the sash for both sliding sash and casement windows.

3.07.02 Windows should be kept well-maintained as they can quickly become a source of draughts, heat loss and water and damp penetration. Wooden frame windows are especially liable to deteriorate if they are not regularly painted and repaired. Once the paint begins to crack and peel the timber becomes much more exposed to the humidity changes of the air, causing it to swell and shrink, which eventually loosens the joints. There is also an increased likelihood of attack from dry rot and woodworm (see 3.23.00). Metal frame windows (other than aluminium) should also be regularly painted both inside and out - the danger being that the metal will rust, especially from water condensing on the cold glass on the inside and running onto the metal frame.

3.07.03 Wooden framed windows that have been badly neglected should be repaired before being repainted or reglazed. The thoroughness of this depends largely on the life of the house and on the general condition of the windows; under certain circumstances it may be better to replace the entire window with a new one.

3. 08. 00 <u>WINDOWS: REPLACING SASH CORDS</u>

Remove side beading

Remove old sash cords

3. 08. 01 Sliding sash windows have an iron counterweight - one on each side of the sash contained in the side of the main frame - which balances the weight of the sash and allows it to be moved easily and makes it stay in the position it's moved to. The counterweights are connected to the sash by cords which run over a pulley at the top of the main frame. These cords need replacing periodically and, should you break one, must be replaced for the window to operate easily and safely. If one cord breaks, the other cords may be in a similar condition, and it's worth changing all the cords at the same time.

3. 08. 02 Use proper sash cords as they are specially waxed, prestretched and rot-proofed, as well as being the correct size to fit the pulley wheel. They are available at most ironmongers or D. I. Y. shops; also buy clout nails, which have large heads, to secure the cords to the sashes.

3. 08. 03 Remove the beading from both sides of the frame, prising it off with an old chisel or heavy screwdriver. Take care not to damage the beading.

3. 08. 04 The lower window will now swing out of the frame held only on its sash cords.

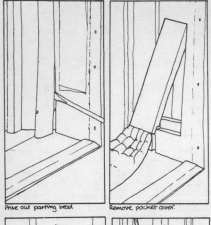

Prise out parting bead   Remove pocket cover.

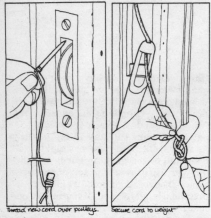

Thread new cord over pulleys.   Secure cord to weight.

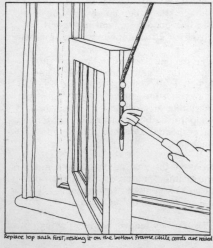

Replace top sash first, resting it on the bottom frame while cords are nailed

These can now be cut or prised off the sash and the window removed. The centre beading can now be prised out and the upper window removed in a similar manner. If the sash windows are large this operation is best done by two people.

3. 08. 05 On the inside lower face of the outer frame are two wooden caps, or pocket covers - one on each side - which can be removed so that the counterweights can be lifted out. These caps are usually not screwed or nailed in, but fitted loose, and they can easily be removed by lifting them from the bottom. However, they may have been painted over and may need a few light taps to loosen them.

3. 08. 06 Remove the old cord from the weights and use it as a guide for cutting the new cords to length. Tie a nail to a piece of string and feed it over the pulley - do the outer (top sash) pulleys first - and down into the frame and out of the weight pocket. Tie the new cord to the string and pull it through. A temporary knot will prevent it from slipping past the pulley.

3. 08. 07 Tie the counterweight onto the new cord and replace the weight back into the pocket. Thread the cord and attach the weight to the other side in a similar manner.

3. 08. 08 While someone holds the top sash in the lower part of the frame, but with one end held outwards, undo the temporary knot, and pull the weight, now in the pocket, up the frame as far as it will go. Nail this end into the existing groove in the end of the sash frame. Take care not to nail the cord any higher than where it will go over the pulley when the window is in position at the top of the frame. If you do, it will prevent the window closing properly. Nail the outer cord to the other side of the sash in a similar way and then move the sash back into position. Replace the centre beads but test that the sash moves properly before nailing them in.

3. 08. 09 The lower sash is attached in a similar manner, the pocket covers replaced and the front beading nailed back into position.

3. 09. 00 WINDOWS: TEMPORARY REPAIRING OF LOOSE JOINTS

3. 09. 01 For temporary or short-life repairs of loose joints on a wooden window frame metal 'L' - shaped brackets are the simplest to use.

3. 09. 02 The quickest method is to leave the sash frame within the main frame. Cut four small wedges that can be driven between the two parts of the frame - this will help to force the mortise and tenon joints back together as well as making the window more steady to work on. The outer beading on sliding sash windows may have to be removed to do this (see 3. 08. 03).

3. 09. 03 Hold the metal 'L' brackets against the joint and mark the position of the screw holes. Use brass or galvanised brackets and screws if they are being used on the outside, to prevent rusting.

3. 09. 04 Using a bradawl, or small drill, make pilot holes and screw the brackets in place. Use screws about $\frac{3}{4}$ of the thickness of the frame. Remove the wedges and repaint (see 3. 26. 00 to 3. 29. 00).

3. 09. 05 If the wood of the sash is badly split or rotten, then a more extensive repair may have to be made. To give additional strength the joint can be glued as well as secured with a bracket.

3. 09. 06 Drill small holes through the joint but not all the way through the sash. Squeeze wood glue from a plastic container into the holes, forcing the glue to run into the interior of the joint. Small lengths of dowels can be pushed into the holes but don't make them too tight as you may split the wood even more. It may be possible, if the holes are carefully placed, to use the pilot holes for the 'L' bracket screws to get glue into the joint.

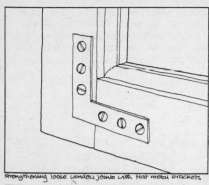

Strengthening loose window joints with flat metal brackets

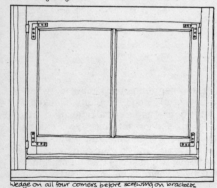

Remove beading and wedge frame to tighten joints

Hold bracket against frame and mark screw positions

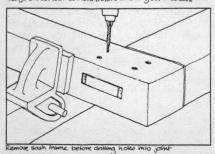

Wedge on all four corners before screwing on brackets

Remove sash frame before drilling holes into joint

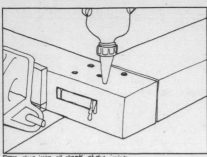

Force glue into all parts of the joint

3.09.07 This method of glueing is best done with the sash removed from the frame, and sash cramps used to cramp the joint together. If you do this while the sash is in the main frame then take care that glue does not ooze out of the joint and stick the sash frame to the main frame.

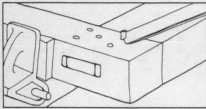

Tighten cramps and plug up holes. Remove excess glue and trim off plugs.

3.09.08 It is possible to hide the metal brackets by cutting a notch in the bottom or top edge of the sash and screwing a flat metal plate across the joint.

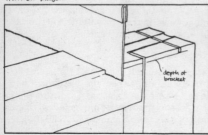

depth of bracket

Mark depth of metal bracket onto frame

3.09.09 Yet another temporary method, which is especially good for badly cracked or rotted joints, is to cut a triangular or 'L' - shaped gusset plate from exterior quality plywood, the same width as the sash frame, and to glue and nail it over the joint. A gusset plate on both sides will be stronger, but make sure it doesn't interfere with the sliding or opening of the window before you do it. This can also be combined with forcing glue into the joint (see 3.09.06). Again it is best to do this with the sash out of the frame, clamped or wedged so the joints are closed.

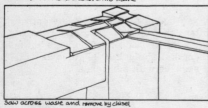

Saw across waste and remove by chisel

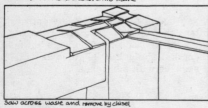

Clamp joint together, and screw on metal plate

3.09.10 Any small cracks can now be filled (see 3.28.06) and the windows painted.

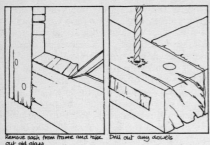

Remove sash from frame and rake out old glass

Drill out any dowels

3.10.00 WINDOWS: PERMANENT REPAIRING OF LOOSE JOINTS

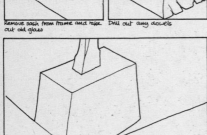

Soften glue with boiling water and tap joints apart

3. 10. 01 For a more permanent repair to loose wooden sash frames it is necessary to remove the glass and take the frame apart.

3. 10. 02 It may be difficult to remove all the glass intact from the sash, however, if the window has been neglected, and if neglected, it is also likely that the putty will be dry and loose. Hard putty can be softened with a blow lamp, but there is a danger of cracking the glass and care should also be taken not to scorch the wood.

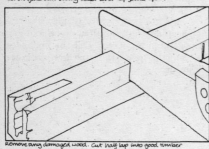

Remove any damaged wood. Cut half lap into good timber

3. 10. 03 Still firm joints may be loosened with boiling water but only if they are glued with animal ('scotch') glues. Dowels may be drilled out using a matching sized drill, and wedges can be removed by partly drilling and partly chiseling out with a small chisel. These joints were never screwed or nailed; however, screws and nails may have been added later in an attempt to strengthen the joint - so keep a look out for them.

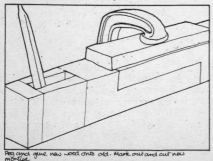

Peg and glue new wood onto old. Mark out and cut new mortise

3. 10. 04 Once the frame is taken apart the pieces can be cleaned and repaired. Glazing bars that are damaged or rotten can be replaced. Take a piece of the old glazing bar to a timber merchant to match the exact shape of the moulding.

Remove damaged tenon

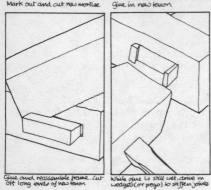

Mark out and cut new mortise   Glue in new tenon

3. 10. 05 If any of the tenons are badly damaged these can be replaced with a hardwood tongue. This is done by cutting a piece of hardwood that is the same width and thickness as the tenon, but slightly longer than twice its length. The old tenon is sawn off and a mortise cut in its place. The new tongue is glued and pegged (see 3. 06. 06) into the new mortise and when the window is later reassembled this provides the new tenon for the old mortise. The sligh extra length is trimmed off once the frame is back together.

3. 10. 06 If part of the frame is too rotten or damaged to make a secure joint, a new length of timber may be lap jointed onto the existing frame. Cut out the damaged section of wood and match its size as near as you can from the timber yard. Cut a half lap (see 3. 06. 10) into the existing piece and the new piece and glue and peg them together. Cut the necessary joint into the new end using the old piece as a guide.

Glue and reassemble frame. Cut off long ends of new tenon   While glue is still wet, drive in wedges (or pegs) to stiffen joints

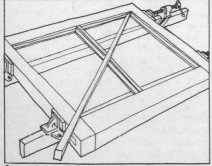

Cramp whole sash; check for squareness and leave to dry

3. 10. 07 When reassembling, it's important to ensure the frame is square. This is best done by measuring the diagonals (see 3. 05. 05). The joints should be glued and cramped and small hardwood wedges driven into each edge of the mortise and tenon joints.

3.11.00 <u>WINDOWS: FITTING NEW FRAMES</u>

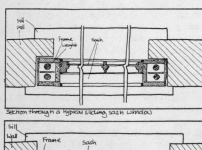

Section through a typical sliding sash window

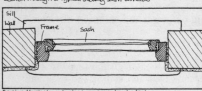

Section through a typical casement window

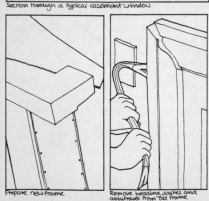

Prepare new frame   Remove beading, sashes and architraves from old frame

3.11.01 Windows are made in standard sizes and in many styles, so it is usually possible to match a new frame with the existing ones. If it is not possible, one can be made to match the original. The critical measurements for sliding sash windows are the height and width of the opening on the outside. The inner dimensions of the main frame can be no bigger than these, and should indeed be slightly smaller so there is at least 1" - 2" (25 - 50mm) of frame showing inside the brick opening. Casement windows are usually fitted into brick-work that is not recessed so the overall frame measurements should be only $\frac{3}{4}$" - 1" (20 - 25mm) smaller than the opening. Metal windows also, usually, fit into an unrecessed brickwork or onto a wooden sub-frame. Before buying check the suitability of the windows for your purposes with the manufacturer.

3.11.02 New wood frames should be given two coats of wood primer and allowed time to dry. If there are any knots, these should be covered with a knotting compound first. The frame head may also project (horns) and these may need to be cut flush with the frame sides also.

3.11.03 Remove the sashes, any window furniture (handles, etc.) and any beading or mould-ing from the main frame. You may need to cut back plaster to free the frame, but try to avoid removing outside render. This may be necessary for casement and metal windows. Cut through the frame with a saw, at least as far as possible without catching the teeth on brickwork, and, using a crowbar, lever the pieces of framing out of the opening.

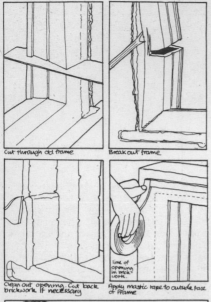

Cut through old frame.   Break out frame.

Clean out opening. Cut back brickwork if necessary.   Apply mastic tape to outside face of frame.   line of opening in brick work.

Place frame in opening, adjust and hold frame in place with wedges, make sure frame is level and vertical.

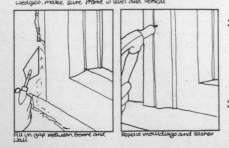

Fill in gap between frame and wall.   Replace mouldings and sashes.

3. 11. 04 Take note of the 'tying in' that was used to hold the previous frame to the wall. In most cases simple friction between wood and mortar is used, but this may be combined with large nails driven through the frame into the brickwork or into wooden plugs cemented into the brickwork. Metal windows are usually bolted to special 'ties' built into the brickwork. The frame can be unbolted from these and they can be re-used for the new frame.

3. 11. 05 For recessed windows, check that the frame fits into the recess - some jambs are wider than others - and if not cut away equally on both sides.

3. 11. 06 It is wise to insert a weather, or water-proof strip around the frame just inside the recess. This can be done using a horsehair rope soaked in tar, putty or, better, mastic tape or compound. Apply this round the outside of the frame an inch or so in from the opening dimension. The window can then be lifted into the opening and pressed against the recess, ensuring the mastic strip makes a waterproof seal all round. Use small wedges to secure the window and adjust it for levelness and uprightness.

3. 11. 07 For openings without a recess the mastic may better be applied after the window is in, while held in position with wedges, and before it is cemented in. Test that the sashes will open before finally fixing the frame.

3. 11. 08 'Tie' the windows in, using the same method as was used on the original frame. If the wedges are small and do not project past the level of the plaster, these can be left in place, and will also help tie the window in. If not, remove them only after the frame has been partly cemented in.

3. 11. 09 Using a mix of four parts sand to one of cement, fill in the gaps around the frame, pushing the mortar well in. Fill the gap between frame and wall on the outside with this mixture. The inside can be finished with plaster.

3. 11. 10 Fit any window boards or sills that are required, or make repairs to existing ones.

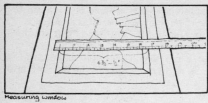
Measuring window

3.12.00 GLAZING

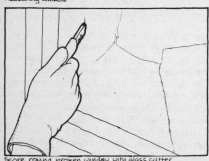
Score round broken window with glass cutter

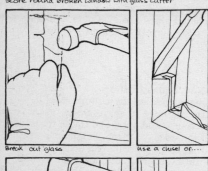
Break out glass   Use a chisel or....

3. 12. 01 Be as accurate as you can in measuring the size of windows. If the panes are too small you won't be able to fit them, if too large, they will not fit in, or only so tightly that expansion and contraction are not allowed for. Measure it from the side edge of the putty on one side to the outside edge on the other (i. e. include the thickness of the putty) and subtract $\frac{1}{4}$" (5mm) from this overall size.

3. 12. 02 Remove the broken glass, wear gloves and work from the top down - if you have a glass cutter score round the edge of the glass first. With a hammer and old-wood chisel or hacking knife, clear away the old putty down to the wood on both faces of the frame. Take care not to dig into the wood and watch out for tacks (sprigs) buried in the putty. Test the fit of the new pane (it can be trimmed down with a glass cutter if too big). There are two types of putty, one for wood and one for metal window frames. Apply it in blobs along the back face of the frame. Don't try to smooth it down, keep it in fairly regular ridges. Rest the bottom edge of the glass along the bottom edge of the frame and push it into position (don't press in the centre) squeezing it out at the back. Use a gentle even pressure, applied all the way round the edge of the glass. Hammer in a small tack halfway up each side of the frame to hold the glass in place. Apply putty around the four sides of the frame, building up a triangular wedge, smooth this down with a scraper blade.

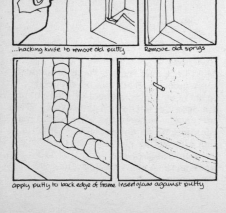
...hacking knife to remove old putty   Remove old sprigs

apply putty to back edge of frame Insert glass against putty

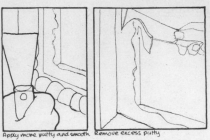

Apply more putty and smooth   Remove excess putty

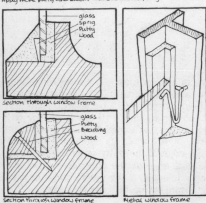

glass
sprig
putty
wood

Section through window frame

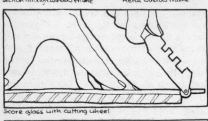

glass
putty
beading
wood

Section through window frame   Metal window frame

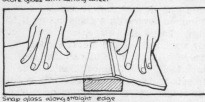

Score glass with cutting wheel

Snap glass along straight edge

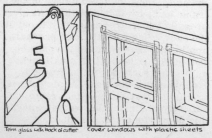

Trim glass with back of cutter   Cover windows with plastic sheets

3. 12. 03 Instead of putty, a piece of $\frac{1}{4}$" (5mm) round beading can be tacked on the four sides of the frame. First set the glass in the putty as above, apply a thin strip of putty into the angle between glass and frame, press the beading into this and nail.

3. 12. 04 Try to repair windows when it is warm; on cold days glass is more brittle and will break more easily. Sheet glass comes in 24 and 32 ounce weight and $\frac{1}{4}$" plate (3mm, 4mm and 6mm metric); as a general rule, 24 ounce (3mm) glass is used in windows whose combined width and length is less than 60 - 80" (1700mm); for 80" and more 32 ounce (4mm) is used. Quarter-inch plate (6mm) is used for shop size windows. Reinforced glass and various types of frosted glass are available - take a broken piece if you want a match.

3. 12. 05 Using a glass-cutter - Single wheel glass-cutter: Use a straight edge to score along, use a firm pressure and start and finish the score to the edges. Place the glass over a straight batten with one edge in line with the score, hold down one side of the glass and apply pressure on the other other until the pane snaps. Use the notches in the back of the cutter or pliers to break off smaller bits (after scoring a line).

3. 12. 06 Heat loss - Most heat loss from a room is through the windows. This can be reduced greatly by taping a sheet of clear plastic over the window on the frame. The air caught between the window and the plastic acts as an insulator. Plastic can also act as glass where the house is of such short-life or money is so scarce as to make buying glass un-economic.

3.13.00 REPAIRING OF LOOSE HINGES

3.13.01 Loose or worn hinges can be the source of jamming on both casement windows and doors. This may be due to the screws coming loose in their holes, or to damage of the frame or door wood, or to the hinges themselves being worn.

3.13.02 Removing screws from door or window hinges can be difficult as they are often rusted, covered with paint or so loose that they can neither be tightened or removed.

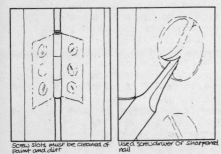

Screw slots must be cleaned of paint and dirt

Used screwdriver or sharpened nail

3.13.03 Clear the screw slot of paint or rust, preparably using a large bent nail that has been filed to a suitable point to fit the slot. Use a screwdriver that is the correct size and one that has a good clean square end to it. The worst danger is that the slot will become damaged by repeated slipping of the screwdriver before it is sufficiently loose.

3.13.04 If the screw won't turn with reasonable pressure try loosening it by other methods rather than risk damaging the slot.

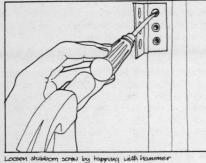

Loosen stubborn screw by tapping with hammer

3.13.05 Put the screwdriver into the slot and give it a sharp tap with a hammer. Try to loosen again, and repeat the tap if it still sticks.

3.13.06 If the screw is rusty, loosen it by putting a light machine or penetrating oil onto it. This method needs time for the oil to soak in.

3.13.07 The screw may also be loosened by heating with a blow lamp or soldering iron. The heat expands the metal and makes a slightly larger hole. Remove the screw when cool.

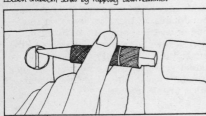

Using a punch to loosen stubborn screw

3.13.08 For very large screws a punch can be inserted into one end of the slot at a tangent to the screw head, and the screw slowly tapped round a quarter of a turn. A screwdriver can then be used to remove it.

3.13.09 If you do damage the slot then the screw head has to be drilled off. Use a twist drill of roughly the same diameter as the screw head, or slightly smaller. Once the other screws have been removed and the hinge lifted away the shank can be removed using a self-gripping mole wrench (file two sided of the shank slightly flat to ensure a good grip) or by cutting a new slot into the shank. If it is impossible to remove the shank the hinge may have to be moved slightly up or down the frame.

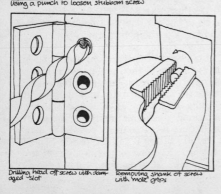

Drilling head off screw with damaged slot

Removing shank of screw with 'mole' grips

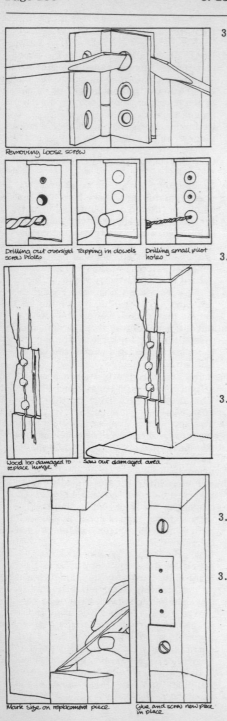

Removing loose screw

Drilling out oversized screw holes | Tapping in dowels | Drilling small pilot holes

Wood too damaged to replace hinge | Saw out damaged area

Mark size on replacement piece | Glue and screw new piece in place

3. 13. 10 If the window or door sticking is a result of the screws being too loose then this can be remedied by putting in larger screws, or by packing the holes. It's often very difficult to remove loose screws as the pressure needed to keep the screwdriver in the slot also stops the screw from coming out as it's turned. The only method is to force a second screwdriver behind the hinge so there is an outward pressure as the screw is turned. Remove all the other screws you can before doing this. Once the head is out, slightly remove the second screwdriver and push the hinge back into its recess, leaving the screw projecting enough to grip it with a self-gripping mole wrench or pliers.

3. 13. 11 Once removed, the loose holes can be patched with filling compound, or the screw threads wound with thread and dipped in a shellak-based varnish (not polyurethane). Larger screws cannot usually be used with hinges, as the holes in the hinge predetermine the size of screw used. The best method is to drill out the screw holes and glue dowels into their place. These can then be drilled with smaller pilot holes for new screws.

3. 13. 12 It's preferable to use non-ferrous or brass screws on windows and exterior door hinges as there is always a likelihood of water seeping in and rusting steel screws. However, brass is quite soft and the slot easily damaged, so use a steel screw of the same size and length to make a good hole, and then replace it with a brass screw.

3. 13. 13 It may be preferable to move the hinges altogether (see 3. 14. 00) or you may need to cut out badly damaged sections and replace them with new wood.

3. 13. 14 Cut back into the frame at a slight angle on each side of the damaged section. Make slightly less deep cuts between these (to stop splitting) and chop out the section with a chisel. Cut a new piece, matching sizes and profile of the existing frame as closely as possible, and carefully tailor it to fit into the removed section. Glue and screw, or dowel it into place, when a good fit has been made.

3.14.00 HANGING A DOOR

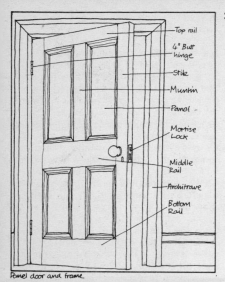

Top rail

4" Butt hinge

Stile

Muntin

Panel

Mortise Lock

Middle Rail

Architrave

Bottom Rail

Panel door and frame

Fitting door to frame   Plane off excess

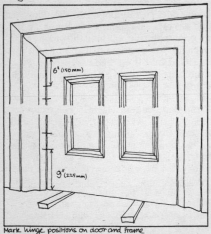

6" (150mm)

9" (225mm)

Mark hinge positions on door and frame

3.14.01 Doors are made to standard sizes and to three different basic patterns - the flush door, the panel door and the battened door - with many variations of construction and appearance. Generally, outside doors are heavier than internal doors and are often made of hardwood.

3.14.02 Doors need to be fitted as accurately as possible to exclude the weather and sound. They may also be required to be fireproof or have a specific fire resistance (measured by how long it takes a fire to burn the door down, $\frac{1}{2}$ hr, 1 hr, 2 hrs, etc.) Carefully check the size of the new door before buying it as it is not possible to take off more than $\frac{1}{2}$'' - $\frac{3}{4}$'' (12 - 20mm) from the edges without cutting into the joints and seriously weakening the door. Give a new wood panel door time to acclimatise to the humidity of the room before fitting.

3.14.03 The only accurate way of fitting a door is to 'offer it up' to the frame and carefully mark each edge with the curves and twists of the door frame. Plane it down, test fitting as you go until there is about 1/16'' (1.5mm) clearance all round. The clearance at the bottom will

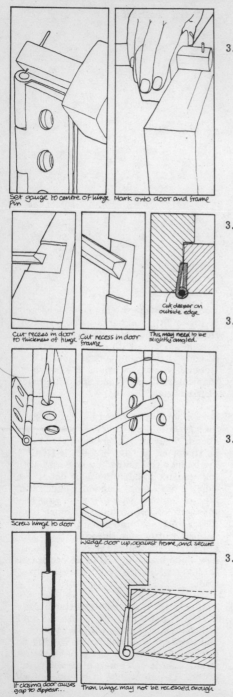

Set gauge to centre of hinge pin

Mark onto door and frame

Cut recess in door to thickness of hinge

Cut recess in door frame

This may need to be slightly angled.

Cut deeper on outside edge

Screw hinge to door

Wedge door up, against frame, and secure

If closing door causes gap to appear...

Then hinge may not be recessed enough

depend on whether there is a carpet, etc.

3. 14. 04 Make allowance for general weather conditions: if it is wet, the wood will have swelled and the door should be made to fit as tightly as possible; if dry, then give slightly more clearance for when the wood swells again, or be prepared to make minor adjustments later. The amount of swelling depends on many things - the construction of the door, the size, whether it is painted, how well the wood is seasoned, etc. - so it's not possible to say how much should be allowed for these moisture movements.

3. 14. 05 Once the door is fitted, place it into the frame, and, using two wedges, raise it until it is at the correct clearance off the floor. The hinge positions can now be marked on both door and frame - about 6" (150mm) down and 9" (225mm) up.

3. 14. 06 Set a marking gauge on the hinges from the outer edge to the centre pin. Transfer this to the edge of the door and the frame. The depth of the recess cut is the same as the thickness of the metal of the hinge; however, the recess cut into the frame should be slightly angled out to allow for the slight wedge shape the hinge makes when fully closed.

3. 14. 07 Using the hinge as a guide, make pilot holes for screws in both the frame and door. Secure the hinges to the door with two screws and then place the door in an open position against the frame, wedging the bottom until the hinges can be fitted into their recesses. Secure each hinge with a single screw and test the swing of the door.

3. 14. 08 If the door seems slightly reluctant to close at the very end of its swing, and if, on close examination of the hinge as the door is shut, the hinges are seen to be pulling slightly away from the wood, the recesses have not been cut deep enough or too deep, or the one on the jamb is at too steep an angle. Remove the door and correct these faults before finally driving all the screws in.

3. 15. 00 <u>DRAUGHT-PROOFING</u>

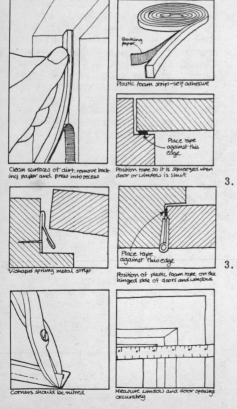

Clean surfaces of dirt, remove backing paper and press into recess

Plastic foam strip-self adhesive

Place tape against this edge

Position tape so it is squeezed when door or window is shut

V-shaped spring metal strip

Place tape against this edge

Position of plastic foam tape on the hinged side of doors and windows

Corners should be mitred

Measure window and door openings accurately

3. 15. 01 Badly-fitting doors, windows and floor-boards are all a source of draughts and heat loss. There are many simple ways to improve the sealing of these and therefore to improve the general insulation of the house.

3. 15. 02 There are several types of draught seals on the market. The easiest to apply is the plastic foam strip backed with adhesive tape - though it is expensive and quickly loses its spring-iness and therefore some of its benefits. Make sure surfaces are clean before applying the tape. It must also be placed in a position where it is squeezed between two parts of the frame. Don't forget to do the hinged side of windows and doors also.

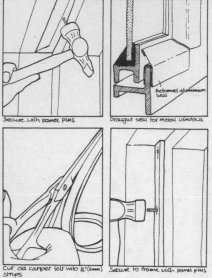

Secure with panel pins

Draught seal for metal windows

Preformed aluminium seal

Cut old carpet felt into ¼"(6mm) strips

Secure to frame with panel pins

Pour boiling water onto torn up paper and stir till it becomes a thick paste then add wallpaper paste

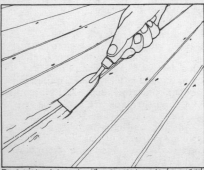

Force mixture into cracks with a scraper, leave to dry and rub down with glasspaper block

3. 15. 03   'V'-shaped metal strips are better for doors and large windows but must be nailed with panel pins, preferably using a 'pin push'. These are placed on the frame at right angles to the closing of the door or window and need at least 1/16" (1. 5mm) clearance between frame and door. They must also be cut round locks and door catches. Special aluminium strips are also available for sealing metal windows.

3. 15. 04   There are also several types of draught-proofing strips for the bottom of doors. The spring felt seal is attached to a spring which closes the seal only when the door is closed, thus allowing the door to be opened over a carpet. Felt ribbons are cheaper but do not make such a good seal.

3. 15. 05   An alternative method is to make your own draught seals. Cut old carpet felt into $\frac{1}{4}$" (6mm) strips and nail these to the inside of door and window frames. Choose the thickness of felt you use according to the size of gap you wish to seal. If the felt is too thick the door will not close properly, or the hinges may be strained. For smaller, better-fitting windows use display felt. This can be backed with double-sided tape first, then cut into strips using a straight edge and sharp knife.

3. 15. 06   Many floorboards have small cracks running between them due to shrinkage over many years. This is often made worse by central heating or electric fires. The best method to fill gaps under $\frac{1}{4}$" (6mm) is to use papier mâché. Use white unprinted unglazed paper. Tear into small pieces (about the size of a postage stamp). Pour boiling water over the pieces while pounding them with a stout stick, until they make a thick paste. Allow to cool (2 - 3 hours) and add a packet of wallpaper paste (cellulose-based) or starch, and mix. The mixture can also be coloured with water soluble colourants, wood stains, etc. , to match the colour of the boards. Using a scraper, force the mixture into the crack, smoothing it down. Let it set for three days then give a final rub down with fine sandpaper.

3. 16. 00 WOOD FLOORING

3. 16. 01 In most pre-war houses the floors, including the ground floors, were constructed of wooden boarding - floorboards - on wooden beams - floor joists. The size of the joist depends on the 'span' - the unsupported length over which the joists run - and the number or frequency or spacing of the joists. Joist sizes vary from $1\frac{1}{2}$" (38mm) to $2\frac{1}{2}$" (60mm) thick and 6" (150mm) to 9" (225mm) or even 12" (300mm) deep, and the spacing between joists, which may vary also on a single floor, from 12" (300mm) to 18" (450mm). Where possible the joists are run across the smaller dimension of the room, and the floorboards will always run at right angles to the joists. The direction and the spacing of the joists can therefore be seen from the direction of floorboards and the spacing of the floor nails.

3. 16. 02 The joists are supported at each end by the house walls, either on a wall plate, or by being built into the brick-work, or by a metal joist hanger. Ground-level floors with no basement are often supported by an extra wall, a sleeper wall, which allows smaller timbers to be used. On upper floors the ceiling of the room below is attached to the joists either by wooden laths, nailed onto the floor joists and then plastered over, or more recently, as plasterboard nailed directly to the joists.

3. 16. 03 Floorboarding is usually square edged, between 7/8" (22mm) and 5/8" (16mm) thick, and between 4" (100mm) to 6" (150mm) wide. Two nails or brads secure each board at each joint, and boards usually run the full length of the floor, ending just under the skirting board. If they are joined, it should be over the centre of a joist. On occasion boards may continue under a partition wall into the next room or passage.

3. 16. 04 More recently, floorboards have been tongue and groove, which allows them to be secret nailed, lessens the problems of cracks between boards and also generally adds to the strength of the floor, allowing slightly thinner boards to be used. Chipboard is also used, put down in large sheets and covered with tiles or carpet.

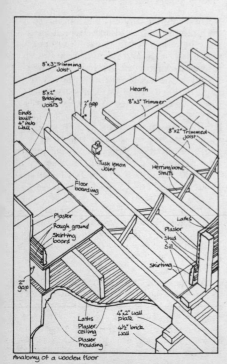

Anatomy of a wooden floor

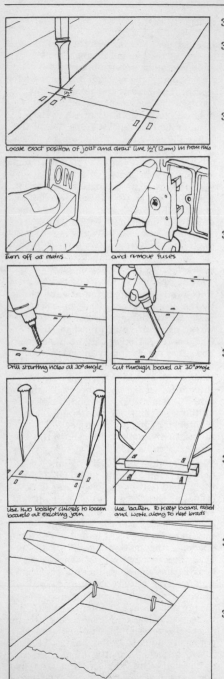

Locate exact position of joist and draw line ½"(12mm) in from this

Turn off at mains

and remove fuses

Drill starting holes at 30° angle

Cut through board at 30° angle

Use two bolster chisels to loosen boards at existing join

Use batten to keep board raised and work along to next brads

Removing boards from under skirting

3.17.00 LIFTING FLOORBOARDS

3.17.01 Lifting floorboards is necessary for many repairs, for inspection and laying new services. It must be done carefully to avoid creating more repair work than you already have.

3.17.02 Many floors have loose boards, or short boards that have been removed previously and screwed rather than nailed back, often dating from the house's conversion to electric lighting. Even if these are not in exactly the place where you need them, it is much easier to remove boards once the first has been lifted.

3.17.03 If there is no convenient loose board or joist to work from, then the appropriate board must be sawn out. Find the edge of the nearest convenient joist by slipping a thin blade between the boards and moving it back towards the joist. Mark this point on both sides and draw a line $\frac{1}{2}$" (12mm) nearer the centre of the joist between them.

3.17.04 Before making any cut remember to turn off the mains electricity. It is very easy to cut into a cable without realising. Gas and water pipes are less of a danger as one can hear the sound of the blade on metal; however, if plumbing is in plastic or polythene pipes, take care not to damage these.

3.17.05 Drill three small holes 1/8" (3mm) close together on the line but at an angle of about 30 degrees. Using these as starting holes, saw across the board keeping to the line, but again at about 30 degrees to the vertical.

3.17.06 Insert a bolster chisel, or suitable thin, wide blade lever and prise the board up, working along the board on both sides towards the next joist and lifting it off each set of brads.

3.17.07 If the board is to be removed right up to the skirting board you might find it pulls out fairly easily, or, if not, it may be necessary to split it up to free it - though this means it will have to be replaced by a new piece. Otherwise you may have to remove the skirting

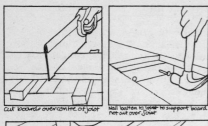

Cut boards over centre of joist   Nail batten to joist to support board not cut over joist

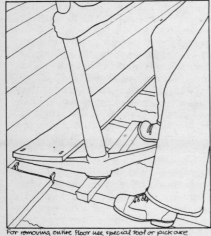

For removing entire floor use special tool or pick axe

One person keeps the board taut while the other lifts the board off the brads

to get at the nails holding the end of the board. Avoid doing this if possible, as skirting is easily damaged, can be difficult to match and will require repainting when replaced. At worst the board may run under the skirting and wall into the next room.

3. 17. 08 In this case, the board must be cut, either over the centre of a joist, or near enough the edge for it to be supported on a 2" x 1" (50 x 25mm) batten nailed to the side of a joist. Or - and this is the least satisfactory method - at an angle such that the remaining board will support it when put back.

3. 17. 09 For removing whole floors, either to re-lay them or in preparation for laying new floors, hire a special floorboard removing tool. A pick can also be very effective for prising boards off their brads. Start by removing a loose or short board (this can be broken out with a pick if it will not be needed again). If necessary remove all the skirting boards - again these can be levered off the wall using the pick or crowbar, and remove one complete length of floorboard. It is then easy to get the pick head under the board, as close to the nails as possible, and lever the board up. It helps if a second person pulls the loose end of the board upwards, keeping a constant pressure on the nails, as the pick is inserted by each joint to make the final pull.

3. 17. 10 Removing tongue and groove boards is more difficult. In most cases it's necessary to cut between the boards, as well as across them, before the board can be removed. Use a pad saw and keep the angle low to avoid cutting electric cables.

3. 17. 11 Remember, take care when removing floorboards - there are pipes and cables under virtually every floor. Turn off at the mains and work carefully, listening for telltale sounds as you saw. Most cables and pipes are run between two floor brads when going across the joists. And, most importantly, don't step off the joists onto the ceilings - these aren't strong enough to support any weight.

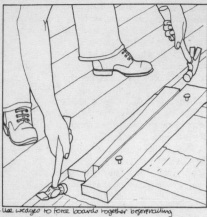

Use wedges to force boards together before nailing

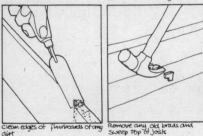

Clean edges of floorboards of any dirt

Remove any old brads and sweep top of joists

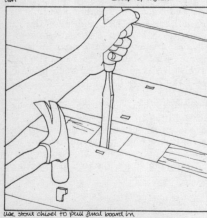

Use stout chisel to pull final board in

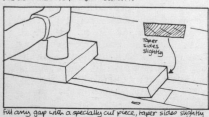

Taper sides slightly

Fill any gap with a specially cut piece, taper sides slightly

3. 18. 00 REPLACING FLOORBOARDS

3. 18. 01 When replacing short lengths, cut a piece of 2" x 1" (50mm x 25mm) softwood batten slightly longer than the width of the board and nail this flush with the top edge of the joist. Short lengths of board are often screwed back in place, as they give access to electrical connections, like a ceiling rose, that may need to be reached on another occasion. It may also be necessary to add a small fillet of wood to replace the length lost on the board by the thickness of two saw cuts.

3. 18. 02 To replace a whole floor, cut two or three sets of wedges out of 1" x 2" x 18" (25mm x 50mm x 450mm) softwood. Clean the edges of the boards of dirt, and plane if uneven. The boards should be dry, and if possible lay floors in dry weather. Clean tops of joists and remove any old brads left. Lay four or five boards against one edge of the floor and place a pair of wedges every 3 or 4 feet (900-1, 200mm) against the edge of these. Push a piece of scrap board against the wedges and the board, and nail it down firmly but leave the heads protruding for easy removal.

3. 18. 03 Using two hammers, go along the wedges and tighten them up until no cracks can be seen between the floor-boards. Starting at the board nearest the centre wedges, nail each board to the joists.

3. 18. 04 Remove the scrap board, and continue to lay boards in fours and fives over the whole floor in a similar manner. On the opposite edge lay a single board under the skirting and cut a special piece to fill any gap left between this and the rest of the floor.

3. 18. 05 To replace a short length of tongue and groove board use the same method as for square-edged boards, but remove the lower lip on the grooved side first so that it can be slotted over the existing tongue.

3. 18. 06 Large areas of tongue and groove board can be laid in a similar manner as square-edged boards; however, remember to protect the tongues by using an off-cut of tongue and groove board. If you're using secret nailing, then the boards must be fitted one by one.

3.19.00 FLOOR SANDING

3.19.01 The cheapest way to make an old floor look respectable is to sand off the years of dirt and grime down to the bare wood, and to varnish or polish it.

3.19.02 To do this you must hire a floor-sanding machine. These are large drum sanders with a built-in vacuum dust collector - like an oversized vacuum cleaner. The sanding belts are usually sold in the same shop, a hire shop or building plant hire shop, that provides the machine. They do cost extra, and this can mount up quite unexpectedly as you usually pay for the ones you've used when the machine is returned. It's often cheaper to buy sanding belts from a builders' merchant than a hire shop, and this is worth looking into, but you must know the correct size.

3.19.03 Sanding machines always leave a small area around the edge that they cannot get to, so it's also worth hiring an edge sanding machine (usually a disc sander). An electric drill with a disc sander attachment can be used but you may seriously overstrain the motor if it is a large area.

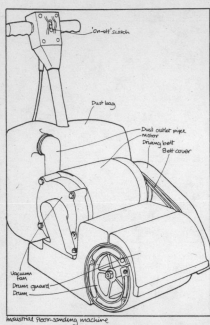

industrial floor-sanding machine

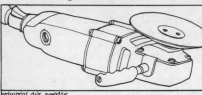

industrial disc sander

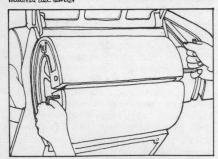

Tip machine back, lift drum cover and engage allan keys

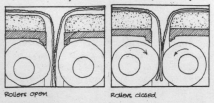

Rollers open   Rollers closed

3. 19. 04   It's important to plan the hiring properly, and to do as much as you can in the shortest time. Hiring is done by the day or by the week (which is much cheaper than for seven daily charges) and in some places, a special weekend rate is charged. Hire the edger after the floor-sander, as you can't do both at the same time, unless several people are helping. A deposit will also be required. Inspect the machine before taking it, ask for a demonstration of fitting the belts, make sure you have the appropriate keys and chucks for opening the drum, check the electrical socket type (must be used with 13 amp square-pin or 15 amp round-pin plugs only), and if possible get the assistant to show you it working.

3. 19. 05   Prepare floors beforehand. Remove all furniture, curtains, carpets, etc. You can't push things to one side - even though the machine has a vacuum attachment, it still makes a lot of dust. Inspect the floor and remove all the odd nails left from lino, etc. Make sure none of the brads are left above the surface of the wood. A stray nail will rip a belt to pieces. If the floors have been painted try to remove as much of this as possible using a chemical paint stripper and scraper, or a blowlamp and scraper. Paint will simply clog up the sandpaper on the sander.

3. 19. 06   The sanding belts are held on the drum by two eccentric (off-centre) rollers that are turned by allen keys, one on each side. One end of the belt is pushed into the slot in the drum, then threaded round the drum and the second end threaded in the same slot. Get the belt as tight and as square on the drum as possible, then rotate the two rollers until they grip the ends of the belt. It occasionally helps to slot an extra thickness of belt into the slot, 1" (25mm) or so wide, cut from a torn or worn-out belt. This allows the rollers to grip more tightly.

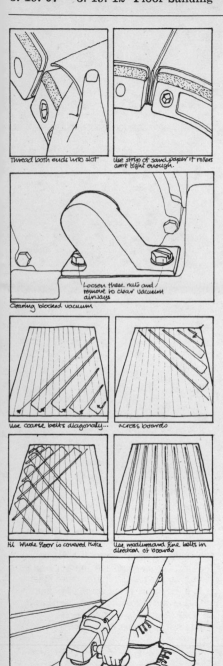

Thread both ends into slot

Use strip of sandpaper if rollers aren't tight enough.

Loosen these nuts and remove to clear vacuum airways

Clearing blocked vacuum

Use coarse belts diagonally...   across boards

til whole floor is covered twice   Use medium and fine belts in direction of boards

Use disc sander to finish the edges

3.19.07 Occasionally a part of a torn belt will lodge in the vacuum tubes and stop the dust being sucked in. If this happens, remove the bag or the inspection plate at the side, and remove the obstruction.

3.19.08 Remember to unplug the machine while changing the belts or handling it in any way other than when actually sanding.

3.19.09 Use the coarsest belt first, sanding at 45 degrees across the boards, starting in the centre and covering each strip twice. If necessary, repeat sanding at 90 degrees to the first direction. When the floor is level and clean, change to a medium belt and sand in the direction of the boards, again doing each strip twice. Finally, change to the fine belt and sand in the same direction until all signs of diagonal scratching have been removed.

3.19.10 The edges can now be done with a disc sander, but keep clearing up the dust, as these usually don't have a vacuum attachment.

3.19.11 Don't try to remove deep cuts or damage with a sanding machine. Badly damaged boards should be replaced, prior to sanding. Don't stand in one place with the drum rotating against the floor - it is quite capable of grinding its way through the thickness of the boards! Start the motor before bringing it into contact with the boards and stop it after lifting the drum up. Wear a gauze smog mask (from most chemists).

3.19.12 Use polyurethane varnish to protect the bare wood. Apply three thin coats, letting each coat dry before applying the next. The boards can be stained, but remember the varnish will also make them slightly darker.

3. 20. 00 ROOFING

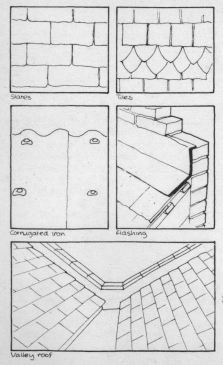

Slates

Tiles

Corrugated iron

Flashing

Valley roof

3. 20. 01 Sloping roofs can be covered with tiles, slates, shingles, corrugated iron, plastic or asbestos. The edges of these coverings, where they meet walls or each other, are covered by flashing. Flashing can be made of lead, copper, zinc or roofing felt. Often lead flashing is ripped off from empty houses, damaging surrounding tiles, letting in rain and generally adding to the deterioration of the house.

3. 20. 02 Be careful while working on roofs. Wear soft shoes and don't walk on slates, tiles, etc. as you may damage them. Walk on gutter valleys or on climbing boards (see 3. 04. 06).

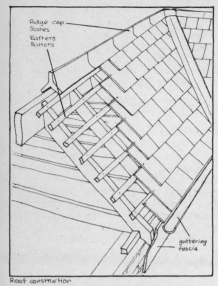

Ridge cap
Slates
Rafters
Battens

guttering
fascia

Roof construction

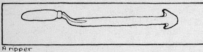

A ripper

Removing a slate with a ripper

Remove damaged slate

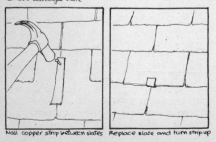

Nail copper strip between slates   Replace slate and turn strip up

3.20.03 Slates, Tiles and Shingles -

The roof is constructed of rafters which
form the slope of the roof, joining at
the top to a ridge board, and held across
the bottom by the ceiling joists. At
right angles to the rafters, battens run
along the roof. There may be a covering of roof felt between the battens and
the rafters. A fascia board is attached
to protect the end of the rafters and
carry the gutters. The tiles are hung
or laid on the battens. The distance
between three battens is roughly equal
to the size of the tile used.

3.20.04 Tiles are laid from the bottom of the
roof to the top, each row is laid side
by side, the next row covers two-thirds
of the one below, but so the join between
each tile is over the centre of the tile
below.

3.20.05 Slates and shingles are nailed to the
batten while ceramic tiles have hooks
(or nibs) which hook over the battens
with only the fourth or fifth row being
nailed as well.

3.20.06 Large sheets of corrugated iron are
generally used on roofs with a shallow
slope. A special nail (with a washer)
is used to secure them through the top
of a ridge to the horizontal rafters. The
washer seals the hole made for the nail.

3.20.07 Replacing a single slate -

New slates cannot simply be nailed in
place as the row above has to cover the
fixing holes. A special tool known as
a ripper is used to remove the old or
broken slate. Pass it under the broken
slate and hook it onto the nails, and
break them to remove the slate.

3.20.08 Use a strip of lead or copper about
1" by 9" (25 x 230mm) - or a stout
piece of copper wire - and nail it to the
batten between the two exposed slates.
Gently lift the slates above and slide
the new slate into position, it should
leave one or two inches of the lead strip
poking out beneath the slate. Bend this
over to hold it in place.

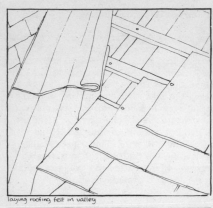
laying roofing felt in valley

Score cement

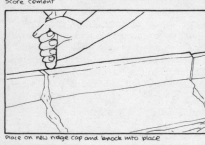
Place on new ridge cap and knock into place

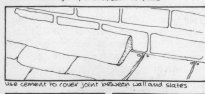
Use cement to cover joint between wall and slates

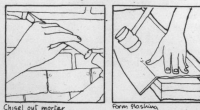
Chisel out mortar   Form flashing

3. 20. 09 If you're covering a large area, clear away all the damaged or broken slates. If there are any gullies or valleys in the roof which are adjacent to the area to be covered, or if these areas are also damaged, recover them before relaying the slates.

3. 20. 10 Clear away any old covering, remove any slates which cover the edge of the gully or valley boards. Lay the new roofing felt down the gully and turn the edge of the felt over. Make sure the new slates cover the edge of the felt. Don't nail the felt in any place that is not eventually covered by slates. It's best to lay two layers. Roofing felt is quite cheap. You can paint roofing felt with mastic or any brand of roof sealer.

3. 20. 11 If you have to join roofing felt make sure there's a good 12 or 18" (300 to 400mm) overlap and that the higher piece overlaps the lower piece.

3. 20. 12 If the existing valley is in reasonable condition you could simply paint it with a coat of sealer.

3. 20. 13 Replace the slates working from the bottom of the roof to the top. Integrate them into the existing slates and use the lead strips to put in the last layer (unless it's right to the top of the ridge).

3. 20. 14 The ridge is usually covered with ridge tiles cemented in place. Replace any that are missing or broken.

3. 20. 15 Where the tiles meet a wall or go round a pipe there needs to be flashing. For fairly short-life flashing, cement will do, but for a fairly long-life house, use a strip of zinc cemented between a course in the bricks and bent down to cover a third of the first slate.

cement flashing into wall

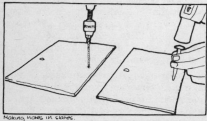
Making holes in slates.

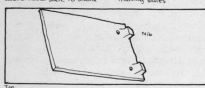
Second hand slate to avoid   Trimming slates

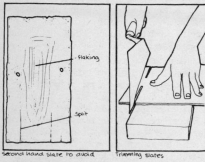
Tile

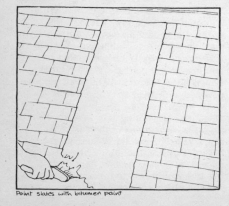
Paint slates with bitumen paint

3. 20. 16 Always buy similar slates or tiles to the ones on the roof, it's almost impossible to integrate two different types. They are usually available second-hand, especially in demolition areas where the houses being pulled down are similar to the one you are in. Make sure slates are in good condition, without splits or flaking surfaces.

3. 20. 17 Holes can be made in slates with a drill or by hammering a blunt nail into the slate while it is on a flat surface. Slates can be trimmed by sawing, by using a special slate cutting tool (worth having if you're doing a lot of slate repairs), or by using the edge of a trowel. Support the slate on a flat surface with the line of trimming over a square edge. Chip with the edge of the trowel till the slate is cut.

3. 20. 18 Repairing a tiled roof -

Tiled roofs are repaired in the same way as for slates. Removing the old tiles may be easier as they are not always nailed down. Replacing new ones can be done by lifting the ones in place and hooking the nibs over the batten. If not, break off the nibs and use the lead strip method   (see 3. 02. 08).

3. 20. 19 Mastic Treatment -

Mastic treatment is a method of waterproofing slate roofs, asphalt, asbestos, cement, concrete, corrugated iron, lead, zinc, and similar surfaces which are in poor condition. It has the advantage of holding loose slates or crumbling concrete in place.

3. 20. 20 Replace any cracked tiles (a square of stout roofing felt may do in place of new slates). Remove any loose debris, moss, etc.. Lift any flashings so it can go under them.

3. 20. 21 Paint on the first coat of Aquaseal (or Synthapruf) - allow 1 gallon for every 6 square yards. Brush upwards, making

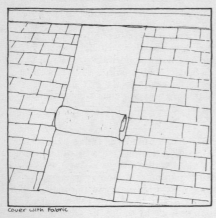

Cover with Fabric

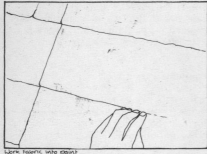

Work fabric into paint

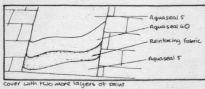

Aquaseal 5
Aquaseal 40
Reinforcing fabric
Aquaseal 5

Cover with two more layers of paint

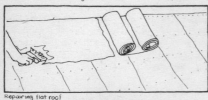

Repairing flat roof

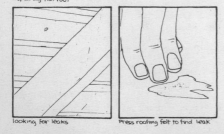

looking for leaks   Press roofing felt to find leak

sure the mastic goes under the lip of each row of slates. The area covered must be in a strip running from top to bottom of the roof and as wide as necessary to cover the poor area. While still wet, cover the area with Aquaseal nylon reinforcing fabric. Bed it well into the sealer, moulding it to the ridges of the slates. Overlap by 3" where two pieces join. Cover this with Aquaseal 40 (or another coat of Synthapruf - allow 1 gallon for every 4 square yards). When dry, apply a third coat using Aquaseal 5 or Synthapruf. Ridge capping can be treated in a similar method.

3. 20. 22 It's important that the end result be a continuous covering over the nylon mesh, with no open holes through the mesh. If there are still holes, give another covering of Aquaseal or Synthapruf. In areas where water collects (like in a valley gutter) it may be necessary to do the whole process, including the reinforcing fabric, up to three times.

3. 20. 23 Repairing a flat roof -
Use roofing felt either laid on existing felt and stuck with a coat of mastic or lay three layers of felt on the boards. (Make sure the boards are smooth and nails are removed or hammered in flat.) Nail the first layer down and stick the second layer and third to the first with mastic (roofing felt adhesive) and nail at the joints. Two layers may be enough to last a couple of years. Change the direction you lay the felt for each layer. Some local authorities say that the last layer should be of a mineralised roofing felt, or covered with sand or stone chippings to lessen the risk of fire.

3. 20. 24 Tracing leaks in roofs can be difficult. Water often runs down the rafters so water stains may be some distance from the leak. Note any pinholes of daylight that can be seen from inside the loft, look for water courses down timber. Leaks often occur in valleys or gutters covered with lead or roofing felt. After rain, when the roof has just dried, try pressing the roofing felt with your fingers. Water that has leaked under the felt will be forced back through the holes, showing them up. Brick parapets should be kept repaired, as water soaking into crumbling bricks and cement can also be a source of persistent leaks.

3.21.00 GUTTERING AND DOWN-PIPES

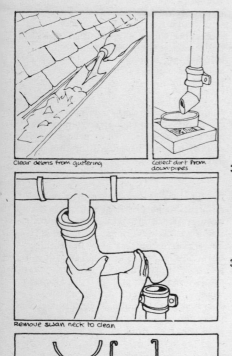

Clear debris from guttering

Collect dirt from down-pipes

Remove swan neck to clean

half round   square

moulded   ogee

Types of guttering

3.21.01 It's fairly important to keep gutters and down-pipes working as they can lead to damp conditions. On most old houses the guttering and down-pipes are of cast iron, and although it is still available for minor repairs, it has been largely superceded by plastic.

3.21.02 Clean out the gutters using a scraper and brush. Put a tin under the down pipes and using a rag tied to a can or long stick clear away any obstructions from them. The swan-necks (the bit between the gutter and the top of the down-pipe) can often be removed and cleaned separately. Clear out any hopper heads.

3.21.03 When replacing or repairing guttering, buy the same type as is already in place: it may be half round, square, moulded or 'ogee'. Cast iron gutters overlap and are held together by a single

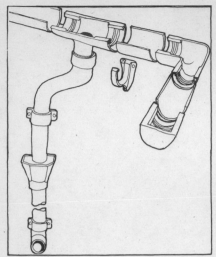

Plastic guttering

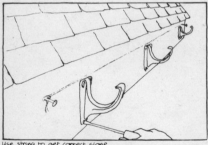
Use string to get correct slope

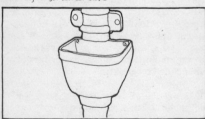
Hopper head

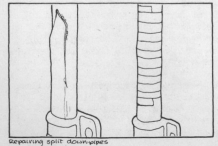
Repairing split down-pipes

nut and bolt, and are sealed with putty. Ogee uses a special union clip. There's a special support for each type of gutter which can be easily screwed to the facia board to support new or sagging gutters.

3. 21. 04 If a lot of work needs doing on gutters it may be best to use new plastic gutter- ing. It is light and much easier to fit. The joints are rubber sealed, and sim- ply push or snap into place. You can replace one section and use the old gut- tering to patch up another less damaged section. Avoid trying to join two types of guttering.

3. 21. 05 When laying new guttering make sure you get a slope towards the down-pipe. Use a string nailed at one end and a spirit level to get a gentle slope. Screw the gutter supports in line with the string. The guttering is then clipped into the supports. Attach a stop end at each end and a down-pipe outlet for the down-pipe.

3. 21. 06 Plastic gutters can be run into cast iron down-pipes, and cast iron gutters into plastic down-pipes. The swan-neck is usually a loose fit and allows this use of differing materials.

3. 21. 07 Replace any broken down-pipes with plastic. They are light and easy to erect. There are several makes which come with instructions. If there is a hopper head you may need to replace only the length to the head (or from it), as you can use this as a junction between the two materials. There are occasions when a caulked joint can be made between plastic and cast iron pipe. Re- place any cast iron grates in open gut- ters (you can often buy plastic grates).

3. 21. 08 If down-pipes are split or have small holes in them, repair them with Sylglas or Aquaseal tape wrapped around the pipe in a spiral. You may be able to repair larger holes with a bit of tin under the tape to reinforce it.

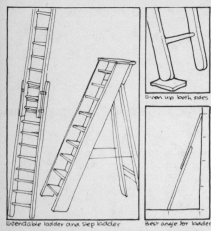
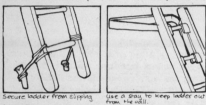

Extendable ladder and step ladder   Best angle for ladder

Even up both sides

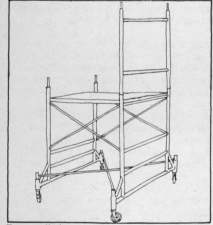

Secure ladder from slipping   Use a stay to keep ladder out from the wall.

Tower scaffolding

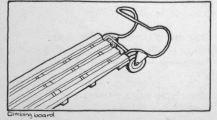

Climbing board

3.22.00 LADDERS AND SCAFFOLDING

3.22.01 Ladders and scaffolding are both fairly easily hired, though they tend to be
quite expensive. If you're doing a lot
of work, scaffolding in the end may be
worth the extra cost, as it's safer and
more convenient.

3.22.02 Ladders come in many types: step
ladders are ideal for decorating and
interior work, while extendable ladders
are needed for exterior work. Over
16 ft (5m) you need a rope operated ex-
tending ladder which is best operated
by two or more persons.

3.22.03 Always set the ladder on level ground,
or use wedges to even up the low side -
a stake can be driven into the ground
and tied to the bottom rung to stop the
ladder slipping outwards or it can be
tied through an open window or to a
strong nail driven into the wall.

3.22.04 If the eaves have a large overhang, a
special stay can be fitted to the top of
the ladder (hire it with the ladder) to
bring the top of the ladder out from the
wall. The ideal position of the base
of the ladder is about $\frac{1}{4}$ the distance
out of its height against the wall.

3.22.05 The cheapest and easiest scaffolding to
erect is the tower. It comes in sections
which are easily put together and
can be fitted with wheels to move it
from one place to another. They can
be built up to 30 or 40 feet (10 - 13m)
and give a working platform of about
8 by 4 feet (2.5 x 1.5m). They should
always be levelled, the wheels locked and
tied to the building before climbing on
them.

3.22.06 Climbing boards are essential when
working on pitched roofing. They can
be hired or you can make one by nailing struts across two lengths of timber.
Secure a lip at the top which can be
hooked over the roof ridge.

3. 23. 00 DRY ROT

Dry rot

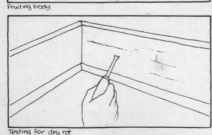

Fruiting body

Testing for dry rot

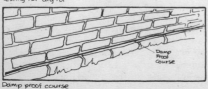

Damp proof course

3.23.01 Dry rot is a big problem in old houses. It is a fungus infection which attacks damp timber, removing the timber's strength and finally turning it into dust. Often the first time people know about dry rot is when the leg of a chair breaks through a rotted floorboard.

3.23.02 Make a specific search for dry rot - if an infection is left unchecked it will weaken the whole floor and could be potentially very dangerous. There are several distinct conditions to look for:

3.23.03 Rotted wood - the wood appears dry and easily crumbles to dust between fingers. There are cracks running along and across the grain giving the impression that the timber is divided into small cubes.

3.23.04 Fruiting body - a severe attack produces a type of mushroom usually hanging off the ceiling or wall into the open air. They are usually brown in colour.

3.23.05 Test with a small knife or screwdriver by pushing it into the wood. If it meets little resistance then you've found dry rot. Wood is often rotted behind paint work without it showing through the paint. Long deep cracks in painted wood are a sure sign.

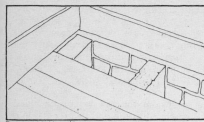
Dry rot in joist ends

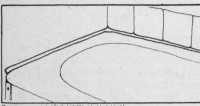
Sealing round the back of the bath

Sealing round the back of the sink

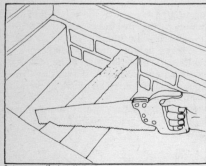
Cut away affected timber

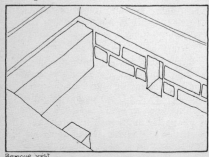
Remove joist

3. 23. 06 Dry rot is helped by dampness so any area where water or damp are likely to be is suspect. Under sinks, baths, washbasins, and W. C. bowls, where wooden floors touch outside walls, especially if the walls feel damp or if guttering and down pipes are in bad condition.

3. 23. 07 Old houses, built before 1900 are particularly prone as they did not have a damp course - water rises up the walls and provides the damp condition for dry rot to attack the end of the joist buried in the wall.

3. 23. 08 Roof spaces are less liable to attack because they are usually well ventilated, but small continuous leaks will lead to the roof timbers being attacked.

3. 23. 09 Any springiness or creaking in the floor should be investigated - lift one floorboard near the external wall.

3. 23. 10 Although called dry rot, the fungus actually needs a moisture content of over 20% in the wood before it can grow. The most common form of fungus is able to penetrate brick walls and travel under plaster. It is also capable of carrying its own water through special water-carrying threads.

3. 23. 11 What to do with your dry rot -

It is almost impossible to completely eradicate the fungus; people spend thousands of pounds and still don't succeed. So don't try, in short-life properties especially.

3. 23. 12 What you can do is first to remove the conditions under which it breeds. Attend to any leaking pipes quickly, try to prevent water from constantly seeping down the back of sinks and baths. Keep the roof, gutters and drain pipes in good condition. If you have got rising damp it is more difficult. Keep the space between the joists well ventilated. Don't lay lino over a wooden floor if water is going to seep under it. The lino will prevent the floor from drying.

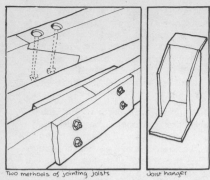

Two methods of jointing joists   Joist hanger

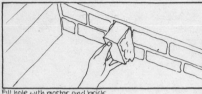

Fill hole with mortar and brick

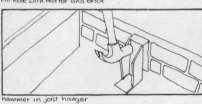

hammer in joist hanger

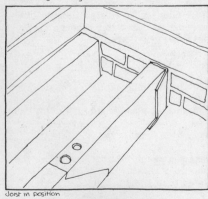

Joist in position

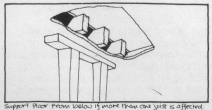

Support floor from below if more than one joist is affected.

3. 23. 13 Secondly, remove all the infected wood; especially if it has weakened the structure; replace with treated timber (you can buy timber treated for dry rot) or buy a fungicide and paint or spray this onto replacement timbers and all surrounding timbers and walls.

3. 23. 14 The most common and dangerous place for dry rot is in the end two feet or so of floor timber where they enter an external wall.

3. 23. 15 Remove the floorboards as far back as the affected timber goes. Burn any floorboards which show any sign of attack and paint the rest with fungicide. Remove the rotted part of the first joist, cutting 12" (350mm) or so back from where the infection seems to end.

3. 23. 16 If it is an upper room, the ceiling below will be joined to the base of the joist. It may be possible to carefully chisel the joist out leaving the laths and plaster or ceiling board - but it's likely you will get some plaster falling. If more than one joist is to be replaced, the ceiling will have to be replaced.

3. 23. 17 Cut a half lap joint in the joists and new timber. Drill two holes (about 3/8 to $\frac{1}{2}$" - 10mm - in diameter) through the two pieces of wood and bolt them together. The other end of the joist should be cut to fit into the hole or support that held the original timber.

3. 23. 18 If this is unsuitable, metal joist hangers can be bought and cemented into the wall.

3. 23. 19 Replace each affected joist one at a time in this way. If there are several weak joists, support the floor from underneath with temporary posts till repairs are done.

3. 23. 20 As long as you keep timber dry and perhaps spray with fungicide every 6 months in areas of high risk you will keep the dry rot from doing too much harm and can extend the life of timber for years. if dry rot is left and the conditions are right, it can destroy thick timber in a matter of months.

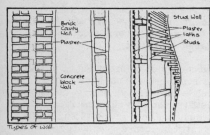
Types of wall.

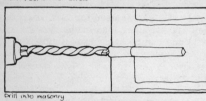
Mark position for screw

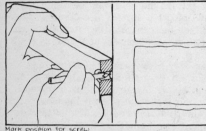
Drill into masonry

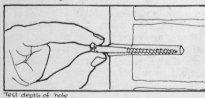
Test depth of hole

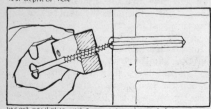
Insert rawl plug and engage screw in rawl plug

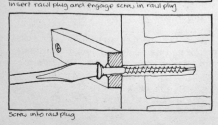
Screw into rawl plug

3.24.00 <u>WALL FIXINGS</u>

3.24.01 There are three types of wall found in most houses in which you may want to make a fixing.

3.24.02 All outside walls and major internal walls will be brick, probably covered in $\frac{3}{4}$ - 1" (20 - 25mm) of plaster.

3.24.03 Partition walls may be made of concrete blocks covered with plaster, or timber frame covered with laths and plaster or plasterboard (stud walls).

3.24.04 Brick and concrete block walls can be fixed by using Rawlplugs or filling compound and screws. Stud walls can be screwed into directly, provided you locate the main upright or cross beams and screw into them.

3.24.05 Masonry walls -

Holes should be deep enough to go through the plaster into the brick ($\frac{3}{4}$" - 1" or 20 - 25mm thickness of plaster) as the plaster isn't strong enough to make a secure fixing. The minimum length of screw is about $1\frac{1}{4}$" to $1\frac{1}{2}$" (35 - 40mm) but if the fixing is heavy they should be longer. The thickness of screws varies and is differentiated by a number. The larger the number the thicker the screw. Number 8 is a good universal size suited to most jobs - and it's best to stick to as few sizes as possible, for each one requires the appropriate masonry bit, or rawl chisel ('rawl tool') and Rawlplug. Rawl plugs, as well as being the same number as the screw you're using, should be the same length, minus the thickness of the piece being fixed. They come in plastic or fibre - the fibre ones are best. Special compound fillers can also be used to fill irregular holes and for any size screw, but they take longer to use.

3.24.06 Mark the position of the fixing holes on the fitting onto the wall, drill the correct size and depth holes. Check that the screw goes in all the way. Push in a Rawlplug or compound (a plug of soft wood will do if you don't have Rawl plugs). Push the screw into the centre

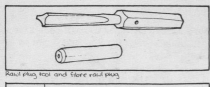

Rawl plug tool and fibre rawl plug

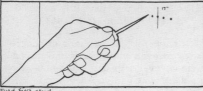

Find first stud.

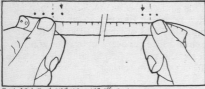

Find next stud and measure off stud centres

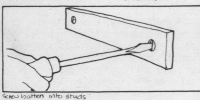

Screw batten into studs

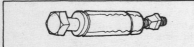

A rawl bolt

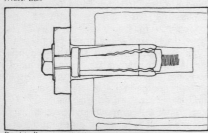

Rawl bolt in masonary

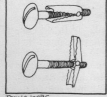

Toggle bolts

of the Rawlplug and screw it in. It should go in fairly easily and tighten up to the end and become solid when up against the fitting.

3. 24. 07   If it seizes up before going all the way in, remove it and put some soap or grease on the screw and try again. If it still doesn't go right in, redrill the hole and put in a new Rawlplug. If it can still be turned when screwed up to the fixture the hole was too big or the rawl plug too small, or the screw missed the centre of the plug. Remove the screw, replug the hole and try again.

3. 24. 08   For very heavy work, like attaching floor joists, or stair supports, etc , use rawl bolts. A large hole is made and the bolt inserted; when it tightens against the fixture, the side of the bolt expands in the hole against the masonry.

3. 24. 09   Steel nails can be used for light fixtures; they are stronger than ordinary wire nails and can be hammered straight into the masonry.

3. 24. 10   Stud walls -

The main uprights (studs) in a stud wall are usually between 16" to 18" (400 - 460mm) apart. Start at one end of the wall and measure 17" (430mm) out, push a sharp point through the plaster, move it 1" (25mm) to each side and repeat until you locate the stud. When found, locate the next one in the same way and measure the distance between them - this should be the centre for the remaining studs.

3. 24. 11   If the fixture has to go in a certain position and there is no stud in that particular place, then fix a batten across the two nearest studs, screwing directly through the plaster into the studs. The fixture can then be attached to the batten.

3. 24. 12   There are special screws (Toggle bolts) which can be pushed through the plaster and hooked onto the laths. When screwing against the screws they open out at the back giving a secure fix. These are only suitable for things like light shelves, etc..

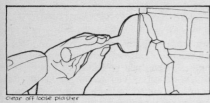

clear off loose plaster

Wet old plaster and wall

Put plaster on the float

and smooth over wall

A hawk

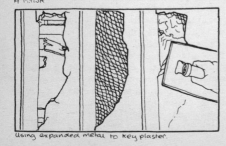

Using expanded metal to key plaster.

3.25.00 PLASTERING

3.25.01 For large areas of plaster-work, use Sirapite which will do as an undercoat and a finishing plaster. Always use clean buckets and trowels and clean water when mixing plaster. Never mix more than you can use in a half an hour. Start by mixing very small quantities, increasing as you get more adept. Clean your trowels each time so that the plaster doesn't set on them. It's good to have a mate to mix plaster for you. It should be mixed to a consistency of dough. Sirapite can be re-wetted for smoothing over after it's been applied but before it has dried.

3.25.02 Clean away any old loose plaster, and if the area to be covered is smooth, score it to give the new plaster something to hold on to. If it's a hole (like in a ceiling) you'll need to fix something on which to 'key' the plaster - wire-netting, expanded metal, wooden battens will do. Wet the wall before applying the new plaster.

3.25.03 Apply the plaster, starting at the bottom and working upwards; keep the layers fairly thin and apply two or three coats; you don't have to wait for the previous one to dry, but do score it. If you're using an undercoat plaster (e.g. Sirapite Browning, which contains sand) then do a finishing coat with pure plaster (Sirapite).

3.25.04 Keep the float wet when plastering. Lift the plaster onto the underside of the float and press it onto the wall and smooth it across the surface holding the float at an angle of about 30-degrees from the wall.

3.25.05 A good metal float will do for most jobs, an old paintbrush for wetting the walls, and a plastic bowl for mixing. A stout piece of plywood fixed to 9" (200mm) of broom handle makes an excellent 'hawk' for holding plaster.

3.25.06 Use Polyfilla or Alabaster for small holes or cracks.

3.26.00 <u>PAINTING: TOOLS AND MATERIALS</u>

3.26.01 Buy the best paintbrushes you can afford, and then look after them. If you buy the cheapest then you're likely to forget them as soon as you no longer need them, having to replace them when you need to do more painting. The best bristles are pig or hog hair, which have a natural taper, giving a good shape to the brush and being able to hold more paint. All brushes lose some hair to start with, so break a new brush in on undercoating.

3.26.02 Depending on the type of painting you're doing, you'll need some or all of the following sizes; $\frac{1}{2}$" (12mm) for window frames and edging; a $1\frac{1}{2}$" (38mm) or 2" (50mm) for general woodwork and small flat areas; a 3" (75mm) for edging large areas and covering smaller flat areas; and a 6" (150mm) for covering large areas. A 'cutting in brush' is specially shaped for painting up to edges and corners, and is useful when doing a lot of windows, etc. A crevice brush, used for getting to awkward areas, can easily be made by cutting the handle off a 2" (50mm) oldish brush and attaching it to 2' (600mm) of coathanger wire to form a long bendable handle.

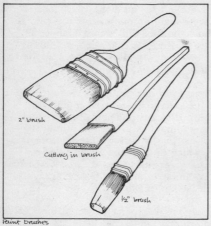
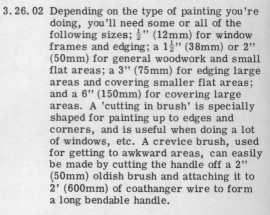

2" brush

Cutting in brush

$\frac{1}{2}$" brush

Paint brushes

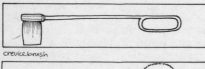
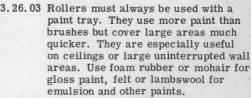

crevice brush

3.26.03 Rollers must always be used with a paint tray. They use more paint than brushes but cover large areas much quicker. They are especially useful on ceilings or large uninterrupted wall areas. Use foam rubber or mohair for gloss paint, felt or lambswool for emulsion and other paints.

3.26.04 Other tools that may be needed: a blow-lamp for softening paint; a stripping knife for removing flat areas of softened paint, and also useful for scraping off loose paint, wallpaper, and filling holes and cracks; shave hooks are needed for stripping mouldings and difficult corners; a wide mouth plastic bucket, or paint kettle, is useful when working high, as the paint can be held on the steps or ladder with an 'S' hook; glasspaper and a sanding block; rags; appropriate solvent; stirring stick and paint can opener.

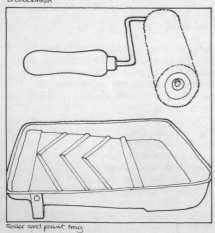
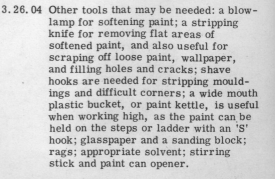

Roller and paint tray

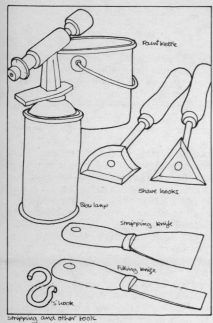

Paint kettle

Shave hooks

Blow lamp

Stripping knife

Filling knife

's hook

Stripping and other tools

Step ladders, scaffold board and strong box

3. 26. 05 Where possible provide yourself with good ladders, steps or trestles and scaffold boards. Always test their stability and safety, and nail down retaining strips where possible. If you use a table, make sure it's strong and steady. Take care when standing near the edge, especially if the legs are set back, as it may suddenly tip up.

3. 26. 06 Emulsion paint is widely used for most surfaces, but is best on walls and ceilings. It's water-based, which means it can be thinned with water, brushes cleaned in water, and used on damp surfaces - providing there is no stain- ing - without harm. Emulsion has good covering power, and while it may take three coats of a light shade to cover a dark one, two are more normal. It comes in a matt or semi-matt (eggshell) finish.

3. 26. 07 Gloss paint is more durable, but more expensive and difficult to apply than emulsion. It is oil-based and must be applied to absolutely dry surfaces. Gloss paint covers less well than emulsion (that is, it's slightly trans- parent), needing an undercoat and two coats of gloss for best effect, but it's for this reason that the colours are much clearer and brighter. Gloss is best used on woodwork - which it helps to protect - on metals that are likely to rust, and occasionally on bathroom and kitchen walls.

3. 26. 08 The price of paint is largely related to its quality, the fastness (amount colours fade) and brilliance of colours and the covering power and thickness of the paint. Painting is a long hard job, and it pays to do it properly and with the best- quality paints, if you don't want to repaint too frequently. It's often difficult to tell how a colour will look from a small colour card, so if you're buying a lot of paint it may be worth getting the smallest quantity to test it out before final commitment.

3. 26. 09 Buy all the paint you'll need at one time; if you don't, you run the risk of finding the colour out of stock, or small differ- ences in colour between one paint batch and the next. As a guide for gloss paint, one side of a door will use 1/10th of a pint (or 1/20th of a litre) for one coat.

3.27.00 PAINTING: CARE OF TOOLS

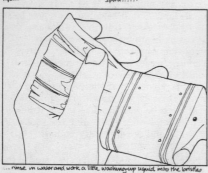

Method of suspending brushes in liquids   Clean gloss paint off with white spirit......

3.27.01 When painting with gloss paint you should not leave the brush unused for more than a few minutes. Brushes can be left without a proper cleaning for short periods if wrapped in polythene or aluminium foil. A better method is to drill holes through the base of the handles so they can be suspended in a jar, without the bristles resting on the bottom and becoming distorted and misshapen. For short periods keep the brushes in water - just shake it off and paint out the paint left in the brush on some scrap hardboard. For overnight storage suspend in an equal mixture of linseed oil and white spirit (or other turps substitute).

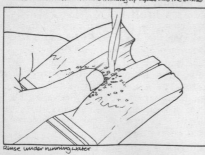

..... rinse in water and work a little washing-up liquid into the bristles

3.27.02 Proper cleaning before storage, or just clearing the brush of excessive paint, should be done first in white spirit, using the fingers to work the paint out of the upper inner bristles, and then in warm water and soap or detergent. Pour a small amount of washing-up liquid into the bristles, work in with the fingers and rinse. Repeat until the brush is clean, wrap up in paper and store flat.

3.27.03 Emulsion paint is easier to remove than gloss, and only requires washing with warm water and detergent. For short periods, suspend in water and shake and paint out before re-use.

3.27.04 If a brush becomes misshapen or ragged, soak in a water soluble glue (starch- or cellulose-based wallpaper glue) and reform the bristles. When the glue is dry, trim the bristles into their proper shape. This method can be used to convert an ordinary brush into a cutting in brush. Leave overnight to soak and wash out glue the next day.

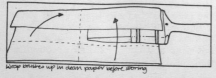

Rinse under running water

Wrap brushes up in clean paper before storing

3.27.05 Rollers and paint trays should be cleaned immediately after use. Use the same methods as described for cleaning gloss or emulsion out of brushes. It's more difficult to leave rollers and trays for short periods; they are best cleaned properly between each use.

3.28.00 PAINTING: PREPARING SURFACES

3.28.01 To get the best our of paint it must be applied to a sound surface. In general this means one free of loose or cracked material, of dust, grease and moisture. Most unpainted surfaces require a special primer to ensure good bonding, and already painted surfaces should be rubbed with glasspaper.

3.28.02 New plaster can be painted with emulsion paint even if slightly damp. The first coat can be thinned to help seal the surface for second and third coats. It should need no other preparation. Before gloss paint is applied to new plaster it must be completely dry - this may take six months - and a coat of thinned emulsion may be applied before the normal undercoat. One coat of gloss should be sufficient.

3.28.03 Painted plaster should be washed with sugar soap and warm water to remove all grease, and then rinsed with warm water to remove all soap. Cracks and holes should be filled with filler, and any loose paint removed. Very marked surfaces can be improved by brushing on thin plaster using an old brush. This does not give a flat surface, but does improve appearance, without the need for complete replastering.

3.28.04 New wood should be lightly sanded and any knots covered with knotting compound (shellac), leaving half an hour between first and second coats. Rub smooth when dry and apply a coat of wood primer. This can be fairly thin, but should be well worked into the wood, especially corners. Leave for 12 - 24 hours to harden. Primer should be applied before glazing so all rebates in glazing bars are primed. Undercoating should be done seven days after putty is applied, and left for twenty-four hours to harden. Rub down with wet and dry glasspaper, damping the surface beforehand. Dabbing a bit of soap onto glasspaper also helps. Wipe all rubbings off afterwards with a clean damp cloth. Apply one, or preferably two, top coats, especially to outside woodwork.

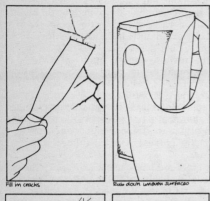

Fill in cracks

Rub down uneven surfaces

Scrape off loose paint

Rub down metal with wire brush

Use old brush to remove dust and loose dirt

Wash surfaces with sugar soap and clean water.

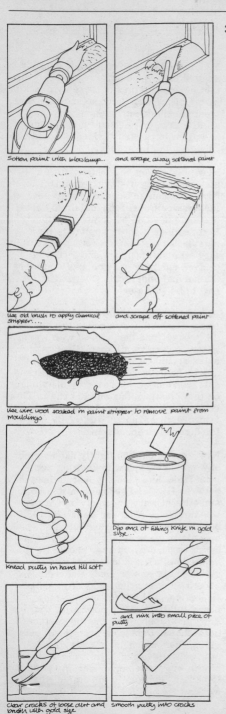

Soften paint with blowlamp...

and scrape away softened paint

Use old brush to apply chemical stripper...

and scrape off softened paint

Use wire wool soaked in paint stripper to remove paint from mouldings

Knead putty in hand till soft

Dip end of filling knife in gold size..

... and mix into small piece of putty

Clear cracks of loose dirt and brush with gold size

smooth putty into cracks

3. 28. 05 Painted wood should be washed and rubbed down before a new undercoat and gloss coat are applied. Emulsion paint can be used on wood, but does not give such good protection. If applied over gloss paint, it must be rubbed down first. If the existing paint is cracked or flaked then it's best to strip it back to the wood. A blowlamp is the fastest method, but must be used with care. Do the more difficult bits first, the mouldings and corners, working from the bottom up, using a shave hook. The large flat areas are done last, using a stripping knife. Don't use a blowlamp on glazing bars as it will crack the glass. Chemical stripping should be done working from the top down. Leave stripper on until paint softens (5 - 10 mins.) but don't leave too long as it will begin to harden again. Several coats may be needed, depending on the thickness of paint. Wash all paint stripper off before repainting. For removing paint from mouldings using a chemical paint stripper, soak a wire-wool pad in stripper and (wearing rubber gloves), rub mouldings with this.

3. 28. 06 If the wood has shrunk and split, these cracks should be filled before repainting. Putty can be used, but a better result is obtained by mixing putty with a little gold size. Work a small piece of putty in hands until warm and soft (add linseed oil if too dry - add whiting (powdered chalk) if too soft). Dip a putty knife into gold size and work it into the ball of putty. Also brush size into the cracks before pressing the prepared putty into them and smooth down with a putty knife.

3. 28. 07 Metal should be cleaned of all rust - use a liquid rust remover, or rub with a wire brush. Paint bare metal with a metal primer before giving it a normal undercoat/gloss coat treatment. If the metal is already painted and is in good condition, simply remove all grease with sugar soap, rinse, and undercoat and topcoat in normal way.

3. 28. 08 Concrete must be primed with special primer. All loose material must be removed, and cracks filled before undercoating and topcoating. Paint can be removed from brickwork, but not plaster, with a blowlamp.

3. 29. 00 <u>PAINTING: GENERAL TECHNIQUES</u>

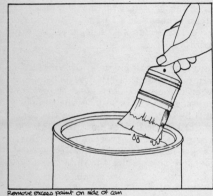
Remove excess paint on side of can

3. 29. 01 Don't over-fill the paintbrush, immerse
in 1" - 1½" (25 - 38mm) and remove
excess paint on sides of tin. When
covering flat areas, work from the
right hand top corner down. With gloss
paint make three downward strokes,
about half the size of the brush apart
and about three times its size in length,
then work back and forth filling in from
the bottom up until a square is filled in.
Do several light upward strokes to
remove any brush marks before re-
charging the brush to do the next lower
square. Don't use a brush bigger than
3" (75mm) for gloss work.

3. 29. 02 Emulsion paint can be applied in the same
way but covering a bigger area with a
larger brush. Brush marks don't show
in emulsion. Work horizontally in strips
about 10" (250mm) deep.

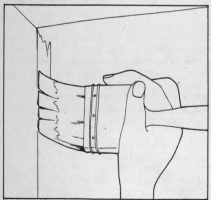
Making a straight edge

3. 29. 03 Always paint the edges first, using the
long edge of the brush well-charged with
paint. Place it near the corner or edge
and slowly move it down, wiggling it
slightly to keep the bristles moving and
slightly bent so you can see the paint
edge the brush is leaving. It may help
to put an elastic band round the bristles
about two-thirds of the way up, or to
use a 'cutting in brush'.

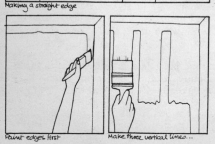
Paint edges first   Make three vertical lines...

3. 29. 04 Paint edges and corners with a brush
first, when using a roller. Cover the

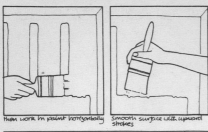

then work in paint horizontally   smooth surface with upward strokes

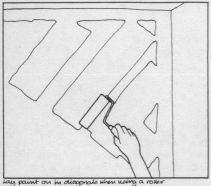

Lay paint on in diagonals when using a roller

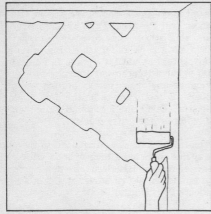

Finish with vertical strokes

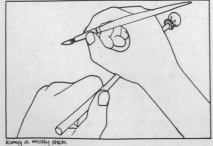

Using a molly stick

roller evenly with paint by rolling it in the tray several times. Apply paint in diagonal strokes, about 2" - 3" (50 - 75mm) apart, one way then the other. Finish off with straight strokes filling in the gaps.

3. 29. 05 It's better to finish a particular area all in one go, joining at corners or edges, than to start in the middle of a wall. This is especially important when using gloss. Try to work with lighter colours first, as it is almost impossible to clean brushes of all paint. Some painters have a separate set of brushes for white paint.

3. 29. 06 Exterior painting is best done in late summer after a fairly dry spell and when one or two more clear days can be expected. This will be when wood will be at its driest and when the sun is unlikely to blister new paint. Don't use gloss paint if frost is likely. Dust can be laid by sprinkling water around, just before applying the final gloss coat.

3. 29. 07 Remove all fittings, handles, bolts, etc., before painting. Protect surrounding areas with brown paper or several sheets of newspaper, as paint will go through a single thickness of newsprint. Use masking tape to give straight edges or to protect from over-painting. Make sure it's well stuck down, and remove before the paint has entirely dried. When painting stairs that are in use, paint every other stair, leave to dry, then paint the rest.

3. 29. 08 When painting mouldings in more than one colour, paint the whole moulding in the most predominant colour first, and pick out other colours with a small sable brush when this has dried. In difficult areas use a molly stick to rest your hand on. Use brushes that are the correct width when doing edges; or, if not available, use the brush side on.

3. 29. 09 Store paint that is left over with the lid firmly in place and upside down. This reduces the tendency of the paint to skin over, and if it does, then the skin is at the bottom. If old paint is used, it can be strained through an old silk stocking to remove lumps and skin.

3.30.00 GETTING THINGS CHEAP

3.30.01 Demolition contractors are one of the best sources of material. Most things you need they are busy tearing out of houses and burning or smashing. But don't forget that they are in it for the money, so once they know you need something, it gains in value. Prices vary tremendously. Often if you chat to the men demolishing the house, they will sell you things really cheap: one may ask £3 for an Ascot, the scrap value, whilst another may ask £10 - more than the value you would pay in a shop.

3.30.02 If you want to get old pipe (e.g. copper) to reuse, you will do best to get it out yourself, as the contractors will only be selling it for scrap, and so won't bother not to kink it. Compression fittings (see 2.11.04) can be bought in the same way, or go to a scrap merchant who may have a load of second-hand fittings. You will have to buy new olives for these (but don't forget that old copper will be $\frac{3}{4}$" pipe or fittings, not 22mm, and you may find it difficult to get new olives or other pipe fittings if you have to buy anything new).

3.30.03 Empty houses in the area, and especially if they are of the same design, are very useful. It is illegal to take things from derelict houses: whatever is in them belongs to the owner of the house. If the owner is a council it is often difficult to get anyone to admit to being in a position where he can allow you to take the stuff. Demolition men make money by selling off the bits - they get comparatively little for actually pulling the house down - so they are likely to get mad if they find you ripping stuff out of a house they regard as theirs.

3.30.04 People dump the most incredible stuff on waste ground and at council rubbish tips, and in skips in the street. Keep your eyes open for furniture, sanitary fittings, wood, etc.

3.30.05 Local junk shops are useful. They will often keep an eye out for something particular that you need.

3.30.06 The local builders' merchant, timber merchants and electric wholesalers are useful sources of things you can't get free, and also of information, although you sometimes get a rough time if you don't know what you need. Sometimes wholesalers may be reluctant to serve you unless you can produce evidence that you are 'trade' (e.g. by printed order). Others will give you a trade discount anyway. Never buy at D.I.Y. shops unless you really have to - they are expensive.

3.31.00 USEFUL ADDRESSES

The following addresses are of places that might be useful for you to visit or to telephone if you want help or advice:

3.10.01 The Building Centre
26 Store Street
London W. C. 1
Tel (01) 637-1022
Has a permanent exhibition of building materials, an index of manufacturers and their addresses, a library, and a very useful bookshop selling books on building, including plumbing and electricity.

3.31.02 Advisory Service for Squatters
2 St Paul's Road
London N. 1
Tel. (01) 359-8814
For information about forming lawful squatting groups, and for legal and other information about squatting.

3.31.03 Shelter (National Campaign for the Homeless)
157 Waterloo Road
London S. E. 1
Tel. (01) 633-9377
For advice on housing and housing rights generally.

3.31.04 Release
1 Elgin Avenue
London W. 9
Tel. (01) 289-1123; and 24-hour service for emergencies only,
(01) 603-8654
For advice on most legal problems.

3.31.05 London Squatters' Union
c/o 5 Huntley Street
London W. C. 1
Tel. (01) 580-0855
(or contact c/o A. S. S.)
The organisation of London squatters.

3.31.06 Her Majesty's Stationery Office (Government Bookshop)

Shop	Mail Order
49 High Holborn	P. O. Box 569
London W. C. 1	London S. E. 1
Tel. (01) 928-6977	Tel. (same)

For Government circulars, statutes, and government leaflets.

3.31.07 Polythene pipe (see 2.13.12) is probably easier to get hold of outside London than in London. People who stock it in London include:

B. C. T. Cadel
45 Duck Lees Lane
Ponders End
Tel.(01) 804-7121

George and Co.
645 b Holloway Road
Tel.(01) 272-2157

Nicholls and Clarke Ltd.
3 Shoreditch High Street
London E. 1
Tel.(01) 247-5432

Graham (Builders Merchant) Ltd.
Hawley Mill
Hawley
Dartford, Kent
Tel. Dartford 27233
(they deliver to London)

You can also get it from Student/ Community/Housing (see 3.10.03) sometimes. Ring your supplier first and check that they have definitely got it in stock, as they tend to be out of stock very frequently. If still in difficulty, contact Yorkshire Imperial Plastics, the manufacturers (see 3.10.07).

3.31.08 uPVC pipe is available rather more widely. If you have difficulty, get in touch with the manufacturers who will tell you who they supply:

Yorkshire Imperial Plastics Ltd.
(they make 'Polyorc')

Head Office
P. O. Box 166
Leeds LS1 1RD
Tel.053-2 (Leeds) 701107

London Office
C. P. House
9th Floor
97/107 Uxbridge Road
Ealing, London W. 5
Tel.(01) 579-1601

3.31.09 Your local library will have some books on building and on the law.

3.32.00 SOME BOOKS FOR FURTHER INFORMATION

3.32.01 General -

Readers Digest Repair Manual
Readers Digest Association - £6.30
Good on general repairs (plastering, papering, etc.) but leaves off plumbing and wiring when it starts getting interesting.

Readers Digest Complete Do-It-Yourself Manual
(same publishers)
Much less useful. Consists largely of projects for the consumer-minded, although 'techniques' section can be useful for carpentry for instance.

Building Construction
W.B. McKay
Longman - £1.50 per volume
Four volumes designed as a text-book, which means that things sometimes come in a funny order (1st year, 2nd year, etc.). However it says all you are ever likely to want to know about drains, brickwork, plasters, roofing and the construction of a building. But not very detailed on plumbing or wiring.

Advisory Leaflets
Department of the Environment
(ex. Ministry of Public Building and Works) - about 4p each
The DOE publishes cheap leaflets on various aspects of building - e.g. single-stack plumbing, plastic pipes, drainage, dry and wet rot, ring mains, plasters, dampness, etc.   They are written in very simple and clear language and can be bought from bookshops, from H.M.S.O. (see 3.10.05), or from the Building Centre (see 3.10.01) or may be stocked by your local library.

3.32.02 Electricity -

I.E.E. Wiring Regulations
Institute of Electrical Engineers
(Savoy Place, W.C.2) - £1.50
from I.E.E.
These are the regulations to which electrical installations in the U.K. should conform. They are in rather technical language and are quite difficult to understand. Also they contain a lot of information which is of no relevance to domestic wiring.

Guide to the I.E.E. Wiring Regulations
M.A. Miller
Peter Peregrinus Ltd. - £1.50
may help but is still technical.

'Rewiring a House' , 'Ring Circuits' , and 'Electrical Installations'
Geoffrey Arnold
Burdett - 45p each
These are simply written books for the layman and you may find them useful as a back-up to the information in Part One.

Electric Wiring (Domestic)
A.J. Coker (ed.)
Newnes-Butterworths - £1.80
Comprehensive and consequently somewhat heavy going. Not completely metric, which is confusing.

3.32.03 Plumbing -

Plumbing
F. Hall   MacMillan - £1
Easy to understand, but does not go into enough detail to really do the job. No index and so difficult to refer to. The metrication is mostly wrong - 15mm pipe is called 13mm throughout

The Plumber's Handbook
Lead Development Association
34 Berkeley Square, London, W.1
free from the L.D.A.
A publicity handout (on a lavish scale) for lead. Tells you everything you could ever want to know about using lead in all its forms, except that lead is too expensive.

Plumbing (Vols. 1 & 2)
A.L. Townsend
Hutchinson Educational - £2 & £1.25
Academic book aimed at passing exams. Difficult book with little practical help on installations and no index.

Plumber's Companion
James Hastings
David & Charles - £2.50
A glorified dictionary of plumbing words you would never guess existed.

3.33.00 THE LAW AND THE SQUATTER

3.33.01
Society has not yet recognised that it is less anti-social for squatters to occupy empty property than it is for landlords to keep it empty for profit or convenience when so many people are homeless. The laws affecting squatting have recently been altered. The changes make squatting more perilous, and could lead to squatters being jailed. But, as these laws have not long been in force and as their actual impact will depend on how they are interpreted by the courts, it is not possible at the time of writing to give an accurate picture of their effect. Nevertheless, it's important to be informed about the law and up-to-date on how it is being applied. The law can be used in a limited way on your behalf as well as against you.

3.33.02
This, briefly, is how the law stands and how, as far as it is possible to say, it will affect squatting.

3.33.03
The forcible Entry Acts, which protected all 'trespassers' against eviction except by court order, have been repealed. Instead it is now a criminal offence to use violence (or threat of violence) to gain entry to property where an occupant opposes entry. However, this doesn't prevent an owner from breaking in while no one is at home. Equally, it seems that squatters can gain entry into unoccupied property without fear of criminal prosecution, provided they don't cause any criminal damage and provided their entry is not opposed by people on the property (e.g. security guards or caretakers, etc.) (see 3.33.09).

3.33.04
It is now an offence not to leave premises when a 'displaced residential occupier' or his or her representative asks you to do so. This is intended to protect genuine residents or owner-occupiers from being 'displaced' by squatters, and if it is not abused will not affect squatters. But there is also an additional section which gives similar protection to a 'protected intending occupier' - who may be the owner or a tenant of a council or housing association. 'Protected intending occupiers' need only a sworn statement to prove their interest in the property and that it is their intention to occupy the property as a residence for themselves. This could well be used fraudulently to evict squatters. Although it is an offence for an intending occupier to give a false statement about when he or she wishes to move in, since there is no time limit this would be hard to follow up or prove. It should be noted that it is a legitimate defence if you can prove that you did not believe that the persons requiring you to leave the premises were displaced residential occupiers, protected intending occupiers of their authorised representatives.

3.33.05
The offence of forcible detainer at common law has been abolished and it is now an offence to resist or intentionally obstruct a bailiff evicting under the 'squatter's procedure' Court Orders.

3.33.06
It is also now a criminal offence to trespass with an offensive weapon. In such cases almost anything can be seen as an offensive weapon - a bread knife, a milk bottle or even a bag of flour, as well as crowbars, hammers and other tools - if it is intended to use them offensively.

3.33.07
So, these are criminal offences - using violence to enter against the wishes of an occupier; not leaving the premises when requested to do so by a 'displaced residential occupier' or a 'protected intending occupier'; offering resistance to a bailiff; carrying offensive weapons while trespassing. They all carry a maximum penalty of six months in prison and/or a £1,000 fine (except

for the last, for which it is three months and/or £1,000 fine). If you are charged with any of these offences, you will be tried before a magistrate, but you can appeal either to the Crown Court on a point of law and/or fact, or to a Divisional Court on a point of law only.

3.33.08

You can no longer be charged with conspiracy to trespass, although you can be charged with conspiracy to commit any of the above offences (or indeed any criminal offence). However, the penalty for conspiracy can generally no longer be greater than that for the actual act itself. It's possible that conspiracy charges may be used more often against squatters than in the past, as they are easier to bring than the actual charges. Any agreement, verbal or otherwise, between two or more people to commit a criminal offence can be seen as conspiracy. Any charges of conspiracy will be tried before a judge and jury, which may give you a chance of a fairer hearing.

3.33.09

The laws governing theft and criminal damage remain unchanged, and they are often used against squatters. It is an offence to enter a house with intent to commit unlawful damage. It is an offence to dishonestly use electricity or gas and could be an offence to take anything you find in the house (e.g., to burn coal left there). Damage to doors and windows, and even painting or repairs, could also be taken as criminal damage, if the owner is intent on harassing the squatters.

3.33.10

Court Orders or Posession Orders - Order 113 (High Court) and Order 26 (County Court) - 'special procedure against squatters' - have been simplified and speeded up. It's no longer necessary for an owner to take 'reasonable steps' to ascertain the names of squatters, although if the owner does know your names (if you sent a letter or letters telling him) and he fails to include them, then the case will be dismissed. The minimum period for

obtaining a Court or Posession Order has been reduced from seven to five days.

3.33.11 Eviction -

If none of the above methods are used against you, you can still be evicted by Court Order. If you are unnamed you have to ask the court to join you as a defendant, though you can defend the case by turning up in court whether the owner has your name or not. The only real reason for defending an eviction order is the hope of gaining time - unless you can show that you are a tenant. However, you do have some chance of a favourable verdict if you can show that:

(1) The plaintiff (owner) has not included all the names of the squatters that you can prove were known to him or her.

(2) There has been insufficient time between the serving of a summons and the hearing (usually less than five days).

(3) The plaintiff is not the owner or the person entitled to possession; you should ask him or her to provide evidence of the latter.

(4) The plaintiff has agreed to occupation, verbally or in writing, or has accepted payments (rent) or approved repairs and has not issued a notice to quit (see 3.33.20).

(5) The defendants have at some stage had a lawful tenancy, in which case the ordinary procedure for eviction should be used, though it is not clear that the new procedures cannot be used against ordinary tenants.

(6) The plaintiff does not have the authority to bring the action. For instance, in a local authority, an officer may not be allowed to act on his or her own, but may have to get authorisation from a committee or from full council. Check the council standing orders in the local library or with a friendly councillor. But the onus is on the defendants to

prove that there is no authority to take the action.

You can ask for a High Court Action to be transferred to a County Court (which is cheaper) under the County Courts Act 1929 s25. If this is refused, it may help to argue that your costs should be taxed on the County Court Scale (s27) if costs are awarded against you.

3. 33. 12 Time to leave -
The court has no discretion to give you time to leave once a Possession Order has been given against you (i. e. the landlord can evict you straight away). However, the landlord will often agree to allow you a certain period of time, in which case the court can suspend an order for that period (usually 28 days).

3. 33. 13 Appeals -
Appeals are generally not worth the cost and trouble. Before contemplating such action you should take expert legal advice. Contact a local group of the Advisory Service for Squatters (address, 3. 31. 02) and remember the results may affect all squatters.

3. 33. 14 Moving out -
When a family has been moved out by bailiffs after an order, and the property is officially empty, and another family move in quite independently, then fresh possession proceedings must be taken. However, there is some legal argument on this score and bailiffs may need to be dissuaded from using the same order again.

3. 33. 15 Legal representation -
Civil legal aid can be granted but not in squatters' cases. Lawyers may sometimes give free help, and you have the right to have a friend with you in court to advise you (a 'McKenzie'). Sometimes courts will allow you to be represented by non-lawyers, e. g. a councillor.

3. 33. 16 Homeless families -
If you are a family and have been evicted, the local authority has a responsibility to see that you have a roof over your head (as a homeless family). If you find it difficult to get the local authority to

agree, contact local housing advice centres (see 3. 31. 02).

3. 33. 17 Compulsory purchase -
It may be possible to persuade the local authority that it should use its extensive powers for purchasing property to buy your house (if it doesn't already own it) and if the owner has left it empty for a long time.

3. 33. 18
As a squatter you are liable to attract the attention of the police, and should therefore take care not to give them any excuse to arrest you: being arrested could lead to eviction as, while you are in the station, the owner could repossess the squat. As well as knowing the laws relating to squatting, be careful, for instance, to keep any cars taxed, insured and M. O. T. 'd. Making a nuisance of yourself, playing loud music late at night, being drunk or leaving rubbish on the street could all annoy the neighbours and bring the police round. Neighbours are often suspicious at first sight of squatters, but if you take reasonable care not to antagonise them, they can become sympathetic and even helpful - especially when they realise the advantages they gain from the renewed 'life' in their area. In several cases the support of neighbours has been decisive in winning legal and publicity battles. Moreover, they can become more active themselves, seeing that they too can stand up to local authorities and demand their rights.

3. 33. 19
Disconnection of services has been used to discourage squatters and at the moment the law is interpreted so that squatters may be refused connection unless they have the owner's consent. In reality, it is difficult for a Board to know whether you are squatting - unless your address has received local publicity or the owner has informed them. The best thing is to call in at your local showroom as soon as you move in, fill in a reconnection form and pay the deposit. If it seems excessive, you can arrange to pay it in instalments or make representations to have it reduced once you are connected. It

could be illegal to reconnect the supplies
yourself, although some squatters in
this position have not been prosecuted.
Water supplies are not usually termin-
ated while someone is in occupation as
this would contravene the health regulations, but they can be turned off
temporarily for repairs or to prevent
wastage (e.g. from broken pipes) or
for non-payment of water rates.

3.33.20 Licensees -
The idea of a 'licence' has been
established in the courts as an agreement to 'tolerate a trespass'. As the
law now stands, this gives a little
more protection to straightforward
squatters. Not only groups and individ-
uals who have signed agreements with
councils, etc., but some ordinary
squatters can be seen in law to be
licensees. As a licensee, you cannot
be evicted without a Court Order and
without being given reasonable notice
to quit - although you are not allowed
to resist a bailiff. A 'licence' can be
made verbally - either gratuitously
(e.g. 'You can stay a few days') or in
return for having done repairs suggested
or agreed by the owner.

3.33.21 Rates -
It is not a criminal offence not to pay
rates. On the other hand, it does not
prove that the local authority is accept-
ing your occupation if it takes rates
from you. However, it is good policy
to pay rates, so that you are seen in
the public mind as a normal resident.

3.33.22 Note -
The information given here has been
carefully checked and, as far as we
can tell, is correct at the time of
writing. Should you become involved
in legal matters, get in touch with
Release or the Advisory Service for
Squatters (see 3.31.02 to 04). They
may be able to help you - and you will
be able to help them by keeping them
up-to-date with what is going on.

APPENDIX 1
GAS SAFETY REGULATIONS 1972

The following material is extracted from the British Gas Corporation Gas Regulations S.I.1879/1972.

PART IV
INSTALLATION OF INSTALLATION PIPES

34.　(1) Any person who installs an installation pipe or installation pipe fitting on any premises shall comply in so doing with the following provisions in this Part of these regulations.

(2) Where such a person carries out the installation in the performance of a contract of service his employer shall ensure that the following provisions in this Part of these regulations are duly complied with.

(3) Where a person installs an installation pipe or installation pipe fitting on any premises forming part of a factory, the occupier shall ensure that the following provisions in this Part of these regulations are duly complied with.

35.　(1) All installation pipes and installation pipe fittings installed shall be of good construction and sound material and of adequate strength and size to secure safety.

(2) All installation pipes and installation pipe fittings shall be installed and jointed by competent persons in a sound and workmanlike manner and so as to be gastight.

36.　(1) An installation pipe shall not be installed in any position in which it cannot be used with safety having regard to the position of other nearby services and to such parts of the structure of any building through which it is laid as might affect its safe use.

(2) A person who installs an installation pipe shall ensure that any necessary electrical bonding is carried out by a competent person so as to connect the pipe electrically to any other nearby services.

37.　(1) No installation pipe shall be installed in a cavity wall nor so as to pass through a cavity wall otherwise than by the shortest practicable route.

(2) Where an installation pipe is installed so as to pass through any wall or is installed so as to pass through any floor of solid construction –

(a) the installation pipe shall be enclosed in a sleeve; and
(b) the installation pipe and sleeve shall be so constructed and installed as to prevent gas passing along the spaces between the pipe and the sleeve and between the sleeve and the wall or floor and so as to allow normal movement of the pipe.

(3) No installation pipe shall be installed under the foundations of a building or under the base of walls or footings.

38.　Every installation pipe installed, which passes through or is in contact with or is likely to be exposed to any material liable to cause the corrosion of the pipe, shall be constructed of material which is inherently resistant to corrosion or shall be protected against corrosion.

39.　Where installation pipes are installed with changes in pipe levels and condensation of water is likely to occur, a suitable vessel for the reception of any condensate which may form in any pipe shall be fixed to the pipe in a conspicuous and readily accessible position and means shall be provided for the removal of the condensate.

40.　All installation pipes installed shall be properly supported and so placed or protected as to ensure that there is no undue risk of accidental damage to the pipes.

41.　No installation pipe shall be installed in such a way as to impair the structure of any building nor so as to impair the fire resistance of any part of its structure.

42.　Where installation pipes supplied from primary meters are installed in a building for the supply of gas to which a service pipe of internal diameter of more than two inches is installed and the supply of gas is required for purposes other than domestic use –

(a) a valve or cock shall be properly fixed in a conspicuous and readily accessible position in the following cases:

(i) in the case of a building having two or more floors to which gas is supplied, in the incoming installation pipe to each such floor; and

(ii) in the case of a floor of a building having self-contained areas to which gas is supplied (whether or not the building has more than one floor), in the incoming installation pipe to each such self-contained area;

(b) a line diagram shall be attached to the building in a readily accessible position as near as practicable to the primary meter indicating the position of all installation pipes, meters, meter controls, valves or cocks, pressure test points, condensate receivers and electrical bonding.

43. A person who has installed an installation pipe or installation pipe fitting shall ensure –

(a) that it is forthwith after installation adequately tested to verify that it is gastight and examined to verify that it has been installed in accordance with the foregoing provisions of this Part of these regulations;

(b) that after such testing any necessary protective coating is applied to the joints of all installation pipes installed;

(c) that after complying with the provisions of sub-paragraphs (a) and (b) purging is carried out throughout every installation pipe installed through which gas can then flow; and

(d) that immediately after such purging every installation pipe which has been installed and is not to be put into immediate use is temporarily sealed off, capped or plugged at every outlet of it with the appropriate pipe fitting.

PART V
INSTALLATION OF GAS APPLIANCES

44. (1) Any person who installs a gas appliance on any premises shall comply in so doing with the following provisions in this Part of these regulations.

(2) Where such a person carries out the installation in the performance of a contract of service his employer shall ensure that the following provisions in this Part of these regulations are duly complied with.

(3) Where a person installs a gas appliance on any premises forming part of a factory, the occupier shall ensure that the following provisions in this Part of these regulations are duly complied with.

45. (1) All gas appliances shall be installed by competent persons.

(2) No gas appliance shall be installed unless –

(a) the appliance and the gas fittings and other works for the supply of gas to be used in connection with the appliance,

(b) the means of removal of the products of combustion from the appliance,

(c) the availability of sufficient supply of air for the appliance for proper combustion,

(d) the means of ventilation to the room or internal space in which the appliance is to be used, and

(e) the general conditions of installation including the connection of the appliance to any other gas fitting,

are such as to ensure that the appliance can be used without constituting a danger to any person or property.

46. (1) A person shall not install a gas appliance if the appliance and the gas fittings and any flue or means of ventilation to be used in connection with the appliance do not –

(a) if in Greater London, other than an outer London borough, comply with any such provisions of the London Building Acts and any byelaws made thereunder,

(b) if in any other part of England or Wales, comply with any such provisions of the building regulations, or
(c) if in Scotland, comply with any such provisions of the building standards regulations,
as are in force at the date of installation of the appliance.

(2) A person who has installed a gas appliance shall forthwith after installation test its connection to the installation pipe to verify that it is gastight and examine the appliance and the gas fittings and other works for the supply of gas and any flue or means of ventilation to be used in connection with the appliance and make any necessary adjustments in order to ensure –
(a) that the appliance has been installed in accordance with the foregoing provisions of this Part of these regulations;
(b) that the heat input and operating pressure are as recommended by the manufacturer;
(c) that all gas safety controls are in proper working order; and
(d) that, without prejudice to the generality of sub-paragraph (a), any flue system or means of removal of the products of combustion from the appliance and any means of ventilation and of supply of combustion air provided in connection with the use of the appliance are in safe working order.

PART VI
USE OF GAS

47. No person shall use or permit a gas appliance to be used if at any time he knows or has reason to suspect –
(a) that there is insufficient supply of air available for the appliance for proper combustion at the point of combustion;
(b) that the removal of the products of combustion from the appliance is not safely being carried out;

(c) that the room or internal space in which the appliance is situated is not adequately ventilated for the purpose of providing air containing a sufficiency of oxygen for the persons present in the room, or in, or in the vicinity of, the internal space while the appliance is in use;
(d) that any gas is escaping from the appliance or from any gas fitting used in connection with the appliance; or
(e) that the appliance or any part of it or any gas fitting or other works for the supply of gas used in connection with the appliance is so faulty or maladjusted that it cannot be used without constituting a danger to any person or property.

48. (1) If at any time any person supplied with gas by an Area Board knows or has reason to suspect that any gas is escaping in the premises supplied with gas he shall immediately shut off the supply of gas at such place as may be requisite to prevent the gas from escaping.

(2) Where any gas continues to escape in any premises after the supply of gas has been shut off, the person supplied with gas shall as soon as practicable give notice to the Area Board of the escape.

(3) Where any gas escapes in any premises supplied with gas and the supply of gas is shut off, the supply shall not be opened until all necessary steps have been taken to prevent the gas from again escaping.

PART VII
REMOVAL, DISCONNECTION, ALTERATION, REPLACEMENT AND MAINTENANCE OF GAS FITTINGS, ETC.

49. An electrical connection shall be maintained by means of temporary continuity bonding while a gas pipe, pipe fitting or meter is being removed or replaced until the work of disconnecting or connecting the gas pipe, pipe fitting or meter, as the case may be, has been completed, except, in the case of a

meter, when its inlet and outlet form a continuous single pipe.

50. A person who disconnects a gas fitting or any part of the gas supply system on any premises shall seal it off, cap it or plug it at every outlet of every pipe to which it is connected with the appropriate pipe fitting.

51. (1) No alteration shall be made to a gas fitting or to any part of the gas supply system on any premises (whether it has been installed before or after the date of coming into operation of these regulations) if as a result of such alteration there would have been a contravention of or failure to comply with any provision of Parts II to V of these regulations if the gas fitting or part of the gas supply system in question had been installed at the date of the alteration.

(2) On every replacement of a gas fitting or of any part of the gas supply system on any premises (whether it has been installed before or after the date of coming into operation of these regulations) the provisions of Part II, III, IV or V (as the case may be) of these regulations shall apply to its replacement as they apply to its installation after the said date:

Provided that where, in the case of the replacement of a meter in a building having two or more floors above the ground floor of the building, the said meter was installed on or under a stairway or in any other part of the building, where the stairway or other part of the building provided the only means of escape in case of fire, the replacement meter may be placed in the former position if the meter and its connections would comply with the requirements of regulation 22(2) relating to meters installed in buildings having less than two floors

above the ground floor or the replacement meter may be placed in another position if the meter would not contravene the provisions of regulation 22(1).

(3) A person who makes any alteration to or replacement of a gas fitting or any part of the gas supply system on any premises subsequent to installation shall ensure that it is forthwith adequately tested to verify that it is gastight.

(4) A person who makes any such alteration of a gas fitting or of any part of the gas supply system on any premises shall ensure that it is forthwith after such testing examined to verify that there would have been no such contravention of or failure to comply with any provision of Parts II to V of these regulations as is referred to in paragraph (1).

(5) A person who makes any such replacement of a gas fitting or of any part of the gas supply system on any premises shall ensure that it is forthwith after such testing examined to verify that it complies with such requirements of Parts II to V of these regulations as apply to the replacement by virtue of paragraph (2).

52. An Area Board supplying gas to any building shall at all times at their own expense keep all service valves inserted in the service pipes in proper working order.

**PART VIII
PENALTIES**

53. Any person offending against these regulations shall be liable on summary conviction to a fine not exceeding £100.

Dated 2nd August 1972.

INDEX